RE-THEORIZING
DISCIPLINE
IN EDUCATION

COMPLICATED

A Book Series of Curriculum Studies

William F. Pinar
General Editor

Vol. 34

PETER LANG
New York • Washington, D.C./Baltimore • Bern
Frankfurt • Berlin • Brussels • Vienna • Oxford

RE-THEORIZING
DISCIPLINE
IN EDUCATION

Problems, Politics, & Possibilities

EDITED BY *Zsuzsa Millei,*
Tom G. Griffiths, & Robert John Parkes

PETER LANG
New York • Washington, D.C./Baltimore • Bern
Frankfurt • Berlin • Brussels • Vienna • Oxford

Library of Congress Cataloging-in-Publication Data

Re-theorizing discipline in education: problems, politics, and possibilities /
edited by Zsuzsa Millei, Tom G. Griffiths, Robert John Parkes.
p. cm. — (Complicated conversation: a book series of curriculum studies; v. 34)
Includes bibliographical references and index.
1. School discipline. 2. Classroom management. 3. Critical pedagogy.
I. Millei, Zsuzsa. II. Griffiths, Tom G. III. Parkes, Robert John.
LB3012.R45 371.5—dc22 2009050145
ISBN 978-1-4331-0966-9
ISSN 1534-2816

Bibliographic information published by **Die Deutsche Nationalbibliothek.**
Die Deutsche Nationalbibliothek lists this publication in the "Deutsche
Nationalbibliografie"; detailed bibliographic data is available
on the Internet at http://dnb.d-nb.de/.

© 2010 Peter Lang Publishing, Inc., New York
29 Broadway, 18th floor, New York, NY 10006
www.peterlang.com

Printed in the United States of America

This book is dedicated to Joska Millei, my father.

Table of Contents

Preface

Being in Trouble: Autoethnography of a Not-Really Bad, White, Middle-Class Jewish Girl

Shirley R. Steinberg

If I had been told thirty years ago that I would be associated with schools and writing a preface for discipline in schools…I wouldn't have believed it. Discipline was always a word that was about me when I was in school; then became a word pertaining to some of my kids when I became a mother. It was a word that meant there was a disconnect between the expectations of the school and the expectations of either me, or my own children. Most of the time, I was quite sure that the school was the party with the inappropriate expectations.

As a daughter, I was *in trouble* most of the time. A very literal mother, one who did not understand nuance, or negotiate, raised me. My mother had many rules: most were absolutely ridiculous. Indeed, my own mothering was formed in becoming everything my mother was not. Mom also had an uncanny ability to choose a punishment, which *never* fit the crime (sort of like school teachers and administrators). I muse at the fact that the two institutions, which are known for punishment and discipline: parents/caregivers and schools, often delegate a consequence, which has nothing to do with a rule infraction. Possibly my mother was a frustrated educator. I went away to school at 17, and I knew that I would not have to follow arbitrary rules.

As a student, I was *in trouble* a lot of the time, for interrupting in class, for arguing, or for speaking out of turn. As a girl, I was considered weird; girls weren't supposed to talk out, to talk too much, or too loud…so I was often a weird, *in trouble* girl. In those days teachers made sure that everyone in the class was privy to the discipline meted out. I was never a *bad* kid; the bad kids sat in the corner or got taken into a closet and spanked with a paddle. When I got older, detention became a reality for many of us, mine was usually for talking back to a teacher, while others were there for cutting class, getting into fights, or picking on others. I never fit in with the other kids in trouble, I was never in the *bad* crowd, nor, in the popular crowd; even my detentions and punishments didn't give me status. When I first saw John Hughes's *The Breakfast Club*, I identified with the state of being, but never encountered a kinship in my own experiences with being disciplined. Often, I was chided for not giving *the right* answer. I clearly remember being singled out in my Mass Communications 101 class in the first semester of university. I adored Professor McKinley, a legend at my school. Known as "The Voice of KSL," McKinley had recently retired from radio and was a communications professor. We were discussing the notion of global communications—the whole sender and receiver discussion—and students were giving answers to a question. I raised my hand and made an observation... McKinley paused, sighed, and asked, "Miss Steinberg, why is it that you always have to be different?" I would have preferred a paddle. I couldn't wait to graduate and get a teaching degree; I would finally be free to create my own rules, fair rules.

As a parent, I was determined to facilitate my children through school. I didn't want them to be me...I wanted them to be popular, smart, and not *in trouble*. After several ragged starts, Joe and I realized that we had to tell our children the whole truth. We told them that we knew that they had amazing thoughts and ideas and that they had high energy...*but,* in order to not replicate our school days, we would mentor them behind the scenes. They knew that we felt that public schooling was a failure and that interpersonally, politically, and intellectually, they would learn more out of school than in school. As a family, we had to find a way to negotiate school, for them to feel safe, valued, and to not constantly be *in trouble.* All four of our children had to learn what to say, and what not to say...what to do, and what not to do...and they had to internalise that schools may *claim* to educate and create good citizens, but what is claimed and what is done are clearly two different results. For years, they each would come home blowing off the pedantic steam of instrumentally rationalized lectures and standardized testing; they swallowed their arguments, observations, and played the game. Each one of them was highly successful in school, popular, and ready for higher education. They had escaped getting into *trouble*. They learned how to be good citizens. They learned how to follow rules and how to not get caught.

As a young teacher, I was *in trouble* most of my days. My students were loud, engaged, and my classes appeared disorganized. Other teachers would comment that after attending my class, students would enter the next class arguing or chattering. They would debate in classroom discussions, and be "overly enthusiastic," when participating. While teaching high school drama in Alberta, a parent phoned me and told me that he felt that something was wrong with me...Reverend Erb told me that in his experience, "no teacher should like students as much as I did." My principal called me in for a yearly review and asked: "why can't you get along with your peers?" He went on to tell me that I was trying too hard and doing too much; working with the students in extra curricular drama was threatening athletic programs, and the coaches saw me as a troublemaker. I left my first teaching position realizing that I couldn't follow the rules.

As a university professor, I teach teachers and administrators how to teach. I am told I have academic freedom. And somehow, I fail to follow the rules. After over a decade in higher education, I have not been able to stay out of *trouble*. Not the big *T* kind, but the little *t* kind…the insidious kind of trouble (the kind you don't know you are in, until you are in it). Three of my doctoral students told me that during a required doctoral class, one of them had been taking notes on his laptop. The professor stopped class to single him out and tell him that laptop use was not a part of the classroom's culture. The student was embarrassed and befuddled as he realized he had missed this particular rule. However, there had never been a discussion of the classroom culture—this "rule" was assumed. My department chair told me recently that I didn't seem to know how to fit in, that my views of education were particularly problematic…furthermore, that it was difficult to understand how social justice applied to a faculty of education, that it was apparent that my particular philosophy of teaching (critical pedagogy) was dead. And, that I needed to follow the rules.

My story is that of a privileged, white female who never *really* was disciplined. Yet my memories of school are largely based on the negative experiences I had when I didn't comply with rules. If my reactions and recollections are so vivid, I can only imagine the impact on children and youth who didn't have my social, ethnic, and cultural capital—the kids who were labelled on sight, stereotyped and "ability" grouped the first day of school. If I was traumatized, what could the result possibly be for kids who were lost in the system, without advocates, without voice?

As a critical theorist, it is not hard to identify the theme of power woven into the weft of my narrative. Power serves to arm parent, teacher, administrator, and supervisor with ammunition against those without power. Power allows the powerful to dole out rules and consequences without rationale, safety, or social context. Power makes up rules, changes rules, and trots out new rules to suit it. Power dictates the structures of schools, teachers, students, and families. Power seeks to sustain and reproduce itself. Power insists on discipline to maintain the status quo.

Discipline is a tool of power. Built upon a deficit model, where transgression is expected, discipline is the natural follow-through of getting *into trouble*. Children and youth who are continually *in trouble* are continually disciplined, and often, the cause becomes the effect and the effect, the cause. Pre-service teacher education students often become obsessed with ways to "manage" the classroom, maintain order, and discipline students. Rare is an equal obsession with ways to engage students, excite them, and provoke thinking and learning. It is also impossible to miss the fact that the lower the socio-economic status of a school, the higher the discipline rate; the more non-white the school, the more frequent the punishments. As our students enter teaching, many claim that their primary concern is how to control the classroom…the assumption is that students must be controlled, implying that without this control, the class would not be a success. The more diverse the school, the more control is warranted. When new teachers begin their first term, they fill classrooms with charts and lists of classroom rules that dominate the walls. Initial classes are filled with the discourse of rules, consequences… discipline becomes the mantra of the classroom, and students are quickly divided into the troublemakers or the good kids.

This book is a cutting edge attempt to change the discourse of discipline in schools. The editors and authors problematise the educational paradigm of discipline through critical lenses based on equity and a socially just system of schooling. Traditional education-eased writing relies on models, taxonomies, and behavioural techniques leading to a successful classroom. The book makes no claim to old theories; instead, it re-theorizes and politicises discipline and the classroom. Reading this volume prompted me to revisit my own schooling, and I realized how discipline framed my reality. Zsuzsa, Tom, and Robert have invited us to engage in a new conversation about discipline, and through this conversation, we can begin to find theoretical, pedagogical, respectful, humble, and safe ways to interact with students, and to refocus our attention to what schooling should be about: teaching and learning.

Acknowledgments

This book began as an idea for a single-authored volume. The idea outgrew itself, however, with depth and richness emerging from the collaborative endeavour that this edited volume represents. During an initial meeting of possible contributors we debated and shaped the argument of this book. Co-writing and reviewing each other's chapters stretched our respective thinking, provoking discussions that furthered the distance we took from well-entrenched understandings of discipline.

Zsuzsa Millei has worked on this book under a Fellowship provided by the Faculty of Education and Arts, hosted by The Australian Institute for Social Inclusion and Wellbeing (TAISIW). Kate Bennett was also funded under this fellowship to do a literature review for the volume, thanks Kate. Anna Kaemmerling's meticulous work as a copy editor was also funded through TAISIW. Zsuzsa acknowledges that some data used in chapters were collected by Andrea Kosz, research assistant under Zsuzsa's New Staff Grant project, jointly funded by the Faculty of Education and Arts and The University of Newcastle. The indexing of the book was funded by the Newcastle Institute of Research in Education (NIRE).

The School of Education at The University of Newcastle also supported this project in multiple ways, including reviews of some draft chapters by members of a Friday 'writing (for publication) group', and the provision of resources for the initial meeting and proofreading, thanks Bronwyn Gallagher and Mick Driscoll for the great work. Special thanks also go to Eva Petersen and Jim Jose who provided constructive feedback and insights on chapters, and to Shirley Steinberg, whom we met when she visited our shores during the drafting of our book, and who agreed to write the preface for this volume.

Chapter 1

Opening the Field: Deliberating Over 'Discipline'

Zsuzsa Millei, Tom G. Griffiths and Robert John Parkes

> [I]f power was never anything but repressive, if it never did anything but say no, do you really believe that we should manage to obey it? (Foucault, 1979c, p. 36)

Discipline in education is both central and peripheral in this book. While discipline in education is the focus of investigation, this book deliberately avoids offering any notions of 'best' theories, methods and practices. We invite readers instead to a discussion on discipline in education that moves between focusing on, and de-centring from, its topic in order to bring new insights into 'traditional' and somewhat exhausted and highly loaded understandings of the concept. Such an approach requires us to pose questions, offer new frameworks to think about discipline in education, and so to complicate its understanding, rather than provide explicit and 'easy-to-apply' answers to perceived problems. We do this with a deliberate aim to shake up our well-established routines and ideas on this important subject in contemporary schooling.

Problems with school discipline have been ranked as the most serious problem with schools according to the Phi Delta Kappa/Gallup poll public opinion survey in the past 38 years (Rose & Gallup, 2005 in Edwards, 2008, p. 15). Driven by this importance and triggered by critical events and media reporting, governments around the world have commissioned numerous inquiries into school discipline directly, such as the historical Elton Report (1989) Enquiry into Discipline in Schools or indirectly, such as The National Inquiry into Children and the Legal Process (1995)[1] in Australia, which followed the ratification of the Convention on the Rights of the Child (1989) and includes a large section on discipline in schools. Media panics, government reporting, and professional bodies' concerns triggered various replies to the problem, and the result was the institution of a range of measures from outlawing physical punishment to introducing various policies to tackle identified issues (Slee, 1992). For example, Sweden was the first country

---

[1] Available online: http://www.hreoc.gov.au/Human_RightS/children/teahers.html#7

to outlaw physical punishment in schools, which they did in 1979; and new schools sprang up in places such as New South Wales (such as Concord High School in the inner West of Sydney) during the late seventies that explicitly rested their reputation on disciplining students without using corporal punishment. In contrast, in the United States there were twenty-two states as of September 2003 that still legally allowed corporal punishment in schools, and according to the U.S. Department of Education (2009):

> Nearly all public school districts—90 percent or more—administer in-school suspensions, out-of school suspensions, and expulsions…. Thirty percent administer corporal punishment. Proportionately more districts in the Southeast administer corporal punishment than do districts in any other region.[2]

In Australia, corporal punishment remains lawful in some Australian jurisdictions although most States and Territories have limited the practice by legislation, regulation, policy or philosophy.

The apparent importance of discipline as an aspect of teaching and schooling is also mirrored in the academic literature, in teacher education programs, and in the workshop offerings made available for the professional development of teachers. Professional teaching standards frameworks in state jurisdictions throughout Australia enshrine 'classroom management' as a key feature of initial teacher education and professional competence a classroom teacher (e.g., see the New South Wales Institute of Teachers' Professional Teaching Standards).[3] Classroom discipline, behaviour management, guidance, classroom management, managing the learning environment, and student behaviour, are some of the keywords and phrases under which large bodies of academic and practical literature are situated. Research and practical work in these areas includes critical and theoretical work that interrogates the concept of discipline and in so doing offers new perspectives on identified solutions, such as a highly collaborative approach to discipline that invokes students' autonomy and engagement, and the promotion of pro-social behaviour (e.g., Porter, 2008) or the creation of a personal theory of discipline (Edwards, 2008). However, this broad area of research is dominated by work in the field of educational psychology. The focus of this body of work tends to be on problems with individual students, classroom environments, or the dynamics of 'whole' schools, leading to solutions aimed at these different levels of scale to improve discipline. Discipline in education, in this way remains strongly instrumental and narrow in focus. Since there is limited research that approaches discipline from perspectives outside the educational psychology field, using interdisciplinary theories and ideas, the field of discipline in education remains relatively secure from the effects of critiques that have the potential to invigorate thinking and policy with respect to the concept and practices of discipline in education. Thus, despite their efforts, a whole variety of reform agendas, professional teacher standards, and policy recommendations re-institute, to varying degrees, policies and practices that are already deeply entrenched in systems of schooling.

---

[2]   U.S. Department of Education, Accessed online: 25th of October 2009 http://nces.ed.gov/surveys/frss/publications/92130/

[3]   Available online: http://www.nswteachers.nsw.edu.au/Main-Professional-Teaching-Standards.html

Getting Beyond Discipline as a Zero-Sum Game

This book critically intervenes in the usual ways of thinking about discipline in education, offering fresh perspectives for rethinking the 'problem' of discipline anew. This book approaches and engages with discipline from outside its 'traditional' field, positioning it at the centre of social science inquiries that use alternative theoretical and paradigmatic ideas. The studies present a range of interdisciplinary thinking on both discipline in education, and about the concept of 'discipline' itself, drawing upon methodological perspectives drawn from the fields of sociology, social theory, politics, history, and philosophy, stretching its focus from the classroom to the globe. Our purpose in this volume then is to expand, challenge and further complicate limited, taken-for-granted, instrumental and insular understandings of discipline.

An argument that runs through the chapters in this volume is that the concept of 'discipline' is narrowly understood as control of students' conduct in educational settings (Slee, 1995), something that is also reflected in educational discourses. This idea constitutes understandings that translate into those practices that constrain and/ or restrict students' conduct; practices that have subsequently been critiqued in terms of their potential to dominate students and limit their capacity or freedom to act. Such work has invoked a concern that the underlying principle of discipline involves a binary tension of control versus freedom (Millei, 2007). In order to abide with this idea of control versus freedom, subsequent discipline theories and practices almost inevitably take up a quest to, in some way, 'empower' and 'free' students from the 'controlling' effects of discipline. Based on this pursuit theorists fashion new approaches and practices that ostensibly free children from teachers' domination by advocating that students engage in forms of self-disciplining. In this book, we argue that this quest constrains alternative theorizing that departs from this rationale. The theorizing in this book aims to stretch the boundaries of this sort of thinking and introduce new perspectives and possibilities that unsettle and further complicate the concept of 'discipline'.

As Millei discusses in detail in Chapter 2, the underlying principle of contemporary classroom discipline approaches produces a continuum that ranges from maximum freedom to maximum control. This model also includes some theorization of power that likens discipline in education to something of a tug of war (Ford, 2003). One can quite easily place theories and practices along different points of this axis, as Porter (2007) does in her book that recounts the theories of, and common approaches to, classroom discipline (see p. 19). While Porter (2007) argues that in laissez-faire discipline models the student has the greatest personal power and the teacher has relatively low power, in autocratic discipline styles power is located on the teacher's side and students are relatively powerless. This way of thinking about classroom discipline, as a zero-sum approach to the question of power, constructs a highly particular perspective on classroom discipline, and any disruption that may occur to it. As Ford (2003) describes:

> We talk of avoiding 'power plays' with students, and we wonder what has happened
> to the respect that used to be afforded to people in our positions. Generally, we talk

about power that establishes the means of controlling the behaviour of others, the 'right' to exert such control, and the nature and limit of that 'right'. Questions of students' power and their 'right to exert control', over themselves and others, have also been given increasing weight in contemporary educational discourses. (p. 8)

Ford (2003) suggests the questioning of students' 'rights' and discipline's 'limits', and more recently ideas of children's 'citizenship', are the positions according to which classroom discipline theories and practices are historically examined and critiqued within the field of educational psychology.

The highly problematic nature of conceptions of 'citizenship' generally, and for school children in particular, is taken up by Millei and Imre in Chapter 10. They draw attention to the development of competing understandings of 'citizenship' in political theory, including liberal, socialist, communitarian and cosmopolitan approaches, and their relationship to prevailing discourses of citizenship in national and international educational thinking. The chapter concludes by questioning whether, and through what means, children could be meaningfully involved in the everyday political practices of citizenship as articulated in political theory and considers classroom discipline in the light of this question. Their use of political theory to elaborate the historical development and construction of notions of 'citizenship' more broadly, taken up by educational authorities to conceptualise children's citizenship, effectively questions the very possibility of children's status as citizens in school systems. The concept of 'citizenship' in schooling and the disciplining patterns of associated rights and responsibilities make the concept uncertain at best. Positions like those promoting children's citizenship rights and obligations incite the invention and justification of a host of 'novel' discipline theories and practices.

While before the 1950s discipline involved both corporal and other forms of non-corporal punishment in schools globally (Edwards, 2008; Slee, 1995), after the violent incidents of WWII, more replacing corporal punishment more 'humane' forms of discipline practices were developed. As Edwards (2008) argues, "since the 1950s, a number of discipline models have emerged that represent a full spectrum between student freedom and teacher control" (p. 16) where the need for less autocratic control on the teacher's side is linked to the creation of more democratic societies to avoid the possibility of new totalitarian regimes. Southgate's study on enduring memories of punishment in school life in Chapter 7, documents precisely the kind of angst about discipline that has driven educators to attempt to develop more 'democratic' discipline approaches. Working on this premise over the past 60 years, discipline theorists in education have developed a range of strategies, such as establishing classroom rules, delivering high rates of verbal and non-verbal praise, and introducing counselling strategies, all of which aim to keep students under control without the exertion of explicit, or direct, authoritarian control by teachers. These techniques and strategies strive to regulate students' behaviour to create order in the classroom in ways that often connect with ideas of the classroom as a 'learning space' that must be 'managed' (Gore & Parkes, 2008). One of the critical arguments made in Chapter 2 by Millei is that efforts that draw on this understanding seek to provide greater levels of student freedom or enable students to focus on their learning, but often have the counter-intuitive effect of producing more subtle or insidious forms of regulation of students that deliver tighter control, through the very freedom they desire to reach. Thus, Millei argues that the incapacity of this framework to escape the dilemma of freedom versus control demands a re-theorizing of the problem.

Discipline in education as a body of knowledge is generally instrumental in character, and located in the field of educational psychology in isolation from other fields of inquiry, and at times even from pedagogy and learning, and is often thought about as a separate and discreet form of management. An understanding of discipline as divorced from pedagogy and as a form of management, as Gore and Parkes (2008) argue, "produces a situation in which teachers are likely to desire classroom order over the construction of an intellectually engaging learning environment" (p. 45). Teachers thus take up discipline as a management issue that robs discipline from its potential to directly and productively guide students by enabling or facilitating their engagement in learning. Slee's (1995) reconceptualisation of "'discipline' consistent with an educational as opposed to a management discourse" (p. 17) serves as an opening point to reconnect with the idea of discipline as educational. Other studies that rethink the potential educational nature of discipline include Watkins's (2005) article and Watkins and Noble's (2008) book, which demonstrate the integral role that discipline plays in the formation of learning routines that enable bodily habituations that are conducive to learning. Watkins continues this work in Chapter 5 of this volume, drawing on some contemporary case studies of students' home and school experiences to explore the potentially enabling character of discipline, and students' self-discipline, and its capacity to enhance students' agency and engagement in education. Crucially, the chapter counters work that pathologises student behaviour and scholastic success against generalized cultural backgrounds, rather it opens up avenues for children's agency by offering a more complex and nuanced understanding of students' acquired dispositions in the home and school, and their potential to enable or constrain student engagement and learning. Parkes makes a complementary argument in Chapter 6 through his exploration of discipline in the martial arts dojo. His argument promotes an understanding of discipline as a pedagogical force that builds capacity and agency, precisely through its modes of constraint.

Classroom discipline and its underpinning rationale are almost universally concerned with power as located on individuals' behalf and fought for in a 'tug of war' (Ford, 2003), as noted earlier. Theories and practices thus recommend ways in which that war could be brought to a peaceful conclusion by moving toward more equalized power differentials. By using alternative understandings of power borrowed from social theory, for example that offered by Foucault, it becomes possible to reconsider the knowledge base of discipline as power/knowledge (Foucault, 1980), making its productive—which should not be read as a synonym for 'positive'—nature more visible (see particularly Chapter 5 & 6). From this perspective, the struggle is reformulated in terms of sites of discursive production and contestation, and subject formation and positioning.

One of discipline's roles, closely paraphrasing Foucault, is to produce 'docile bodies' and to constitute the subject of whom it speaks: the disciplined subject. Following Foucault, writings by Hart (2001), Millei (2005) and Gore and Parkes (2008) for example, engage in the work of reconceptualising discipline as fundamentally educational (pedagogical), rather than exclusively something managerial designed simply to keep order. Millei (2005) focuses on the construction of the event of 'disruption' in classrooms and argues that it is frequently constituted as a 'control problem', highlighting alternative ways to understand these situations that are linked to pedagogy or students' cultural background. Simpson (2000) connects discipline more closely with the hidden curriculum through which schools ensure that 'docile bodies' inhabit them, hence discipline's regulative but also 'productive' nature. Simpson (2000) examines the ways in which children's bodies are disciplined during transitions from primary to secondary schools:

> from the moment they entered the school, pupils were introduced to a strict regime of constraint, which not only determined where and when they should be throughout the day, but also how they should comport themselves (p. 77).

In a similar study, Kamler (1994) examines children's transition from the home or preschool to primary school. Branson and Miller (1991) employ a sociological lens and focus on the social relations that school discipline produces by analysing the individualising power of discipline. They argue that these theories shape a unitary subject that ignores difference, "fixed in the logocentric creation of changeless, static concepts" (p. 183).

Another dimension of the work exploring alternative conceptions of discipline involves the critique of characterizations of individual students in terms of their behaviour. Laws and Davies (2000) make visible the constitutive force of discipline through a study of a particular school for 'behaviourally disturbed children'. They examine the construction/ formation of the 'behaviourally disturbed child' as the subject of discipline that positions some children in ways that make them unrecognisable by other discourses. They analyse a particular scenario in which a young boy is viewed as 'delinquent', whose positioning cancels out possibilities for the teachers to see him in other ways, for example as a 'protester', which might be understood in a more positive light, legitimating his 'role' in this situation. Graham's (2007) work on the constitution of 'disorderly objects' continues this theme. She examines individual statements about 'problematic' behaviours in school with a concern about "how this particular statement functions—what does it do and with what effects?" (p. 1). Graham scrutinizes the ways in which the constitution of individuals as particular subjects creates the condition of possibility for the identification and classification of behaviour disorder and disorderly behaviour. Millei and Raby in Chapter 3 trouble in a similar manner the ways in which teachers approach and understand discipline. To make classroom discipline unfamiliar, Millei and Raby recount ideas that inform teachers' behaviours with regards to 'indiscipline' and codes of conduct, and demonstrate that the ideas underlying certain conduct codes are mostly illogical and cursory in nature. In this way, they formulate one of the interesting 'problems' of discipline, that is, the incongruent and temporary nature of teachers' argumentations in regards to the form of discipline they employ in certain situations.

Discipline also has the capacity to produce desire, pleasure, and even suffering (Southgate, 2003). In Chapter 8 Cliff elaborates a critique of unproblematised notions of the 'healthy citizen', and their implication for pedagogical practices in schools. Part of this critique identifies the pleasure that students might receive from their self-disciplined activity directed toward the achievement of desired body shapes, drawing on Foucault's (1979b) work. In Chapter 6 Parkes makes a similar move using Foucauldian theory, exploring the voluntary subjection to the extreme discipline of the martial arts that he argues arises from a desire to attain the perceived benefits of training. Taylor picks up the thread on 'desire' in Chapter 9, and focuses upon the widening gulf between the increasingly sexual-desire-promoting domain of children's popular culture, and the anxiously sexual-desire-denying domain of early childhood schooling. She teases out some of the paradoxical ways in which young children are simultaneously disciplined to become desiring, denying, regulated and self-regulating sexual subjects by these pedagogical discursive domains. Taylor argues that these striking contradictions carry commonly side-stepped and yet very significant implications for early childhood educators. Taylor calls us to move beyond the equally paralysing and exciting, and co-implicated sexual desires of teachers and children, and to rethink desire as pedagogical.

This book continues to re-think the idea and knowledge base of 'discipline' by opening it up to other perspectives originally advanced within Slee's (1995) work, which reconsiders discipline in terms of its educational potential via more complex conceptions of power. Inspired by this earlier work, in this book we necessarily draw on multiple understandings of the concept of 'discipline'.

The Multiple Meanings of 'Discipline'

The word 'discipline' has multiple meanings, many of which are used in the chapters that follow. First, 'discipline' is a synonym for control, and embodies a sense of creating or maintaining order. Understood in this way, discipline often carries a negative connotation in popular and academic understandings. As a means of creating order, 'discipline' may imply the use of practices of punishment, reward and regulation, designed to promote compliance and submission. Freire's (1975) analysis of education reveals how this concept of 'discipline' comes to operate in educational settings. According to Freire, typical curriculum policy implies the transmission of rarefied knowledge produced elsewhere (other than the classroom in which it will be studied). This knowledge is intended to be 'passed on' to learners, and thus constructs classrooms in which learning is understood in terms of 'reception' and conformity. Such a situation generates a condition of passivity in the pupils that may end up in their inevitable disruption of their classes and the resultant invocation by their teachers that young persons simply comply or receive the consequences. The impact of this form of discipline is taken up by Southgate in Chapter 7, in which punishment becomes the means of eliciting compliance, with enduring effects on the learner and their memories of schooling.

A second meaning of 'discipline' that also relates to a form of order, but of a logically different kind (Wilson, 1971), was developed in the context of progressive education by utilizing Dewey's (1916) ideas in which:

> A person who is trained to consider his action, to undertake them deliberately, is in so far forth disciplined. Add to this ability a power to endure in an intelligently chosen course in face of distraction, confusion, and difficulty, and you have the essence of discipline. Discipline means the power at command; mastery of the resources available for carrying through the action undertaken. To know what one is to do and to move to do it promptly and by use of the requisite means is to be disciplined, whether we are thinking of any army or a mind. Discipline is positive. To cow the spirit, to subdue inclination, to compel obedience, to mortify the flesh, to make a subordinate perform an uncongenial task—these things are or are not disciplinary according to the development of the power to recognize what one is about and to persistence in accomplishment (p. 129).

According to Wilson (1971), 'disciplined' activity is driven by implicit reasons and intrinsic values, while 'controlled' activity arises from the adoption of extrinsic reasons and values. Thus, a person who contemplates her or his actions and performs them with consideration may be described as a 'disciplined' person, and it is something of this kind of 'disciplined citizen' that we see emerge from the analysis, provided by Cliff, of the 'healthy citizen' and their calculating, enterprising nature in Chapter 8; the 'composed student' articulated by Watkins in Chapter 5; and the 'disciplined martial artist' depicted by Parkes in Chapter 6.

A related third meaning of 'discipline' implies a specific field of academic study or knowledge, such as the discipline of education (arguably), or economics, physics, psychology, history, or sociology. Disciplinary knowledge (or scientific knowledge) is important and valorised in the government of conduct "in its depths and details" (Foucault, 1979b, p. 19) since it intends to shape or reshape the ways individuals conduct themselves. Knowledge compiled in disciplines, according to Foucault's (1980) understanding, is always enmeshed in relations of power because it was being applied to the regulation of social conduct and is implicated in the questions of whether and in what situations knowledge is to be applied or not. Power, discourse and truth go hand in hand. As Foucault (1980) explains:

> [there are] manifold relations of power which permeate, characterize and constitute the social body, and these relation of power cannot themselves be established, consolidated nor implemented without the production, accumulation, circulation and functioning of a discourse. There can be no possible exercise of power without certain economy of discourses of truth which operate through and on the basis of this association. We are subjected to the production of truth through power and we cannot exercise power except through the production of truth. (p. 93)

Disciplinary knowledge turns individuals into its subjects, because individuals make sense of themselves by referring to various bodies of knowledge. This understanding of discipline is also taken up by Cliff in relation to conceptions of the 'healthy citizen' that circulate within contemporary media, public and policy discourses, that derive from knowledge produced through a range of health science disciplines operating inside and outside the academy (Chapter 8). Likewise, Millei and Raby's analysis of teachers' understandings of 'indiscipline' in Chapter 3 is built on the examination of those discipline knowledges that compose discipline theories and practices and are utilized to evaluate particular disorderly behaviours by teachers.

In a fourth meaning, 'discipline' operates as a form of self-regulation (self-discipline) that permeates modern institutions and is encouraged by them (Foucault, 1979a). Disciplinary power, however, has spread out from modern institutions and 'disciplinary societies' (Foucault, 1979b) and has been arguably overtaken by 'societies of control' (Deleuze, 1992). In 'societies of control', disciplinary power is recoded into a particular form of control. Deleuze (1992) defines it as a "modulation, like a self-deforming cast that will continuously change from one moment to the other…[therefore] in the societies of control one is never finished with anything" (p. 5). Control in 'societies of control' is continuous, infinite and diffuse and is not confined within institutions as disciplinary power was. Thus, in a 'society of control' the disciplining of subjects extends from 'closed' institutions into all areas of life (Deleuze, 1992), and utilizes expertise, such as counsellors, conflict resolution and child development experts, and apparatuses external to the state (Foucault, 1979a), which could be the family, sport clubs, religious organizations, behaviour management advice sites on the Internet or doctors and counselling clinics. These definitions of discipline almost inevitably blur into one another, as described by Raby in Chapter 4. Raby illuminates the ways in which penal ideas originating in legal frameworks for the control of criminals move into school discipline policies and the ways in which ideas, such as social responsibility, disperse through different policy areas for the regulation of subjects in a nation state in general and schools in particular. Cliff also exemplifies the working of 'control societies' where the media and Internet sites deliver control at a distance to regulate students' bodies.

In perhaps a fifth take on discipline, Parkes' chapter draws on an understanding of discipline as pedagogy. Parkes is particularly interested in the way martial disciplines construct different kinds of individuals through the practice of specific techniques of self-styling that emerge when voluntarily applying the rules, regulations, strategies, tactics, and techniques of a specific martial art. Parkes' depiction of discipline shares something in common with Watkins' notion of 'composure' (Chapter 5), and Cliff's understanding of the 'enterprising citizen' (Chapter 8), as noted earlier, challenging us to rethink discipline from the perspective of the foreign, drawing on an example that is both outside regular schooling, and derived from the 'marginal' traditions of Eastern philosophy. The result is an understanding of discipline that is intimately connected with a 'pedagogy of desire', in which willing subjection becomes the means of attaining a certain kind of freedom, albeit within the limits or parameters established by the discipline.

There is clearly no single definition of discipline at play in this volume, and the concern regarding discipline's relationship with freedom recurs at various points throughout the book. Certainly the lack of a single definition of discipline has led Griffiths and Imre in Chapter 11 to problematise the universal character of the 'discipline problem', and its understandings in the globalised age, asking whether substantively different national or local understandings (and with them systems and practices) are possible. They draw on international relations theory to consider the modern nation-state, in an inter-state system, and world-systems analysis in particular that argues for intensified convergence globally in phenomena like education, driven in part by the shared geocultural underpinnings of national governments everywhere. Further, they also point to the constructed nature of educational problems globally, including discipline, and the extent to which they remain unproblematised and taken for granted as common problems to be solved by schools and systems. Whether tied to a (cosmopolitan) world culture of education, or a nation-state's location and participation in a single capitalist world-economy, questions of whether and to what extent we can generate alternative approaches, and their potential to contribute to alternative futures, are raised.

Considerations of the future, particularly in terms of the potential for education, and discipline within education, to construct citizens or subjects who might, perhaps in a Feirean sense, be enabled to act on and change the world in a critically informed way, in the final chapter of this volume. This chapter, by Millei, Imre and Griffiths, works to raise questions particularly about the (im)possibility of discipline as a means of achieving the utopian goals of education. Exploration of education as a utopian endeavour, seeking to produce citizens/subjects for an ideal society, whether socialist or capitalist, to be realized somewhere over the horizon, underpins much of the work in this volume. For these scholars, however, even when discipline is conceptualised as a positive ideal inside a utopian framework, it almost inevitably results in dystopic consequences. Rather than provide easy solutions, this chapter serves to continue the work of rendering education and discipline problematic and unstable.

Critiquing and Complicating Understandings of 'Discipline'

While there are numerous critiques of discipline approaches in education from within educational psychology, those that problematise these approaches from outside it or by using social theory are limited. The focus of this book is firmly in that space, placing 'discipline' at the centre of social science inquiry in order to trouble, multiply and complicate its understandings. One of these works utilizes Foucault's (1979b) notion of governmentality to examine how school rules and conduct codes fashion gendered citizens and produce sites of resistance in neo-liberal regimes (Raby, 2005). Raby articulates forms of resistance also in this volume in Chapter 4. Millei (2007) by adopting the same theoretical stance discusses classroom discipline theories as aligned with different modes of governing citizens and argues that these theories employ more sophisticated forms of regulation with the utilization of psychological discourses and modern forms of government that seemingly work to provide students with relatively more power and freedom than previous theories ensured. This volume should be read as an attempt to contribute to this marginal but important body of work.

Understanding discipline as a force that has the capacity to shape, punish, repress, enable, compose, construct, form, reform, deform, include, and exclude, the authors in

Should you pay prescription charges? Read all the statements in Part 1 opposite. You don't have to pay a prescription charge if any of the statements apply to you (the patient) on the day you are asked to pay. (A valid War Pension exemption certificate only entitles you to free prescriptions for your accepted disablement.) Put a cross in the first box in **Part 1** that applies to you, read the declaration and complete and sign **Part 3**.

Benefits which DO NOT provide exemption. You are NOT entitled to exemption from prescription charges because you receive Pension Credit Savings Credit, Incapacity Benefit, Disability Living Allowance, Contributions based Jobseeker's Allowance or Contributions based Employment and Support Allowance. Only those benefits listed in **Part 1** provide exemption. An HC3 certificate does not entitle you to free prescriptions.

Evidence. You may be asked to provide evidence to show that you do not have to pay. You could show the relevant benefit award notice, or an exemption or pre-payment certificate. If you cannot show evidence at that time you can still get your prescription items free but your Primary Care Trust will check your entitlement later if you do not show proof (see paragraph about Penalty Charges).

If you have to pay a prescription charge. You (or your representative) should put in **Part 2** the amount you have paid and then sign and complete **Part 3**.

Need help with the cost of prescription charges? You can get information by ringing 0845 850 1166 or by reading leaflets HC11 or HC12. You may be able to get these leaflets from your GP surgery or pharmacy. Or ring 0845 610 1112 to get one, or go to www.dh.gov.uk/helpwithhealthcosts

Not entitled to free prescriptions? Pre-pay to reduce the cost. If you think you will have to get more than 4 items in 3 months or 14 items in 12 months it will be cheaper to buy a pre-payment certificate (PPC). Phone 0845 850 0030 to find out the cost, or order a PPC and pay by credit or debit card. You can pay for a 12 month PPC by direct debit instalment payments. Buy on-line at www.ppa.org.uk To pay by cheque get an application form (FP95) from your pharmacy or go to www.dh.gov.uk/helpwithhealthcosts The FP95 tells you what to do.

Do you need a refund? If you are unsure if you are entitled to free prescriptions you should pay for the prescription item(s) and ask for a receipt form FP57. **You must get the FP57 form when you pay for the item(s), you cannot get the form later.** If you find you didn't have to pay, you can claim your money back up to 3 months after paying. The FP57 tells you what to do.

Patient Representative. If you are unable to collect your prescription yourself, someone can take your completed form for you. You must complete **Part 1**. Your representative must complete **Parts 2 and 3. Anyone who collects a Schedule 2 or 3 controlled drug must sign the box in Part 1 when they collect the item(s)** and provide proof of identity if requested.

Data collection. Information about the prescription items on this form will be processed centrally to pay monies due to the pharmacist, doctor or appliance contractor for the items they have supplied to you. The NHS will also use the information to analyse what has been prescribed and the cost. The Counter Fraud and Security Management Service, a division of the NHS Business Services Authority, may use information from this form to prevent and detect fraud and incorrectness in the NHS.

Penalty Charges. If it is found that you should have paid for your prescription items, you will face penalty charges and may be prosecuted under the powers introduced by the Health Act 1999. Routine checks are carried out on exemption claims including some where proof may have been shown. You may be contacted in the course of such checks.

MURPHY, Sean (Mr)

NHS Number: **420 112 3871**   EMIS Number: **8071**

7 Lune Street, Saltburn-By-The-Sea, TS12 1JU

Citalopram 20mg tablets   [:

use as directed, 112 tablet
Last Issue: 08-May-2014 (4/6)   Next Issue Due: 09-May-2014

this book have attempted to open up critical debate around 'discipline', its meanings, its potential to be seen in alternative ways, and its potential to contribute to alternative futures. The contributions to this volume emerge from multiple theoretical positions, and although perhaps 'dominated' by critiques derived from the application of Foucault's work, includes voices drawing on theorists such as Wallerstein, Girard, Bauman, international relations theory, Kant, Deleuze, and Rose albeit sometimes more obviously than others. As we noted at the beginning of this introduction, this book does not intend to contribute to the 'how-to' literature on classroom discipline; it provides no magic solution for teachers; and makes no claim to offer recipes or easy solutions to perceived discipline problems in schools. Rather, this book sets out to encourage us to re-examine 'discipline', to look at it again, from outside its taken-for-granted home in educational psychology. This book seeks to trouble and challenge our ways of thinking about 'discipline', to provoke us to consider what it is we do in the name of 'discipline', and to what effect. We hope you agree that the contributions to this volume incite the reader to rethink 'discipline', provoking a reconsideration of its problems, politics, and possibilities.

References

Branson, J., & Miller, D. (1991). Beyond individualism: A post-structuralist critique of current approaches to school discipline. In M. N. Lovegrove & R. Lewis (Eds.), *Classroom Discipline* (pp. 173–195). Melbourne: Longman Cheshire.

Deleuze, G. (1992). Postcript on the societies of control. *October*, 59, 3–7.

Dewey, J. (1916). *Democracy and Education*. New York: The Free Press.

Edwards, C. H. (2008). *Classroom Discipline and Management* (5 ed.). Hoboken, NJ: John Wiley & Sons.

Ford, M. (2003). Unveiling technologies of power in classroom organization practice. *Educational Foundations*, 17(2). 5–27.

Foucault, M. (1972). *The Archeology of Knowledge and the Discourse on Language* (S. A. M. Smith, Trans.). New York: Pantheon.

Foucault, M. (1979a). *Discipline and Punish: The Birth of the Prison* (A. Sheridan, Trans.). London: Penguin Books.

Foucault, M. (1979b). Governmentality. *Ideology & Consciousness*, 1979(5), 5–21.

Foucault, M. (1979c). *The History of Sexuality volume 1: An Introduction* (Vol. One). London: Penguin Books.

Foucault, M. (1980). *Power/Knowledge: Selected Interviews and Other Writings*, 1972–1977 (Gordon, Colin ed.). Hertfordshire: The Harvester Press Limited.

Freire, P. (1975). *Pedagogy of the Opressed* (M. B. Ramos, Trans.). Ringwood, Vic, Australia: Penguin Education, Penguin Books Ltd.

Gore, J. M., & Parkes, R. J. (2008). On the mistreatment of management. In A. Phelan & J. Sumsion (Eds.), *Critical Readings in Teacher Education: Provoking Absences* (pp. 45–60). Rotterdam: Sense Publishers.

Graham, L. (2007). Speaking of "disorderly" objects: A poetics of pedagogical discourse. *Discourse*, 28(1), 1–20.

Hart, D. (2001). Slip, sliding away: A critical discourse anaylsis of teacher conceptualisations of discipline and behaviour management. In P. Singh & E. McWilliam (Eds.), *Designing Educational Research: Theories, Methods and Practices* (pp. 45–57). Falxton, Qld: Post Pressed.

Kamler, B. (1994). Shaping up nicely: The formation of schoolgirls and schoolboys in the first month of school. A report to the Gender Equity and Curriculum Reform Project, Department of Employment, Education and Training. Canberra, ACT: Australian Government Publication Service.

Kohn, A. (2001). *Beyond Discipline: From Compliance to Community.* Upper Saddle River, NJ: Prentice Hall, Inc.

Laws, C., & Davies, B. (2000). Poststructuralist theory in practice: Working with "behaviourally disturbed" children. *Qualitative Studies in Education,* 13(3), 205–221.

Millei, Z. J. (2005). The discourse of control: Disruption and Foucault in an early childhood classroom. *Contemporary Issues in Early Childhood,* 6(2), 128–139.

Millei, Z. J. (2007). *Controlling or guiding students—what's the difference? A critique of classroom approaches to discipline.* Paper presented at the 2007 AARE Conference Fremantle, Fremantle, WA, Australia. www.aare.edu.au/07pap/mil07410.pdf

Porter, L. (2007). *Student Behaviour: Theory and Practice for Teachers* (3rd ed.). Crows Nest, NSW: Allen & Unwin.

Porter, L. (2008). *Young children's behaviour: Practical approaches for caregivers and teachers* (3rd ed.). Marrickville, NSW: Elsevier Australia.

Raby, R. (2005). Polite, well-dressed and on time: Secondary school conduct codes and the production of docile citizens. *The Canadian Review of Sociology and Anthropology,* 42(1), 71–92.

Simpson, B. (2000). Regulation and resistance: Children's embodiment during primary–secondary school transition. In A. Prout (Ed.), *The Body, Childhood and Society* (pp. 60–78). Basingstoke: Macmillan.

Slee, R. (1995). *Changing Theories and Practices of Discipline.* London and Washington, DC: The Falmer Press.

Slee, R. (Ed.). (1992). *Discipline in Australian Public Education.* Hawthorn, Vic: The Australian Council for Educational Research Ltd.

Southgate, E. (2003). *Remembering School: Mapping Continuities in Power, Subjectivity & Emotion in Stories of School Life.* New York: Peter Lang.

United Nations High Commissioner for Human Rights (1989) Convention on the Rights of the Child. Retrieved August, 17, 2007, from http://www2.ohchr,org/english/law/crc.htm

Watkins, M. (2005). The erasure of habit: Tracing the pedagogic body. *Discourse: Studies in the Cultural Politics of Education,* 26(2), 167–181.

Watkins, M., & Noble, G. (2008). *Cultural Practices and Learning: Diversity, Discipline and Dispositions in Schooling.* Penrith South, NSW: University of Western Sydney.

Wilson, P. S. (1971). *Interest and Discipline in Education.* London: Routledge and Kegan Paul.

Chapter II

Is It (Still) Useful to Think About Classroom Discipline as Control?

An Examination of the 'Problem of Discipline'

Zsuzsa Millei

Introduction

The verb 'discipline' in classroom discipline approaches is understood predominantly in functionalist terms as a form of regulation or control to create and maintain order (Slee, 1995). Power associated with ideas of regulation and control in this context is thought about in structuralist terms, which is possessed and represents a powerful will over the powerless. In this chapter first I make a case that this way of thinking about discipline constructs a central problem that I term in this chapter the 'problem of discipline'. This problem is identified by all approaches of classroom discipline, and they all attempt to address and overcome this problem. The 'problem of discipline' revolves around the opposing ideas of students' freedom/autonomy versus teachers' dominance/control that constructs an axis between maximum freedom and maximum control according to the 'personal power' the teacher exerts and the 'personal power' the students have (Porter, 2007). In this way, laissez-faire approaches to discipline are located on the maximum freedom end, while autocratic approaches on the opposite end (for a graph look at Porter, 2007, p. 19). Other approaches are also lined up on this axis according to the level of freedom they allow for students as well as the teacher control they carry.

With the strong entrenchment of the prospects of democracy, social justice and rights, those approaches are considered as more desirable that endow students with autonomy and freedom. Drawing on students' rational autonomy, self-regulation seems to be the key to students' freedom and is evaluated as more desirable and passionately promoted by theorists (e.g., Francis, 1975; T. Gordon, 1974; Kohn, 1996; Rogers, 1969). The 'problem of discipline', in this way, fashions the provision of students' freedom as desirable and 'control' as negative or repressive. The control end of the axis is considered so problematical by some, that guidance theorists decided to delete the word 'discipline' from their vocabulary (Gartrell, 1998; Kohn, 1996; Porter, 2003). Control is understood in relation to the 'problem of discipline' as externally applied, devoid of logical or moral force and as an impediment in the learning process. The idea of dominance is also implicit in this problem and is thought about as subjection to the will of authority (Wilson, 1971). Dominance and control appears as entangled, therefore in this context freedom is positioned as the opposite to control and dominance, and is described as "the ability and determination to regulate one's life by rules which one has accepted [freely I would add] for oneself" (Peters, 1966, p. 197). Thus, the idea of rational autonomy presumes that external control ceased.

Critiques of classroom discipline approaches also target them at the 'problem of discipline'. These critiques centre upon the failed fulfilment of principles of humanist morality, such as the principles of rational autonomy and freedom of the individual (e.g., Balson, 1991; Kohn, 1996; Rogers, 1969). The main argument of these critiques is that making compliant students through discipline is not a democratic, just or humane way to create order (e.g., Dollar, 1972; Gartrell, 1998; Gordon, 1974; Kohn, 1996; Porter, 2008, 2007, 2003, 1996). While accepting the necessity of such measures in particular cases, these critiques are questioning the high level of control teachers exercise (Charles, 1981; Glasser, 1992; A. Gordon & Browne, 1996; T. Gordon, 1974; Porter, 1996). Democratic discipline approaches, such as Rogers' (1969), not only deliver this critique but also immediately suggest strategies to address this point of criticism. These strategies attempt to reduce teachers' dominance by promoting self-regulation, which, according to Rogers, immediately turns students more 'humane'. Their central tenet is to enable children's freedom through social support, so they are able to regulate themselves according to their own 'individual order'. Guidance theories strive to reduce teachers' dominance to authoritative guidance and as a result to provide students with more autonomy (Gartrell, 1998; Kohn, 1996; Porter, 2003).

The 'problem of discipline' sits at the heart of discipline approaches and shapes the ways theorists of classroom discipline understand and think about discipline and the ways teachers develop practices to maintain order in classrooms. It also constructs particular understandings of power relations that are based on a structuralist understanding of power and forms ideas about 'good' teachers and students; it shapes how they understand and relate to themselves. This chapter, after discussing the particular take up of the 'problem of discipline' by particular discipline approaches, questions whether this idea is still useful to understand classroom discipline.

The chapter develops an analysis using Foucault's understanding of transformations of power and government. This analysis reveals that the quest to produce discipline approaches that aim to solve the 'problem of discipline' actually imposes greater tutelage over students in insidious ways. It is argued that the negative view of 'discipline' as controlling and dominating is predicated on a utopian quest for freedom. Rather than freeing up students from dominance such quests impose a form of control that is masked in students' assumed freedom and autonomy. This line of argument is discussed in four steps. I first (1) briefly outline the recent perspective on classroom discipline approaches and sketch their take on the 'problem of discipline'. Then (2) I focus, following Foucault, on the problem of power and government and their conceptualisation in regards to the school as a pastoral institution of the administrative state and classroom discipline and argue (3) that discipline approaches function as part of a specific power-apparatus. Finally (4) I conclude that rethinking classroom discipline along Foucauldian lines places discipline under a new light that demonstrates its complexity and dynamism besides those readings that are available through the use of the 'problem of discipline'.

Unearthing the 'Problem of Discipline' in Discipline Approaches

Questioning or inquiring into discipline approaches on the 'problem of discipline' has been prevalent since their historical emergence. The end of the Second World War was marked with the production of a number of classroom discipline approaches that aimed to replace coercion and physical punishment in classrooms. These approaches appeared partly as a reaction to the severe human rights violations of the war and sought to create rational and autonomous individuals who were able to resist autocratic control and dominance (Slee, 1995). Intertwined with the creation of democratic or liberal forms of education, such as child-centred pedagogy (Fendler, 2001), discipline approaches were also aimed to free students from the control of the teacher.

Approaches to classroom discipline can be divided into three distinct categories based on the ways in which they encounter the 'problem of discipline': interventionists, non-interventionists and interactionalists (Charles, 1981; Edwards, 1993; Levin & Nolan, 1991; Lovegrove & Lewis, 1991; Wolfgang & Glickman, 1986). Interventionist approaches, such as those of Dobson (1970), Canter and Canter (1992), Jones (1987a, 1987b) or Rogers' (1991), target students' behaviours and self-regulation, and subject these to training through certain practices. Among these practices are the establishment of behavioural rules, giving out praise and rewards, the acknowledgment of good deeds, administering punishment in the form of 'time-out', trips to the principal and so on. The type of self-discipline taught by these approaches is exhibited in a behavioural accommodation to external rules. All these techniques utilize a form of power that is conceptualised as located on the teachers' behalf and to which students have to submit. Critiques of these approaches often target these strategies by using the 'problem of discipline'. They argue that these approaches necessitate a teacher-centred approach to discipline that limits students' autonomy and subjects students to teachers' dominance and control (Lewis, 1991).

Interactionalist approaches carry an outwardly democratic style to discipline. They require the teacher to place the needs of the group as a whole above the needs of individual students and the teacher (Levin & Nolan, 1991). Two major discipline approaches can be categorised here: Neo-Adlerian Theory, which relies on "Adlerian/ Dreikursian interactionalist strategy" (Balson, 1991, p. 23); and Control theory, which presents a whole school approach to discipline devised by Glasser (1985; 1986).

In the Neo-Adlerian classroom discipline theory, two basic principles of individual psychology are evident. First, this theory upholds that there is a desire (fundamental need) in all humans to belong to a social group where the group is built on reciprocal relationships (interaction) and members accommodate to each other. Second, that every action of the individual is seen to be as rational, purposeful and "consistent with a chosen manner of belonging…[which are] attention, power, revenge, or withdrawal" (Balson, 1991, p.28). The Neo-Adlerian discipline theory is more concerned with the intention (motivation) to belong than the behaviour. Discipline, according to these theorists, focuses on how to change the way the individual fulfils his or her intentions without interfering with others or others' needs. It strives to help students in making 'more desirable' decisions regarding the fulfilment of their needs and to exhibit 'appropriate' behaviours in line with social values and norms (Balson, 1991). In sum, this theory builds on the rational autonomy of the individual student and discipline focuses on the creation of an environment and social relations in which the student has the possibility to develop his/her own order in line with social norms and values and acts autonomously or freely according to that order.

The other theory that belongs to the interactionalist group, Control theory (Glasser, 1986) conceptualises disruption in the classroom as caused by a lack of sufficient relationships between students and teacher. Relationship, according to Glasser (1986), is based on rapport that teaches the student to take responsibility for this relationship. Disruption also arises if schools leave students' emotional needs unfulfilled or if they leave students unmotivated. Emotional needs are defined as love, power (need to control what happens to oneself), freedom (need of independence from others' control) and fun (Glasser, 1986). Control theory understands power and freedom as residing in the individual. With this manoeuvre, this theory not only maintains the desirability to fulfil students' need for freedom and power, but also claims that there is a 'natural balance' of power and freedom, which was disturbed by the teachers' dominance and that is the reason why disruption occurs.

According to interactionalist approaches, the teacher should act as a leader rather than as a boss, hence power is supposedly reduced and dominance is tamed. Being a leader, the teacher's superiority is guaranteed by expertise rather than power (Gordon, 1974). The classroom order is kept through 'reasonable' but few rules that rational and autonomous individuals can accept as their own (Glasser, 1992). The teacher passes on to students 'mental tools' to enable them to solve problems rationally and effectively by themselves in consideration of the others and by following liberal democratic values (Balson, 1991; Glasser, 1992). These values are: mutual respect, student participation in decision-making, promotion of student self-discipline, freedom and responsibility (Balson, 1991; Dreikurs & Cassel, 1990; Glasser, 1992).

Non-interventionist approaches use a person-centred (Neville, 1991) or student-oriented model (Lewis, 1991) to classroom discipline. They believe, that "students must have the primary responsibility for controlling their own behavior" and they are "inherently capable" of doing that if given the opportunity to do so (Levine & Nolan, 1991, p. 93). The classroom environment is designed to facilitate self-control. Students develop for themselves 'reasonable' guidelines and classroom rules with the facilitation of the teacher. Proponents see the control of outward behaviour as a necessary but insufficient method. In the resolution of disruptive behaviour the teacher facilitates individually each student to self-monitor and regulate their feelings and thoughts according to their needs and preferences. Some of the better-known theorists are Ginott's (1972) positive communication model, Berne's (1964) transactional analysis model or Kohn's (1996) guidance approach to discipline. Non-interventionist approaches transformed discipline from getting students to comply through the domination of the teacher to producing "morally sophisticated people who think for themselves and care about others" (Kohn, 1996, p. 62), thus acting as rational autonomous and free individuals ready to participate in democratic societies.

Each of these ways of approaching classroom discipline, however, shares some common weaknesses. Firstly, they approach discipline as a zero-sum game. They construct autonomy as 'personal power' possessed by the individual that is greater if domination is kept to a minimum. In this way, by reducing his or her domination over the student the teacher can actually pass on some of her or his power to the students by which they become empowered and more autonomous. Secondly, each category assumes that the rationale and aims of discipline revolve around a freedom–control binary. Proponents and critiques of these approaches consider domination as less desirable, and they strive to free students through different avenues and strategies. These are the utilisation of students' self-discipline, the management of their intentions to belong, the fulfilment of their needs, or the monitoring of their thoughts and feelings. Through these strategies students' autonomy and freedom are ensured while order in the classroom is maintained. Thirdly, this grouping of classroom discipline approaches adopts a Weberian understanding of power as the ability to carry through and to enforce one's own will in a social relation (Weber, 1947). In this understanding power is linked with dominance as an ability to bind obedient people. Power, according to this perspective, is based on and in an individual and his/her ability to use it. Freedom is conceptualised as the absence of power and as an ability of the individual to act on one's own without outside determination. Freedom here is understood as the condition of autonomy. An autonomous individual, consequently conducts one's self according to a self-formulated 'law' of reason and rationality that corresponds with desired ways of being. This conceptualisation of power and freedom allows for the construction of the binary between the opposing states of the obedient individual (be that of trained or automatic obedience), and the self-regulated, rational, autonomous individual. Built on this binary, the problem of 'discipline' repeatedly returns in approaches and critiques of classroom discipline in different formats but with the same quest to free students from teachers' control.

Using Foucault to Rethink the 'Problem of Discipline'

By utilizing an alternative view of power developed by Foucault (1980; 1982), a new perspective opens up to understand classroom discipline. In Foucault's view (1982), power is performed rather than achieved, and it is not simply a form of oppression or repression, moreover "individuals are the vehicles of power, not its point of application"

(Foucault, 1980, p. 98). Therefore, power implies the necessity of 'free' actors for whom the field of possibilities is brought to bear upon. In this way power is productive, something that brings about behaviour and events (Foucault, 1979c). It is conceptualised as relations where "these relations are rooted deep in the social nexus" (Foucault, 1982, p. 222). Since power is not a direct action upon others' conduct, in his later work on governmentality Foucault uses the term 'conduct of conduct' (2008, 2007, 1979b) to describe the exercise of authority, such as that by a government or school or classroom teacher, as the means "to structure the possible field of actions of others" (Foucault, 1982, pp. 220–21).

Wielding power is different from domination. In domination, power is exercised to incapacitate or repress the dominated in order to serve certain ends. In contrast, Foucault sees power as working though the freedom of individuals. Relations of power are always present, and they are only possible if there is a certain freedom or symmetry on both sides. Thus relations of power are "mobile, reversible, and unstable" networks infusing the lives of humans and organizations within which they operate (Foucault, 1994a, p. 292). Foucault (1994c) calls asymmetrical power relations 'domination', such as in the case of marital relationships in the 18th century, where the women had few options to resist the husband's dominations (for example, refusing sex or 'pilfering' money) and these never reversed the situation.

Relations of power are understood in this perspective as productive in relation to the formation of conduct and subjectisation that operate through forms of knowledge, discourses and particular techniques. In *The Order of Things,* Foucault (1970) examines how and in what particular historical moment people became the object of knowledge. By the late 19th century the 'human sciences', such as psychology, philosophy or sociology, produced systems of classification that defined the subjects of these sciences. Through making people the object of scientific knowledge, these sciences produced vast knowledges and discourses about their subjects in order to talk about and deal with these subjects. In the twin processes of objectivation and subjectisation, individuals are also made the subjects of these disciplinary knowledges because individuals make sense of themselves by referring to various bodies of knowledge. Objectivation and subjectisation form a "reciprocal bond" that Foucault calls "truth games" (1994b, p. 315). In these 'truth games', knowledge is produced that "may be considered valid or invalid, winning or losing" (Foucault, 1994b, p. 295). Scientific knowledges that are considered valid or winning have a normalizing power that regulates individuals to work to meet the criteria of being 'valid' and 'winning' through making themselves subjects of these knowledges (Foucault, 1979a). Disciplinary power (the power scientific knowledges wield) that is carried through this normalization impacts on the individual's body and behaviour. It makes the individual regulate her own conduct, it creates new comportments of the body and individuals, it produces novel aptitudes, it increases the individual's performance and multiplies its capacities in order to increase ones utility (Foucault, 1979a). Disciplinary power and subjectisation have a principal role in producing governable individuals by making them docile and by increasing their utility.

In the education context of the classroom then, individuals, teachers and pupils alike, play a part in power's operations where there is action upon oneself in an uneven field of regulated possibilities (Rose, 1999). In this way, government also has an ethical sense, meaning how to conduct oneself appropriately to a situation, thus it also embraces the control of someone's own behaviour, passion or instinct (Rose, 1999). The government of the self is "an exercise of the self on the self by which one attempts to develop and transform oneself, and to attain to a certain mode of being" (Foucault, 1994b, p. 282). If self-government is linked to ethics in this way, then it entails the idea of freedom, the free creation of one's self. According to Foucault, ethics is "the conscious *[réfléchie]* practice of freedom" (Foucault, 1994b, p. 284). Government, by shaping one's conduct through mapping out possibilities for action, attempts to shape how the individual practices one's freedom, but government is not constitutive of freedom. It entails, therefore, the possibility that the 'governed' might act or think differently.

In order to analyse how this specific form of government or governmentality came about and utilizes disciplinary knowledges, and to tie it in with the emergence of schooling, a particular type of administrative-pastoral institution, some ideas of Foucault on political forms of power need to be further elaborated. Governmentality "marks the emergence of a distinctively new form of thinking about the exercising of power in certain societies" from the 16th century (Dean, 1999, p. 19). In his lecture series on governmentality, Foucault (1979b, 2007, 2008) analyses writings on the 'art of government' during the past four hundred years. He counterposes and typifies the varied types of government and outlines a long movement from sovereignty to the 'governmentalized state'. Sovereignty, as he argues, is exercised on territory and its inhabitants with the use of a divine or natural knowledge and its aim is to retain the principality of the sovereign (Foucault, 1979b, 2007). In contrast, government is concerned with the management of the population as a collection of individuals who can be described by particular characteristics or classifications; hence the role of disciplinary knowledge in the classification and management of population. By managing the population, a government's aim is to increase the population's well-being or the common good. The goals of this management can be broken down into specific finalities, that the population multiplies, its wealth increases, assurances are made for general health and well-being and thus, government is fundamentally different to sovereign power in their ends (Foucault, 1979b).

The governmentalisation of the State is born out of the ancient Hebraic conceptions of pastoral power modelled on the shepherd-flock relations during the 17th and 18th centuries (Foucault, 1988). According to the pastoral theme, as it is applied to the 'art of government', the shepherd/God wields power over a flock and gathers them together, guides and leads them, thus they have a specific relation. The 'pastoral technology' in the management of 'men' *(sic)* has developed in line with its three aspects. First, the complex moral ties, where the shepherd is *responsible* not only for each and every sheep's life, but for their *actions* as well. Second, there is a concern of the flock's *obedience* to the shepherd. The sheep must permanently submit to the pastor because it is the sheep's will. Third, the relationship implies a *specific knowledge* between the pastor and each sheep, which in its particularity individualizes each sheep—its needs, its actions and its soul—with the help of the instruments of *self-examination and conscience*. Thus, by this knowledge a link is created between responsibility, obedience, knowledge of oneself and confession to someone else (Foucault, 1988).

Compulsory schooling in the governmentalised state was neither implemented as the hegemonic 'will to govern' nor to serve the principles of emancipating the working classes or realising the ideal of human development (Hunter 1994). Rather, as Hunter (1994) proposes, schooling surfaced as a "tactically improvised institution... serving a mixture of spiritual and worldly ends" (p. xxii). The school, according to this conceptualisation, is an apparatus of the governmental or administrative state (Foucault, 2007) that deployed pastoral pedagogy to serve governmental ends. Consequently, the school as Hunter (1996) argues, and I would add classroom discipline approaches as a technology of the school, "can neither be understood nor reformed as the expression of a coherent set of ethical or political principles" (p. 90), such as the realization of a democratic politics or the provision of liberal education.

This is the context within which I re-consider the 'problem of discipline'. In what follows, I argue that subsequent discipline approaches, that appeared as innovations to address the 'problem of discipline', are themselves trapped within the problematic of the administration of classroom discipline. While claiming to provide more freedom and equality to students in theory, they in effect impose greater regulation and pastoral tutelage. Consequently, egalitarian and dominance-free discipline became impossible because the closer approaches and practices get to these principles the more subtle forms of control and tutelage are imposed. The problem is the nature of the bureaucratic-pastoral school that makes it impossible to realize 'egalitarian' or liberatory classroom discipline. Such egalitarian or liberatory goals remain as utopian as the goal of seeking a domain in which power does not operate (Foucault, 1988, pp. 145–46).

Understanding Classroom Discipline Differently

It was established so far that classroom discipline belongs to a specific power apparatus of the school, which attempts to realize the formation of a particular self-reflecting comportment of subjects to make students available for government. It needs to be noted here, however, that the self-reflecting subject is not given by nature, nor is it "the general form of human being", but rather "is a particular comportment of the person, formed within a highly specialized relationship of self-examination and guidance, self-control and obedience" (Hunter, 1993, p. 89). In this structured space, educators are like shepherds. They exercise pastoral care over their charges by drawing on expert knowledges *(savoirs)* to initiate individuals into the arts of self-concern and self-regulation (Foucault, 1994d). The expert knowledge compiled in classroom discipline approaches is a complex means to form capacities and subjectivities of individuals. The (pastoral) pedagogy attached to classroom discipline delivers principles for individuals to do "ethical work" on themselves in the form of practices of "self-problematization...for taking an interest in [them]selves as the subject of [their] conduct" and to "'work on the self of the self'...disciplining and comporting themselves as the responsible agents of their own personhood" (Hunter, 1996, p. 158). Through this problematisation, individuals learn to relate to themselves as the subjects of their own conducts and capacities and learn to form their subjectivities.

Interventionist approaches translate punishment (coercion) to a specific language utilising behaviourist notions of 'stimulus', 'response' and 'logical consequences' in ways Skinner's (1968) theory did, for example. Slee (1995) argues that through this translation, punishment or coercive regulation was 'tamed' and a scientific knowledge and method to teach students self-regulation was born. Through the problematisation of particular behaviour deemed inappropriate in classrooms and the administration of consequences, individuals learn to monitor and evaluate their behaviour and to relate to themselves as the subject of their behaviour. Thus, if one performs 'good' behaviour, one is considered as 'good' and understands one's self as 'good'. The specific pastoral pedagogy of interventionist approaches promotes the constant self-surveillance and self-discipline of students' own behaviour according to certain behavioural norms. It normalises students' conduct and forms their subjectivities through their concern regarding the self.

It is argued by advocates of interventionist approaches that if a person acquires self-discipline the teacher control decreases and ultimately diminishes. It is also believed that if students self-regulate themselves, power is not applied. Yet the transformation of a subject's capacity to act is not possible without exercising power (Foucault, 1979c). Self-discipline or self-government proceeds according to certain knowledge about "a number of rules of acceptable conduct or of principles" and also knowing one's self, therefore it is principled and not free of power (Foucault, 1994b, p. 285). Interventionist approaches, if examined from this perspective, structure a field of possibilities for 'appropriate' behaviour, assign principles of behaviour and mobilise students to perform self-examination and self-regulation of their behaviour, and to understand themselves according to this knowledge. Thus, power is exercised, it is exercised to shape actions towards desired directions and to form a particular comportment of the individual, the 'self-reflective' subject.

Interactionist and non-interventionist approaches utilize psychological and counselling knowledge. These knowledges constitute a different repertoire of particular faculties and capacities available to individuals than interventionist approaches do. The central set of faculties developed here draws on the idea of 'rational autonomy'. An autonomous individual, according to this idea, has the capacities that enable one to create one's own order and is capable to reflect on, monitor and accommodate one's actual conduct within this order. Conduct here involves much more than behaviour. It contains intentions, needs, feelings and desires and consequently, classroom discipline approaches construct and aim to train these capacities in order to avoid or deal with disruption and to produce obedient subjects.

For example, through negotiation and problem solving, students are taught to explore and monitor their inner ideas, feelings, desires and wishes, and to align those with their partners' in negotiation. Through this process subjects are mobilised to "become active participants in their own social and ethical development" (Kohn, 1996, p. 77). With these approaches the work of the self moves into new territories—to inner ideas, feelings and wishes—and targets directly the individual's morality. By training one's faculties, the individual increases the potential to acquire an appropriate moral code and to conduct one's self according to that. Through this improvement that aligns morality closer and closer with a presumed ideal, as proponents of these approaches claim it, the individual incrementally gains more freedom from outward regulation or the 'facilitation' of the teacher. Power works through these approaches by creating a field of possibilities by assigning moral principles, such as the ones interactionalist approaches do: the principle of social solidarity, respect, responsibility and so on (Balson, 1991; T. Gordon, 1974).

Non-interventionist approaches invent and utilise different capacities again. While interactionalist approaches also draw on knowledges attached to counselling, non-interventionist approaches widen the range of possible targets for personal self-reflection and their scope to the inner, self-guided development of the individual. They target individuals' ethical and moral self-development itself in such a way that autonomy becomes an 'artefact', not something that is possessed by the individual (Hindess, 1996, p. 73). Individuals do not only work to align their morality with external codes of conduct or social allegiances, but particular capacities are talked into being by these approaches to make individuals capable of engineering their own individual ethics and moral development by continuously reflecting on their own conduct. In this way, the student understands herself or himself by reflecting on the deeds he or she did and measures that to moral principles and devises ways for improvements. Personal improvement and continuous self-actualisation (enterprise) appear as intertwined. The individual understands him/herself not only as reflecting an outside morality or the individual's own, but someone whose morality and ethics are in need of continuous improvement.

The continuous improvement of one's ethics and morality is a conscious practice of freedom that happens through a constant monitoring and evaluating in relation to external constraints. So free action is limited by a previous being that is rendered problematic or 'enslaving'. Consequently, continuous improvement is regulated by ideas of 'un-freedom' that are defined in relation to dominance. It is here that the usefulness of understanding classroom discipline in relation to the 'problem of discipline' becomes the most problematic. The principle of free self-realisation maintained by liberal education is best approximated by non-interventionist approaches that provide the greatest freedom to individuals by reducing teachers' dominance to a minimum. However, its principles were fulfilled not through the foundation of a humanist morality but by a constant measuring up and improving on the freedom that freedom from domination espoused. These approaches, thus, enabled the illusionary freedom of the individual from others' dominance and regulation. They actualised the individual to freely create him/herself against constraining relations that were constructed by classroom discipline in relation to the 'problem of discipline'. This illusionary freedom by turning to be instrumental enabled the regulation of individuals through their ethics, their free self-creation and self-induced development by non-interventionist approaches without the use of 'repressive' power. Individuals, however, were not freed from repression but rather freedom was created as an artefact by governmentalised institution of school. This freedom as an artefact provides avenues for the more subtle or insidious regulation of students through the very freedom they desire to reach.

Abandoning the 'Problem of Discipline'

The 'problem of discipline' is constructed through the interplaying of at least two ideas: a Weberian understanding of power and a perspective on freedom that understands it as a condition of rational autonomy. This problem produced critiques that demand more egalitarian or democratic relationships in classrooms and led to the development of innovative ways in disciplining students. By equalizing the power differential or aim to cease the application of power altogether in these relationships, critiques claim that a democratic form of discipline can be reached that enables and at the same time utilizes the rational autonomy of students. The prospect of egalitarian relationship, so they say, also makes this relationship more 'humane'. The quest for students' liberation from teacher control principled by democratic politics and liberatory education thus produced its own conception of 'equality'.

This study of classroom discipline approaches from the perspective offered by Foucault demonstrated the impossibility of a power-free relationship between students and teachers. This relationship is not only unequal but also is bound with shifting power relations where available discourses position and re-position the teacher and the student, as 'facilitator', 'leader' or 'counsellor' and as 'obedient', 'responsible', 'respectful' or 'self-creator'. Moreover, the utopian notion of 'equality' and freedom, as the ultimate goal of discipline approaches, are turned out to be by-products and ends in themselves. The use of 'equality' as an ideal intertwined with the 'problem of discipline' is better understood as a rationale of government that fashioned multiple shifts in the techniques applied to form 'certain kind of people' capable of self-regulating their own conduct. Furthermore, 'equality' between teachers and students is also impossible due to the unequal relationships inherent in pastoral pedagogy that classroom discipline inherited from the school.

I suggest moving away from those frameworks that examine and critique discipline approaches on the axis of the 'problem of discipline'. While the 'problem of discipline' is productive in producing new understandings, discourses and techniques of discipline, these remain contrived with the illusionary rationale of 'equality' and 'freedom'. The application of different perspectives has the potential to see discipline as unlinear, unpredictable and more complex, and that traverses distinctions between freedom and control or autonomy and repression. It also has the potential to depart from its humanistic framework to introduce new insights. A small body of literature has already explored discipline approaches from this new perspective and this book also continues this work. As I pointed out in this chapter the quest for 'equal relationships' that are embedded in discipline approaches has a limited scope and it also restricts the understanding and analysis of these approaches, the social relations they produce and the understandings of disruptive situations in classrooms. As has been demonstrated above, the perspective on power and governmentality developed by Foucault makes it possible to understand classroom discipline with greater complexity and dynamism. Investigations from this perspective enhance our understanding about the production of shifting power relations, their role in 'truth games' and the constitution of subjectivities in relation to those, and possible forms of resistance as well.

References

Balson, M. (1991). An interactive approach to classroom discipline. In M. N. Lovegrove & R. Lewis (Eds.), *Classroom discipline* (pp. 23–42). Melbourne: Longman Cheshire.

Berne, E. (1964). *Games people play: The psychology of human relationships.* Harmondsworth: Penguin.

Canter, L., & Canter, M. (1992). *Assertive discipline: Positive behaviour management for today's classroom.* Santa Monica, CA: Lee Canter and Associates.

Charles, C. (1981). *Building classroom discipline.* New York: Longman.

Dean, M. (1999). *Governmentality: Power and rule in modern society.* London; Thousand Oaks, CA: Sage.

Dobson, J. (1970). *Dare to discipline.* Eastbourne: Kingsway Publications.

Dollar, B. (1972). *Humanizing classroom discipline: A behavioural approach.* New York: Harper & Row Publishers.

Dreikurs, R., & Cassel, P. (1990). *Discipline without tears.* New York: Dutton.

Edwards, C. H. (1993). *Classroom discipline and management.* New York: Macmillan.

Fendler, L. (2001). Educating flexible souls: The construction of subjectivity through developmentality and interaction. In K. Hultqvist & G. Dahlberg (Eds.), *Governing the child in the new millennium* (pp. 119–142). New York & London: RoutledgeFalmer.

Foucault, M. (1970). *The order of things: An archaeology of the human sciences.* London: Routledge.

Foucault, M. (1979a). *Discipline and punish: The birth of the prison* (A. Sheridan, Trans.). London: Penguin Books.

Foucault, M. (1979b). Governmentality. *Ideology & Consciousness, 1979*(5), 5–21.

Foucault, M. (1979c). *The history of sexuality volume 1: An introduction* (Vol. One). London: Penguin Books.

Foucault, M. (1980). *Power/knowledge: Selected interviews and other writings, 1972–1977* (Gordon, C. ed.). Hertfordshire: The Harvester Press Limited.

Foucault, M. (1982). The subject and power. In H. Dreyfus & P. Rabinow (Eds.), *Michel Foucault: Beyond structuralism and hermeneutics* (pp. 208–227). Chicago: University of Chicago Press.

Foucault, M. (1988). The political technology of individuals. In L. M. Martin, H. Gutman & P. H. Hutton (Eds.), *Technologies of the self: A seminar with Michel Foucault* (pp. 145–162). London: Tavistock Publications.

Foucault, M. (1994a). *Michel Foucault: Power.* (R. Hurley, Trans. Faubion, James D. ed. Vol. Three). London: Penguin Books.

Foucault, M. (1994b). On the government of the living (R. Hurley, Trans.). In P. Rabinow

(Ed.), *Michel Foucault: Ethics subjectivity and truth* (Vol. One, pp. 81–86). London: Allen Lane, The Penguin Press.

Foucault, M. (1994c). Technologies of the self (R. Hurley, Trans.). In P. Rabinow (Ed.), *Michel Foucault: Ethics subjectivity and truth* (Vol. One, pp. 223–252). London: Allen Lane, The Penguin Press.

Foucault, M. (1994d). The ethics of the concern for the self as a practice of freedom (R. Hurley, Trans.). In P. Rabinow (Ed.), *Michel Foucault: Ethics subjectivity and truth* (Vol. One, pp. 281–302). London: Allen Lane, The Penguin Press.

Foucault, M. (2007). *Security, territory, population: Lectures at the College de France*. Houndmills, Basingstoke, Hampshire: Palgrave Macmillan.

Foucault, M. (2008) *The birth of biopolitics: Lectures at the Collège de France 1978–1979* (G. Burchell, Trans.). Houndmills, Basingstoke, Hampshire: Palgrave Macmillan.

Francis, P. (1975). *Beyond control? A study of discipline in the comprehensive school*. London: George Allen & Unwin.

Gartrell, D. (1998). *A guidance approach for the encouraging classroom* (2 ed.). Albany, New York: Delmar Publishers.

Ginott, H. G. (1972). *Teacher and child*. New York: Macmillan.

Glasser, W. (1985). *Control theory*. New York: Harper and Row.

Glasser, W. (1986). *Control theory in the classroom*. New York: Harper and Row.

Glasser, W. (1992). *The quality school* (second ed.). New York: Harper Perennial.

Gordon, A., & Browne, K. W. (1996). *Guiding young children in a diverse society*. Needham Hights, MA: Allyn & Bacon.

Gordon, T. (1974). *Teacher effectiveness training*. New York: Peter H. Wyden.

Hindess, B. (1996). Liberalism, socialism and democracy: Variations on a governmental theme. In A. Barry, T. Osborne & N. Rose (Eds.), *Foucault and political reason* (pp. 65–80). London: UCL Press Ltd.

Hunter, I. (1993). The pastoral bureaucracy: Towards a less principled understanding of state schooling. In D. Meredyth & D. Tyler (Eds.), *Child and citizen: Genealogies of schooling and subjectivity* (pp. 237–288). Griffith University: Institute for Cultural Policy Studies, Faculty of Humanities.

Hunter, I. (1994). *Rethinking the school: Subjectivity, bureaucracy, criticism*. St Leonards, NSW Australia: Allen & Unwin Pty Ltd.

Hunter, I. (1996). Assembling the school. In A. Barry, T. Osborne & N. Rose (Eds.), *Foucault and political reason: Liberalism, neo-liberalism and rationalities of government* (pp. 143–166). London: UCL Press.

Jones, F. (1987a). *Positive classroom discipline*. New York: McGraw-Hill.

Jones, F. (1987b). *Positive classroom instruction*. New York: McGraw-Hill.

Kohn, A. (1996). *Beyond discipline: From compliance to community*. Alexandria, VA: Association for Supervision and Curriculum Development.

Levin, J., & Nolan, J. (1991). *Principles of classroom management: A hierarchical approach*. Englewood Cliffs, NJ: Prentice Hall.

Lewis, R. (1991). *The discipline dilemma*. Hawthorn, Vic: The Australian Council of Educational Research Ltd.

Lovegrove, M. N., & Lewis, R. (Eds.). (1991). *Classroom discipline.* Melbourne: Longman Cheshire.

Neville, B. (1991). The person-centred approach to classroom management. In M. N. Lovegrove & R. Lewis (Eds.), *Classroom discipline* (pp. 3–22). Melbourne: Longman Cheshire.

Peters, R. S. (1966). *Ethics and education.* London: Allen & Unwin.

Porter, L. (1996). *Student behaviour: Theory and practice for teachers.* St Leonards, NSW: Allen and Unwin.

Porter, L. (2003). *Young children's behaviour: Practical approaches for caregivers and teachers (2 ed.).* Marrickville, NSW: Elsevier Australia.

Porter, L. (2007). *Student behaviour: Theory and practice for teachers* (3rd ed.). Crows Nest, NSW: Allen & Unwin.

Porter, L. (2008). *Young children's behaviour: Practical approaches for caregivers and teachers* (3rd ed.). Marrickville, NSW: Elsevier Australia.

Rogers, W. (1991). Decisive discipline. In M. N. Lovegrove & R. Lewis (Eds.), *Classroom discipline* (pp. 43–66). Melbourne: Longman Cheshire.

Rose, N. (1999). *Powers of freedom: Reframing political thought.* Cambridge: Cambridge University Press.

Skinner, B. F. (1968). *The technology of teaching.* New York: Appleton Century Crofts.

Slee, R. (1995). *Changing theories and practices of discipline.* London and Washington, DC: The Falmer Press.

Weber, M. (1947). *The theory of social and economic organization.* Glencoe, IL: Free Press.

Wilson, P. S. (1971). *Interest and discipline in education.* London: Routledge and Kegan Paul.

Wolfgang, C., & Glickman, C. (1986). *Solving discipline problems* (2 ed.). Boston: Allyn and Bacon.

Chapter III

Embodied Logic: Understanding Discipline through Constituting the Subjects of Discipline

Zsuzsa Millei and Rebecca Raby

Introduction

This chapter encounters the ways in which thinking about discipline in schools is connected to scientific and popular ideas of human nature, the 'process' of growing up, constitutions of 'the child' and 'the adolescent', and ideas of the modern subject and citizen. It examines some of the ideas that conjoin to inform theories, shape codes of conduct and create discourses of classroom discipline. One of the aims of this examination is to demonstrate the 'polyvalent' nature of classroom discipline discourses (Foucault, 1977). The other aim is to draw attention to their utilitarian use by individual teachers that produces embodied logics, that is, situation-specific, value-laden, shifting and diverse logics, to understand young persons as subjects of discipline and reasons for their disciplining. We will argue that to create this logic might be due to teachers' desiring to be rational or to be looked upon as making rational decisions in regards to issues with indiscipline. In this way, it is possible that this desire for rationality is what makes teachers' decisions sometimes illogical or contradictory.

The vast literature on behavior management presents classroom discipline as governed by principles (theories) and practiced through techniques. Specific discipline theories are commonly composed from coherent sets of ideas that guide the understanding of disruption and disruptive students and are translated into practices of discipline to maintain order in the classroom (Porter, 1996). Here, we introduce 'on the ground' discipline as less principled and more complex. We highlight the ways in which this complexity forms possible temporal and situation-specific statements through which teachers might understand and address students and their misdemeanours. We also study some examples of teachers' temporary assemblages of multifaceted statements, of their 'embodied logic', with which they understand particular codes of conduct and their rationale and necessity. The analysis reveals how these logics are complex, shifting, often inconsistent, contain incompatible ideas and, therefore, are less based on clear principles than theories of disciplines advocated through classroom management literature.

Classroom discipline is understood in our perspective as a technology of the school to deliver social training and to regulate the student population (Hunter, 1994). Consequently classroom discipline approaches are imbued with power and draw on scientific knowledges about individuals and their actions that are mostly borrowed from psychology (Foucault, 1979). Teachers utilise these scientific knowledges of classroom discipline to understand and regulate students and disruption. They also employ technologies and techniques, such as conditioning or forms of counselling, to regulate students that were invented by experts in these fields. Most discipline theories outline a coherent set of ideas about order and disruption, the individual as a subject of discipline and the individual's capacities, often through such scientific knowledges. In practices of classroom discipline, however, teachers use a grab-bag of such available scientific statements about individuals and disruptions, mixed with other discourses, that coagulate to form a particular situation-specific and flexible logic. Through the consequent lens, disorder and disruptive acts are understood and teachers devise strategies accordingly to (re-)create classroom order (Slee, 1995). We demonstrate below, that while particular discipline theories commonly carry a unified subject, in their applications they often draw on multifaceted ideas about 'the child', 'the adolescent', 'growing up', 'development', 'discipline' and so on that are reorganised in a logic that serves to address given scenarios. In other words, these particular and temporary assemblages of statements are flexible and mobile, adapt to situational shifts, and produce diverse ideas about the disciplined subjects and understandings of discipline.

This chapter first studies discourses of discipline theories in order to outline the ways in which they utilise scientific knowledges and produce possible understandings of the subjects of discipline and discipline itself. Then we move on to studying the individual logic school codes of conduct employed to maintain order and that teachers deploy to understand and deal with particular situations to extend the number of discourses under examination and to demonstrate the ways these assemblages play out. The data for this section is drawn from a multifaceted research project into school rules of conduct and disciplinary strategies conducted in several distinct regions of Ontario, Canada, between 2003 and 2009.[1] Finally, our discussion highlights the fundamentally complex and productive nature of these theories and what they might mean in regards to contemporary discipline.

Discipline Theories and Constituting the Subjects of Discipline

Approaches to discipline are intertwined with developmental discourses; discourses of 'the child' and 'the adolescent'; discourses of citizenship; and other pedagogical theories and practices. The assemblage of these discourses comprises a powerful technology to form certain kinds of subjects. While we limit our focus to these, we also note that there

---

[1]   This data is also used in Chapter Four and is described in detail there.

are many other discourses also at play in understanding, dealing with and talking about student discipline, including those addressing safety and risk, reflecting public concerns "about school discipline and mirrored by unruly students, bullying and violence in classroom and on playgrounds" (Fields, 2000, p. 73) or discourses and those surrounding individuals' past experiences in school in relation to discipline (Southgate, 2003 and Chapter 7). In this section of the chapter we single out and discuss particular discourses in the following order: (1) discourses of development; (2) progressive efficiency; (3) objective driven discipline; and (4) autocratic and democratic discourses of discipline. We do this to demonstrate potential understandings of the student subject that are taken up by teachers to understand and deal with disruption.

Discourses of Development

Some discourses of discipline utilize theories of development; such as Piaget's (1965) theory of cognitive development or Kohlberg's (1984) theory of moral development that explains children's rule following and developing skills of moralising. The deployment of these discourses introduces a particular psychological reasoning that constructs and authorizes certain approaches to classroom discipline. For example, as Slee (2003) states: "[s]ociety is intolerant of age-inappropriate behaviour. Early childhood professionals need to recognize *developmental stages* in young children as a standard against which to compare atypical behaviour" (p. 5). Porter (2003) similarly encourages teachers to look at disruption as a result of "behavioural mistakes" comparable to "*developmental errors*" caused by "normal exuberance, normal exploration [or] lack of skills" (p. 18).

Through the deployment and detailed attention to such *developmental trajectories*, discipline theories precisely identify and target certain behaviour. In doing so this meticulous mechanism constructs novel abilities in children, described through developmental principles that were previously not thought of. For example, while earlier it was thought that thinking required language, recently it is accepted that children not only think before they can talk but understand others' intentions (Bloom, 2004). In this way *complex developmental knowledges expand the scope of observable objects* to include the inner child and the soul (Walkerdine, 1984). Motivation, as an example of the ways in which even the understandings of certain capacities are shifting, has been a concept used in educational psychology for decades but has been developed differently depending on the theory it is aligned with (Fendler, 2001). In behaviourism, motivation was cultivated through reinforcement and was understood in terms of cause and effect. In constructivist theory, motivation moved towards the soul of the individual and is understood as a desire to participate in one's learning. Through these understandings of motivation, the subject is constituted in various ways that blend the novel observations of the most up-to-date psychological theories and research with century-old ideas of behaviourist conditioning.

Progressive Efficiency

Developmental thinking also utilises the idea of "progressive efficiency" (Fendler, 2001). This idea involves an assumption that the *more developed* the young person is in the areas of social relations, for instance, the *more efficient* he or she is in negotiating and solving problems, and therefore, the less disruption he or she will cause. Thus, competencies are mapped through developmental norms or stages and discipline approaches aim to foster these competencies. They therefore judge disruption according to developmental norms and institute consequences that are developmentally appropriate or meaningful for children. For example, teenagers' assumed and naturalized hormonal imbalances, and defiance of authority appear here as developmental norms, legitimising their strict control as a form of guidance. Or, young children are assumed to be unable to competently convey their emotions due to the immaturity of their linguistic abilities, immaturity that is sometimes evaluated as the cause of troubles with peers and therefore classroom disruption (Porter, 2003; Slee, 2003). The deployment of developmental thinking and the adoption of the idea of progressive efficiency create particular ways of understanding young persons and training their capacities. As such these are also forms of students' regulation without the use of explicit control (Pongratz, 2007; Millei, 2007a, b).

Objective Driven Discipline

Behaviourism introduced the idea of objectives to discipline theories (Fendler, 2001; Slee, 1995). According to behaviourism, particular behaviours can be achieved through a pre-designed plan of conditioning. Such an objective driven approach has been utilised in different forms of discipline that are interconnected with ideas about the learner and what she or he will become. Objectives thus link discourses of discipline to ideas about young persons in the classroom and their future prospects. One object of discipline is to ensure successful learning, hence the conceptualisation of the child as a learner and discipline as enabling the *objective of learning*. In another example, in interactionist theories (such as Balson, 1991; Dreikurs & Cassel, 1990; Glasser, 1992; Hoover and Kindsvatter, 1997), the *objective is* the creation of a citizen who is a rational and responsible *member of democratic societies*. The citizen is expected to make decisions regarding the fulfilment of her needs in a way that corresponds to social norms. (e.g., Glasser, 1985, 1986, 1992; Balson, 1991). Hoover and Kindsvatter's (1997) democratic discipline connects these objectives to disciplinary and training measures in the classroom: "When we ask what we want our students to act like as future citizens, and when we decide to educate for future citizenship, we begin to establish the agenda for the formative development of our students" (p. 82). Non-interventionist approaches to discipline (Levin & Nolan, 1991), such as Gordon's (1974) teacher effectiveness training or Ginott's (1972) positive communication model, are also interested in fostering democratic citizens, but through democratising the process of discipline in order to contribute to the prospect of raising democratic citizens. Hence, the creation of future democratic citizens is the objective of discipline in these approaches. By drawing on particular constitutions of 'the child' and 'the adolescent' that attribute to them agency, rationality, autonomy and freedom alongside a need for guidance, they consider them as participating members in democratic processes in the present while also preparing them for their future as citizens in liberal democratic societies (Porter, 2003).

There are numerous approaches that restrict students, constituting them as either irrational, irresponsible and in need of authoritarian direction through which they will learn to keep the rules necessary for being citizens in the future. Yet other approaches constitute young persons as rational choice makers who are inherently inclined towards rule breaking and will become the antisocial criminals in the future (Slee, 2003). These latter ones are mostly represented by statements of interventionist approaches (Levin & Nolan, 1991), such as Canter and Canter's (1976) assertive discipline or Dobson's (1970) punishment model that go as far as arguing for strict control over students in order to socialize students through obedience. *Socialization*, thus appears here as the *objective of discipline*. The teacher-centred approach of interventionists (Lewis, 1991) constitutes its subject as ignorant and therefore needing to go through a socialisation process to learn school rules and practices. Built on this presumed and complete socialisation, they understand students as either deliberately oppositional or compliant with the learned rules. Self-discipline, according to these theorists, means accommodation to, and internalisation, of imposed rules (Kohn, 1996; Porter, 2003). This focus on socialization is also about preparing students for the future, such as *future employment* or a *rule-oriented form of citizenship* thus becomes the *objective* of discipline. Dollar (1972) relates this position directly to classroom discipline:

> The majority of…classroom rules, like the rules which govern our society, are designed for the common good. In order for large groups of people to live within a limited area, each individual must be socialized to certain rules of conduct or behavior. The teacher's source of control is directly dependent upon her ability to make rules and enforce the students' compliance with the rules (p. 5).

This functionalist emphasis on the role of socialization in schooling is strongly highlighted in certain disciplinary approaches and emerges frequently in teachers' talk about discipline, as we will explore below. This line of reasoning serves to legitimise teachers' demands for students to obey the rules without question.

Autocratic and Democratic Discourses of Discipline

From the 1970s, different systems of reasoning emerged that re-evaluated the rights of students (arguably due to liberation movements (Balson, 1992; Lewis, 1991) and further problematised in Chapter 4). As a result, "teachers found that they could no longer dominate students" (Balson, 1992, p. 6). Consequently, teachers appropriated more democratic styles of discipline, such as interactionist and non-interventionist ones. Yet a changing political climate, uneasiness with student confidence and rising fears related to safety in schools has concomitantly supported the introduction of the more authoritarian zero tolerance type policies. These popular disciplinary strategies first emerged from the United States in the late 20th and early 21st century as 'get tough' approaches to school discipline. The tension between democratic forms of discipline and tight control still remains in disciplinary practices (as it is discussed in Chapter 2): appearing in school codes of conduct and teachers' thinking about classroom practices, as discussed in the next section.

To partly answer these shifts towards more democratic thinking, disciplinary practices, discipline approaches and associated pedagogies changed to more child-centred or interactive ones (Bredekamp & Copple, 1997; MacNaughton, 2003). This shift included the utilization of a new concept of 'the child', the one who is competent, strong and having particular capabilities from a young age that enables her or him to live with freedom. These capabilities are social competence, negotiation skills and democratic involvement; dispositions, such as the desire to take an active part in one's own self-discipline; and the desire to belong or to develop certain skills (Millei, 2007a). Disruption was (re)constructed as a problem to be solved through flexible and individual solutions and negotiation in order to develop young persons' skills and to utilize their willing attitude to cooperate in their own discipline. While interventionist theories understand self-discipline as the internalisation of behavioural rules, democratic approaches to classroom discipline reconceptualized self-discipline as being considerate to others. Through these dimensions, as Bell, Carr, Denno, Johnson & Phillips (2004) argue, the child is able to "adjust to school limits and expectations and...to negotiate social interactions with other children and adults" (p. 192) and is, consequently, less likely to perform 'inconsiderate' acts (Porter, 2003).

In practice, ideas of development, progressive efficiency, objective driven discipline, and autocratic and democratic approaches to discipline are blended together to form mobile arrangements that constitute particular logics to understand student subjects and to fashion tactics for their discipline. Staff members use temporary combinations of technologies that are produced by distinct discipline approaches as the solution to specific problems with order in school. The student subject is thus constituted and re-constituted depending on the discourses used to address specific situations. In this way, the student subject might encounter the development of a particular ability and be trained towards the objective of future citizenship, directed through a specific process intended to increase efficient self-discipline, and/or understood as in need of direct control. At other times a student's freedom may morally supersede the possibility of the imposition of any control at all. These mobile arrangements in turn create flexible subjects of discipline who may bear multifaceted characteristics at the same time.

Codes of Conduct: Responsibility, Respect and Neo-Liberal Subjects

In this section we continue to study some of the aspects outlined above through examining how disciplinary discourses play out in their practical application in relation to codes of conduct. We also extend these discourses with those of responsibility, respect and neo-liberal subjectivity (Rose, 1996). To carry out this task we discuss a sample of school codes of conduct and commentary from teachers to demonstrate how these discourses play out in policy documents and teachers' thinking. The positions explored here reflect a multiplicity of premises on human nature and aspects of 'childhood' and 'adolescence' as conceptual categories (James and Prout, 1990), including development and becoming, and inherent nature and being.

School codes of conduct are meant to educate students and their parents about students' expected behaviour: they therefore prescribe student behaviour. Codes often include a brief philosophical framework and then a list of rules. The framework commonly discusses developing an independent, autonomous subject through student responsibility and the centrality of respect. For example as one code states: "Our purpose is to assist young people to become self-disciplined, self-directed individuals who take responsibility for themselves and their education." While only a minority of codes reflected this example's specific use of the term self-discipline, the concept of responsibility is a cornerstone of most codes and in itself implies self-discipline or self-regulation. Responsibility is individualised to the student who is exhorted to make sensible choices and to take responsibility for them. The student is thus 'responsibilised'[2] towards self-governance (Hannah-Moffat, 2000). Such language is a nice example of attempts to shift school rules towards the more democratic, interactionist approaches described above, with processes of control consequently blurred through the language of choice.

This finding is consistent with the Australian codes reviewed by Lewis (1999) where he found students' self-discipline to be the primary frame for school codes of conduct. Despite such 'responsibilising' frameworks, codes of conduct then present the rules themselves as a list of negative directives that are non-negotiable, imposed, and frequently unexplained, reflecting an interventionist or custodial approach (Hoy & Weinstein, 2006) that Schimmel (2003) also observed in his review of codes of conduct in the United States. Supporting this claim, a minority of schools even overtly state that students are to defer to authority, particularly when they are being disciplined. The codes construct a scenario through which students are to learn self-discipline through obedience and conformity (Raby, 2008). In this way, students are 'responsibilised' to be active in developing their self-discipline, but until they reach their full potential to discipline themselves according to the particular codes, they are coerced to do so through the authority of the teacher. In this way a certain capacity to handle responsibility for one's own behaviour is assumed to exist from a young age, alongside assumptions of the same person's incapacity to understand rules.

This tension between a democratic framing of self-discipline and a more authoritarian one is addressed though various techniques, which create some points of correspondence. Indeed, schools deploy the concept of responsibility itself by bringing these two goals together in a way that ultimately favours sovereign obedience. As one school lists: "… students have the responsibility to:

Develop self-discipline.
Meet the expectations of the code of behaviour at all times…[…]
Be courteous and respect authority and the people in positions of authority."

Responsibility, on the one hand, can be considered as an individualized tactic that structures the field of possible conducts and deploys the subject as active in her or his self-discipline. It is also used, on the other hand, in order to reinforce the dominance of the rules and authority figures. The person who is taking up this position, the "self-disciplined student," is therefore someone who acts as if he or she is inherently obedient.

Another tactic within some codes of conduct is to focus on respect for self, others, property and authority. The category of "respect for self" is a particularly interesting one as it is a disciplinary technique that suggests care for the self , and yet it is presented through some school codes of conduct in a similar way to responsibility, as contingent on compliance. The same school states that "self-respect is impossible unless students first

---

[2]   The term: 'responsibilised' is invented by Hannah-Moffat (2000).

respect other people's authority and property" while other schools suggest that respect for self is evident through obedience to school rules, such as those against the use of drugs and alcohol. We propose, therefore, that discourses of 'responsibility' and 'respect' are taken up by codes of conduct as tactics that mix ideas of self-discipline, obedience, authority, and so on to serve at least two purposes. First, they produce active subjects who are expected to voluntarily take up particular ways of conducting themselves as if they were their own decision-makers while these behaviours are also ascribed by codes of conduct. Second, they serve to justify and legitimise power relations between teachers and students by re-fashioning the idea of obedience as a responsibility or a contingency of respect.

A similar relationship between self-discipline and obedience becomes visible when schools employ zero tolerance policies. A version of this policy was adopted in Ontario between 2002 and 2008. Zero tolerance reflects a common, behaviourist approach or object driven discipline (Slee, 1995) as it is based on the idea that certain infractions will bring mandatory consequences. Zero tolerance assumes that swift, sure consequences will deter future problems, both in a specific student and in other students. It assumes a rational subject who will weigh the consequences before choosing to break a rule. Punishment is thus framed in the context of student choice: students illustrate their responsibility by making the choice to behave in the face of certain consequences.

In a similar pattern to individual school conduct codes, when zero tolerance was introduced in Ontario it was framed in language of responsibility and respect wherein "… students must demonstrate respect for themselves, for others and for the responsibilities of citizenship through acceptable behavior" (Ontario, 2001). In this example, students are expected to be immediately responsible whereas individual school codes of conduct more frequently suggest that students are in the process of learning responsibility, a distinction that reflects the liminal positional of young people as both in the present and in the future, which we will return to shortly.

In the next section we move on to discuss the ways in which previously explored discourses of discipline approaches, considerations of respect, responsibility, obedience, neo-liberal ideas of the individual and assumptions about 'childhood', 'adolescence' and human nature play out in teachers' commentaries on school codes of conduct.

Constituting Embodied Logics

Embodied logic is a particular and temporary selection of available statements that forms mobile assemblages to understand and reason about student subjects and their discipline. Staff members' comments on school codes of conduct reflect these flexible collections, and here we examine some of these to illustrate how they produce multifaceted understandings.

The following excerpt revolves around considerations of responsibility and self-discipline:

> Jen (teacher): I think it is important to, to discipline for lattés and truancies. Um, again because you need to teach them how to be responsible and to, to be present for learning….

Bill (teacher):…at least give the kids a heads-up warning first. You know like if you see somebody, say "that's really not appropriate to wear today. I don't want to see that outfit […]," you know? For me to deal with it first. Give the kid the opportunity to make the decision to correct it too, some ownership and some responsibility too. Like, to try to give the power to that kid to make that decision.

Jen's comment typically suggests that a teacher-directed form of discipline is necessary in order to teach future responsibility and yet she feels the need to legitimise the use of authority by drawing on classroom discipline's pedagogic role to settle students down to be ready for learning. In contrast, Bill's comments are reflective of a democratic approach in that Bill is interested in the student making a choice. Bill pre-determines, however, the possible options for students and keeps the consequence of not making the 'right choice' in focus. His comments thus illustrate concerns with teachers' dominance explicated by guidance approaches. Guidance, in order to subdue dominance, aims to institute more democratic relations between students and teachers, and therefore the emphasis on control and obedience is subtle in Bill's talk, for it is tamed by the use of ideas of 'ownership', 'responsibility', 'decision making' and the 'handing over of power', but it is still there and perhaps more insidious, belying their more democratic aims. This tendency for guidance approaches to be enlisted in the interest of control has also been observed by Slee (1995), Pongratz (2007) and Millei (2007a, b) and further elaborated on in Chapter 2.

Several comments from Chicago, a vice-principal, discuss young people as junior adults, or adults in training, who can see that a rule is not unreasonable. He also suggests that students today are more mature than in the past and therefore sees a problem when teachers are overly committed to consistency and rigidity. But then he argues that young people are insufficiently mature, so their responsibilities and abilities to make decisions are incongruous with their independence, as evident in the following two quotes:

I think that it's that difference of maturity between a 14 or a 15 year old often than say a 19 or 20 year old, one who is in public school and another who is paying seven thousand dollars a year to be in a program [re: cleaning up own lunch mess].

However I think that it is a natural function maybe of families, that at 14 and 15 and 16 years of age, parents begin to, I dunno if they begin to lose control over children as much as they had before or they assume too much that children are capable of making adult-like decisions because they're asking for adult-like responsibilities and opportunities and then trust that the kids will know what to do is right. […]That is exactly when you <u>cannot</u> let kids, in my opinion, make all those decisions[…]I mean, some kids make some wacky decisions at those ages.

The above examples and quotations, all from one interview with the vice-principal, position students in a number of ways. They are junior adults, on the one hand, who can see reason and are therefore rational, like adults. On the other hand, they are also seen as adults in-the-making (developmental rationality) because they do not always make the right decisions. They are also understood as more mature than students of the past, reflecting proximity to adulthood, desires for independence and recognition of cohort-based generational difference. But they are seen as not mature enough to recognize the need to clean up their own lunch mess, although this decision is then more directly attributed to a rational weighting of having to pay or not pay for their schooling. Following this vice-principal's logic, students possibly need top-down discipline due to their immaturity; guidance towards making the right decisions; and also incentives and consequences based on their presumed rationality.

In these staff narratives, there is a tension between an emphasis on young people's developing autonomy and independence alongside emphasis on obedience. Another related tension is evident between considering young people as beings in the present versus becoming in the future. Further, assumptions about human nature (e.g., as rational) stand in tension with those about childhood or adolescence (e.g., as irrational). The particular circumstances of individual situations and the power relations involved not only mix such contradictory statements into coherent logics, but enable the teacher to use them to underpin the rationality, relevance and benefits of these strategies for students. If we look at the following statement from Bill:

> My juniors and I got into an issue about some classroom rules and so I said to them "you know I've tried to meet you half way and you guys aren't able to meet me half way so I'm going to have to go to the letter of the law here." And with my seniors, I feel that they're at the point where they can have some more responsibilities for their actions.

Bill in his statement seamlessly uses contradicting notions of students being irrational and rational, obedient and autonomous, and as being irresponsible in the present while becoming more responsible with time.

In another example, Iron, a more seasoned teacher was concerned with zero tolerance approaches because "Uh…kids make—and they're kids, 'cause they are in high school and they're still kids—they make bad mistakes." He also talked about how students sometimes forget the rules and therefore need reminders. In light of such developmental assumptions about young people, Iron was also more flexible with first timers. Yet when a student challenged the rules, he interpreted this as defiance of authority, and as therefore in need of suspension, particularly as he felt the rules are clear and simple. Iron recognized young people's errors as 'developmental' mistakes, but ultimately suggested that students need to be punished in the name of authority. Developmentally they may need leeway, but he is the one to determine this. Students both need top-down, non-negotiable consequences, but also ones that can be flexibly interpreted by him to recognize that students are developing and in need of guidance.

Conceptualisations of childhood and adolescence as both being and becoming are evident in the above examples and further complicate understandings of self-discipline. The fluidity of these categories of growing up allows young people to be framed in multiple and conflicting ways: within an immediate context they are prone to irrationality and yet assumed to be rational in response to behavioural strategies; they are in need of present control from others and in need of future internalised control; they are guided by their biologies (e.g., hormones) and yet able to make the right 'choice.' And yet within these conflicting representations, the underlying necessity to discipline through the enforcement of codes of conduct remains intact and unquestioned. Students need discipline because of their irrationality and hormonal excesses and yet also to guide their rational choices, to ensure their present control and their future self-discipline.

In light of the above disciplinary approaches, which foreground developmentalism, and the various comments above that conceptualise students within processes of development, it is somewhat surprising that staff comments rarely flagged the need to shape disciplinary approaches to specific, developmentally appropriate capabilities, even though secondary schools span grades nine through twelve. Some staff did discuss being more lenient with older students because they are considered to be more responsible—a distinction some other staff felt to be unfair. On the one hand, if younger students are assumed to be less able to understand some of the contextual or contingent nature of rules, as Nucci (2001) and other developmentalists suggest, then such a 'black and white' or rigid application of rules in order to learn them reflects some logic. But if students were presumed to be both more mature and more familiar with the rules than younger students are, then it would seem logical to be stricter with older students because they should know better. In this instance, developmental logic can be used to support opposite positions. Only two staff members, Spencer (principal) and Molly (vice-principal), made any reference to the possibility that differences in maturity level over time should lead to increasing expectations in terms of the rules. Rather, any increase in expectations was more likely to be based on the assumption that the longer students are in school the better they will know the rules, due to repeated exposure to the information. This latter idea reflects a behaviourist, rather than a democratic or developmental, approach to pedagogy and learning, with students as shaped by their environment rather than by their active participation in shaping their behaviour or their developing capacities (Millei, 2007a).

Within future-oriented developmental frameworks, young people are also 'trapped' by what they are in the present. Lesko (1996) talks about this irony in reference to youth who are abstracted as timeless, as they are always becoming, but at the same time imprisoned by time in that their age keeps them from representing themselves. This present incompleteness is also defined by various assumptions about adolescence in relation to discipline: e.g., that this is a time when young people are testing boundaries, peer-oriented, present-oriented, risk-taking, and so forth—while developmentalism did not seem to guide staff approaches in terms of incremental skill-building etc., it did emerge in such broader discourses that 'fix' adolescents in a specific mindset that swings between rationality and irrationality, and between dependence and independence.

> Gemini (teacher): It's all about immediate gratification at that age right?

> Iron (teacher): Today they'll follow the rules, tomorrow—I don't know, a hormonal thing—they don't want to follow the rules. The next day, they follow the rules.
> Interviewer: Yeah? So you think it's just because they're teenagers?
> Iron: Yeah! Yeah, I think it's just 'cause they're teenagers.

> Louis (principal): Teenagers need to express themselves in a very different way. They need to, uh…. Yeah, remember. I mean, these are…their hormones are raging! Alright? […]They're in their teenage years. Their hormones are growing, you know? They're leaving the…. They're trying to…the separation from the home. Daddy is no longer the coolest thing, mommy is no longer the coolest thing. Mommy isn't all-knowing, daddy isn't all-knowing anymore. "I don't want to hold their hands, I don't want to be hanging out with mommy and daddy anymore, I'm cool now!" Rules? Rules are the same thing. I know better!

Within this orientation, rather than assuming an immediate rationality or responsibility, it is suggested that young people need guidance from their present immediacy, irrationality and defiance to the future consistency, patience and compliance of adulthood. It is assumed, that armed with scientific knowledges of the adolescent stage, teachers know teenagers better than teenagers know themselves. Yet again we see that there is complexity in how teenagers are represented in their present contexts. First, they are guided by instant gratification, then by inconsistency in how they feel and then by defiance—all this alongside the other, abovementioned assumptions that consequences will be meaningful to them.

Another orientation towards thinking about young people and discipline is to assume certain things about young people not because they are children or adolescents, but because they are displaying inherent human nature and are therefore little different from adults. At the end of his above commentary on student mistakes, Iron noted, "but then, we all make bad mistakes." For Iron, this recognition opened up an opportunity for leeway, yet for others, references to human nature did not. It was far more likely for such references to emphasize inherent rationality and students' consequent choice to misbehave and face consequences. This assumption of rationality was evident in frequent adherence to principles of deterrence through automatic and escalating consequences. It is ironic that such orientations suggest children are competent and yet are concomitantly those most inclined towards seeking obedience to authority through top-down interventions. This emphasis implies little need for flexibility in institutional response to rule-breaking, as do the other two common assumptions about human nature raised by staff: that we have an inherent desire to defy rules and that we have an inherent need for order.

Emphases on human nature conceptualise young people in the present. Another, conflicting present orientation, addresses context. A separate part of the research discussed in this chapter involved conducting focus groups with students on rule breaking. For students, some 'petty' rules are problematic and therefore broken because they do not address their practical, everyday needs: to eat between classes, to wear a jacket for warmth, to hide bad hair with a hat, and so forth. For them, these needs were framed as basic human needs. While staff frequently dismissed such practical concerns, many also made specific contextual allowances for them in their everyday classroom management. For example, students in a large school who had a later lunch break were given more freedom to eat in class, which is usually against the rules. Some staff were similarly attentive to the immediate contextual circumstances of student misbehaviour when they were having problems at home, recognizing that, as for teachers, personal context can influence how one behaves at school. For a teacher, Sarah "Every kid is different and every circumstance is different. It's hard to just use these blanket rules, except for the case of something, you know, really violent. If the kid has a gun, or…"

While these contextual commentaries almost never considered the dynamics of the classroom, the school, or wider political and economic issues (Slee, 1995) such contextual understanding was unusual in that it framed young people as located in the present and having legitimate concerns. In contrast to the above references to human nature, it was frequently used to circumvent zero tolerance type policies.

Interrogating Embodied Logic

Together, the combination of assertions presented here about young people specifically and human nature more generally illustrate sets of ideas that reflect various disciplinary approaches discussed above and that were assembled by teachers to produce a particular and situated logic to understand and discipline student subjects. In these mobile and flexible understandings and discourses, contradicting ideas are used seamlessly, for the most part to justify, legitimate and deploy control over students in sometimes outward and other times insidious ways.

This analysis performed on teachers' commentaries points to some conclusions about reason and rationality. It seems to us that teachers use radically diverse, shifting, multifaceted and sometimes contradicting sets of ideas and values to make codes of conduct reasonable or to justify their approaches to student discipline. These ideas sometimes explicitly, and other times inherently, draw on rationales of discipline approaches, considerations of respect, responsibility, and care of the self, and ideas of 'childhood', 'adolescence' and human nature and so on to support opposing positions. We see these mobile assemblages of statements as a kind of postmodern pastiche of problem responses (Chapter 6 also takes up this idea in part).

Does this indicate that we are living in an everyday, postmodern fragmentation? Is there a mimesis of the desire to reason, order and efficiency? Perhaps this is the Rene Girard (1986) position: that we have a 'scapegoating' of students. Girard argues that human desire is constituted through imitation, thus we learn what to desire through the imitation of others. He maintains that desire is neither rooted in the object nor in the person who desires. To have a desire for rationality, by closely paraphrasing Girard (1986), is learned from a third person, a model whose desire we imitate in order to resemble the model. 'Good' teachers strive to be rational, thus we learn this desire to become a 'good' teacher. However, in this process of learning, a conflictual mimesis occurs that is manifested in the competition between teachers to prove who is rational, a competition which "converge[s] on one and the same adversary that all wish to strike down" (Girard 1987, p. 26). Here, we claim that the competing teachers' adversaries are the students as 'arbitrary victims'. Because of this apprehension that students are the cause of teachers' problems in classrooms and schools, teachers attempt to "deflect their destructive energy" (Wallace, 1994, p. 10) through disciplinary actions such as zero-tolerance policies or punishment, that 'destructs' the victim. Does this mean that we desire reason for desire's sake, rather than for the sake of reason itself? Might our logical explanations and coherent approaches to why we discipline students in particular ways in fact have nothing to do with the 'actual' practice and ethics of regulation?

References

Balson, M. (1991). An interactive approach to classroom discipline. In M. N. Lovegrove & R. Lewis (Eds.), *Classroom discipline* (pp. 23–42). Melbourne: Longman Cheshire.

Balson, M. (1992). *Understanding classroom behaviour* (3 ed.). Hawthorn, Vic: Australian Council for Educational Research.

Bell, S. H., Carr, V., Denno, D., Johnson, L. J., & Phillips, L. R. (2004). *Challenging behaviors in early childhood settings: Creating a place for all children.* Baltimore: Paul H. Brookes Publishing Co.

Bloom, P. (2004) Language: Children think before they speak. *Nature, 430, 410–411.*

Bredekamp, S., & Copple, C. (1997). *Developmentally appropriate practice in early childhood education programs serving children from birth to age 8* (revised edition ed.). Washington, DC: National Association for the Education of Young Children.

Canter, L., & Canter, M. (1976). *Assertive discipline: A take charge approach for today's educator.* Seals, CA: Canter and Associates.

Canter, L., & Canter, M. (1992). *Assertive discipline: Positive behaviour management for today's classroom.* Santa Monica, CA: Lee Canter and Associates.

Dobson, J. (1970). *Dare to discipline.* Eastbourne: Kingsway Publications.

Dollar, B. (1972). *Humanizing classroom discipline: A behavioural approach.* New York: Harper & Row, Publishers.

Dreikurs, R., & Cassel, P. (1990). *Discipline without tears.* New York: Dutton.

Fendler, L. (2001). Educating flexible souls: The construction of subjectivity through developmentality and interaction. In K. Hultqvist & G. Dahlberg (Eds.), *Governing the child in the new millennium* (pp. 119–142). New York & London: RoutledgeFalmer.

Fields, B. A. (2000). School discipline: Is there a crisis in our schools? *Australian Journal of Social Issues, 35*(1), 73–86.

Foucault, M. (1977). *Discipline and punish: The birth of the prison* (A. Sheridan, Trans.). London: Penguin Books.

Foucault, M. (1979). *The history of sexuality volume 1: An introduction* (Vol. One). London: Penguin Books.

Ginott, H. (1972). *Between teacher and child.* New York: Peter H. Wyden.

Girard, R. (1986). *The scapegoat.* (Y. Freccero, Trans.). Baltimore: Johns Hopkins University Press.

Girard, R. (1987). *Things hidden since the foundation of the world.* Stanford, CA: Stanford University Press.

Glasser, W. (1985). *Control theory.* New York: Harper and Row.

Glasser, W. (1986). *Control theory in the classroom.* New York: Harper and Row.

Glasser, W. (1992). *The quality school* (2nd ed.). New York: Harper Perennial.

Gordon, T. (1974) *Teacher effectiveness training.* New York: Peter H. Wyden.

Government of Ontario, Ministry of Education. (2001). *Code of conduct* (pp. 1–11). Toronto: Queen's printer.

Hannah-Moffat, K. (2000). Prisons that empower: Neo-liberal governance in Canadian women's prisons. *British Journal of Criminology, 40,* 510–531.

Hoover, R., & Kindsvatter, R. (1997). *Democratic discipline: Foundation and practice.* Upper Saddle River, NJ: Merril, Prentice Hall.

Hoy, A. W., & Weinstein, C. S. (2006). Student and teacher perspectives on classroom management. In C. M. Evertson & C. S. Weinstein (Eds.), *Handbook of classroom management: Research, practice and contemporary issues* (pp. 181–219). Mahwah, NJ: Lawrence Erlbaum Associates, Publishers.

Hunter, I. (1994). *Rethinking the school: Subjectivity, bureaucracy, criticism.* St Leonards, NSW Australia: Allen & Unwin Pty Ltd.

James, A., & Prout, A. (1990). *Constructing and reconstructing childhood: Contemporary issues in the sociological study of childhood.* Bassingstoke, Bristol: Falmer Press.

Kohlberg, L. (1984). *The psychology of moral development.* New York: Harper & Row.

Kohn, A. (1996). *Beyond discipline: From compliance to community.* Alexandria, VA: Association for Supervision and Curriculum Development.

Laws, C., & Davies, B. (2000). Poststructuralist theory in practice: Working with 'behaviourally disturbed' children. *Qualitative Studies in Education, 13*(3), 205–221.

Lesko, N. (1996). Denaturalizing adolescence: The politics of contemporary representations. *Youth and Society, 28*(2), 139–161.

Levin, J., & Nolan, J. (1991). *Principles of classroom management: A hierarchical approach.* Englewood Cliffs, NJ: Prentice Hall.

Lewis, R. (1991). *The discipline dilemma.* Hawthorn, VIC: The Australian Council of Educational Research Ltd.

Lewis, R. (1999). Preparing students for democratic citizenship: Codes of conduct in Victoria's 'schools of the future'. *Educational Research and Evaluation, 5*(1), 41–61.

MacNaughton, G. (2003). *Shaping early childhood: Learners, curriculum and contexts.* Maidenhead, Berkshire, England: Open University Press.

Millei, Z. J. (2007a). *A genealogical study of 'the child' as the subject of pre-compulsory education in Western Australia.* Murdoch University, Murdoch. http://wwwlib.murdoch.edu.au/adt/browse/view/adt-MU20081002.80627

Millei, Z. J. (2007b). *Controlling or guiding students—what's the difference? A critique of classroom approaches to discipline.* Paper presented at the AARE Conference Fremantle, Fremantle,WA, Australia. www.aare.edu.au/07pap/mil07410.pdf

Nucci, L. P. (2001). *Education in the moral domain.* Cambridge: Cambridge University Press.

Piaget, J. (1965). *The moral judgment of the child.* New York: The Free Press.

Pongratz, L. (2007). Freedom and discipline: Transformations in pedagogic punishment. In M. A. Peters & T. A. C. Besley (Eds.), *Why Foucault? New directions in educational research* (pp. 29–42). New York: Peter Lang.

Porter, L. (1996). *Student behaviour: Theory and practice for teachers.* St. Leonards, NSW: Allen & Unwin.

Porter, L. (2003). *Young children's behaviour : Practical approaches for caregivers and teachers* (2nd ed.). Marrickville, NSW: Elsevier Australia.

Raby, R. (2008). Rights and responsibility: Secondary school conduct codes and the production of passive citizenship. In T. O'Neill & D. Zinga (Eds.), *Children's rights: Theories, policies and interventions.* Toronto: University of Toronto Press.

Rose, N. (1996). *Inventing our selves: Psychology, power and personhood.* Cambridge & New York: Cambridge University Press.

Schimmel, D. (2003). Collaborative rule-making and citizenship education: An antidote to the undemocratic hidden curriculum. *American Secondary Education, 31*(3), 16–35.

Slee, J. (2003). *Managing difficult behaviour in young children.* Canberra: Early Childhood Australia Inc.

Slee, R. (1995). *Changing theories and practices of discipline.* London: The Falmer Press.

Southgate, E. (2003). *Remembering school: Mapping continuities in power, subjectivity & emotion in stories of school life.* New York: Peter Lang.

Walkerdine, V. (1984). Developmental psychology and the child-centered pedagogy: The insertion of Piaget into early education. In J. Henriques, W. Hollway, C. Urwin, C. Venn & V. Walkerdine (Eds.), *Changing the subject: Psychology, social regulation and subjectivity* (pp. 153–202). London & New York: Methuen.

Wallace, M. & Smith, T. (Eds.). (1994). *Curing violence.* Sonoma, CA: Polebridge Press.

Chapter IV

The Intricacies of Power Relations in Discourses of Secondary School Disciplinary Strategies

Rebecca Raby

Introduction

Scholars such as Pongratz (2007), Millei (2007) and Fendler (2001) reflect on a shift in recommended school disciplinary procedures towards "softer" guidance approaches, which seek to act upon the very soul of the child. We also see a concomitant reinforcement of traditionally authoritarian techniques reflected through a reliance on suspensions, for example, particularly within 'zero tolerance' policies. This chapter draws on policy documents and interviews with teachers and administrators from Ontario, Canada, to provide a neo-Foucauldian exploration of how three specific disciplinary strategies, as well as students' potential participation in the creation of school rules, are presented and discussed. The three discipline-related strategies under consideration are escalating consequences, suspension, and social responsibility assessments. How these are addressed both in policy, such as codes of conduct, and by staff suggests that escalating consequences and suspension are primarily understood as disciplinary strategies intended to foster obedience, safety, deterrence and self-discipline. In contrast, social responsibility assessments entail an alternative strategy presented in the language of self-discipline, sociality and, particularly where they overlap with student participation, citizenship development.

Michel Foucault's multifaceted analysis of power relations through sovereignty, disciplinarity, governmentality and ethics of the self provides a framework through which to examine tensions within this complexity of secondary schools' disciplinary strategies as they reflect and produce various understandings of students and their relationship to the school. Through examining these strategies, I explore how forms of power relations interweave and how the resultant web is partly achieved through the dividing practice of producing the 'good' and the 'problem' student, or repeat offender. Finally, I reflect on potential domination embedded within these forms of power relations and disciplinary strategies.

Methodology

Most Western, mainstream schools include a code of conduct to guide student behaviour by explaining expectations of students and outlining specific rules. The codes are usually developed by school boards and by personnel within individual schools themselves, although they also frequently reflect broader political mandate from various levels of government. Commonly those involved in rule creation are administrators, with some input from teachers and occasionally even from students and/or parents. While I reference such documents at the school, school board and provincial levels, this paper primarily draws on thirty-one interviews conducted with teachers and administrators on the creation and application of the rules in their secondary schools. These interviews were conducted as part of a wider research program that worked with codes of conduct and student focus groups to investigate school rules, their enforcement and the rationales behind them. Twenty-one interviews (five vice-principals and sixteen teachers) were conducted with staff in a semi-rural region and ten (two principals and eight teachers) in a large city.

Interviewees were located through asking school principals and vice-principals for referrals, through an advertisement in the Ontario Secondary School Teachers' Federation newsletter, and through word of mouth. They were asked to discuss their schools' rules and enforcement strategies, how this information is communicated to students, and the participants' own roles in the production and/or enforcement of rules. They were then asked to reflect on which rules and enforcement strategies are appropriate or inappropriate; to raise any significant issues they see pertaining to school rules; to discuss their philosophy behind school rules and why students might break or follow them; and finally to reflect on the possibility of student participation in the production and review of school rules.

Escalating consequences, suspensions and student participation were among the strategies that were discussed frequently—this data was then isolated and analysed through the lens of power relations. In contrast, only one interviewee raised the specific technique of using "social responsibility assessments". While such assessments are not widely used in Ontario, they are provincial policy in British Columbia and provide an interesting, innovative strategy to examine.

Escalating Consequences

Escalating consequences refers to the process by which consequences for a given rule violation increase in severity with repeated violations. This discipline strategy was espoused by staff interviewed both during the mandate of Ontario's "zero tolerance" framework of automatic suspensions under the Conservative Party (Ontario, 2000) and later, with the new, Liberal government's shift to "progressive discipline," which formally espoused escalating consequences alongside suspensions (Ontario, 2008).[1] Escalating consequences

---

[1]   The Safe Schools Act, introduced in 2000 by the then Conservative government, was interpreted by many as zero tolerance because it required suspensions and expulsions for specific rule infractions, although it also included two potential mitigating circumstances: if the pupil cannot control his or her actions or foresee their consequences, or if the pupil is not a threat to anyone. The Safe Schools Act allowed teachers to give suspensions, a right that had previously only

are advocated primarily to address issues such as lateness, dress code violations, or the use of cell phones and tend to have a common progression: 1) communication with the student in order to explain rules or give a warning, 2) confiscation, in the case of hats or phones, 3) detention, which can escalate in length and number, 4) contact with parents, 5) suspension, which in turn can escalate in number of days, and 6) expulsion, which was rarely addressed in the interviews. Several staff also used community service or written reflection within escalating consequences.

Teachers and administrative staff, from those advocating custodial or hierarchical disciplinary strategies, to those more liberal staff members who were attentive to the context of infractions and student motivations, embraced escalating consequences. The approach was logical to most staff as they felt an offence should be treated differently when it is repeated over and over again. They felt that offenders needed to realize that the more they repeated an infraction, the greater the consequences would be. A result of this is that a student could eventually be suspended for a very minor infraction, such as wearing a hat.

Teachers and administrators discussed the tactic of escalating consequences through alternatively or concurrently drawing on sovereign, disciplinary and governmental understandings of power. Sovereign rule involves an understanding that legitimate, sovereign authority is maintained through hierarchical applications of power that are ultimately about its perseverance (Foucault, 1978a). The aspiration to have obedient subjects through the exercise of sovereign power is directly reflected in many school codes of conduct, which emphasize obedience to authority and compliance through extended lists of rules and their dissemination to students. Within this broader context of a sovereign exhortation to obedience represented by the listing of rules and the endpoint of suspension resonating with behaviourism (Slee, 1995), escalating consequences also involve many features that Foucault presented as integral to disciplinary power, a non-sovereign form of power that flourished with the modern need to govern a population "in its depths and its details" (Foucault, 1978a, p. 102). Disciplinary power is a force that operates at the most micro-levels of interaction through processes such as surveillance, categorization and normalization as people watch, evaluate and categorize others and

---

been held by the principal. New strict discipline schools were introduced for students who had been expelled. Popular criticism of the zero tolerance portion of the Act began to grow when the new policy was seen as linked to a steep rise in suspension rates disproportionately affecting visible minorities and students with learning disabilities (Hoffman, 2001; Gabor, 1995). In response to these criticisms, in 2006 the new Liberal government introduced a review of the Safe Schools Act and its application, resulting in a new Safe Schools Act, "Safe, Caring and Restorative Schools." This new Act drew on the language of "progressive discipline," emphasizing the promotion of positive student behaviour and allowing principals to determine the most appropriate consequences for student misconduct. The new policy maintained a list of offences that should lead to suspension or expulsion, but expanded the mitigating circumstances to include things such as the student's age, family situation and special needs. Furthermore, the new Act required schools to offer educational support for students suspended or expelled for more than six days and removed responsibility for suspending students from teachers. Beyond suspensions and expulsions, the new Act recommended that schools consider a much wider range of preventative and progressive alternatives, including peer mediation and anti-bullying initiatives.

themselves, and are concomitantly watched, evaluated and categorized, thus creating and reproducing certain beliefs or knowledges about them (Foucault, 1977).

Embedded within escalating consequences are such processes of observation, evaluation and remediation. Inherent in escalating consequences is a need for surveillance and record keeping, for example, in order to keep track of the number and type of student infractions:

> Maria (teacher):…I'm a stickler for lates, so I have a late book to sign if they come in late. […]So the first late, it's a detention, they come in, they fill this out and then when they get to the third late, they get a detention and—the first detention is five minute, the second ten, fifteen, that sort of thing.

> Sarah (teacher):…you start off with warnings, you take action, you talk to the kid, you— um—consult parents, family. So you document everything, so that the kid has a chance to improve instead of just, you know, arbitrarily suspending.[2]

For many, this process of record keeping posed challenges within the school as there needed to be a successful way to keep track of student infractions across various classes as well as during non-instructional time (e.g., in hallways). Many teachers were frustrated with other teachers' non-enforcement of rules, or failure to adequately keep track, resulting in various school strategies for better record keeping and a process of surveillance between teachers, as well as of students.[3]

Record-keeping in turn creates and evaluates new categories of people, in this case, "repeat offenders":

> Louis (Principal): And, you know what? Some kids who are chronic rule-violators, you know what? […]Obviously we're going to focus on them a little bit more than the kid who's never been in trouble. But you know what? With any rules—and I think it's good practice—is, are there any mitigating circumstances? If a kid is chronically not following the rules and chronically not respecting our policies, then that kid is going to get hammered. Okay, I'll change my word. That kid is going to get consequenced, the full discipline.

Louis gestures towards the possibility of mitigating circumstances in chronic rule-breaking, but then prioritises that chronic repeat offenders will be "hammered," or punished, although he then corrects his language to refer to consequences. In this instance, once a student is categorized as a chronic problem, the rigidity of enforcement escalates towards more direct and severe displays of administrative domination. For staff members like Louis, the importance of escalating consequences is that it ensures a sovereign application of ultimate or "real" consequences for students who have been categorized

---

2   It is interesting that Sarah talks about providing students with an opportunity to improve, a goal which would seem to better correspond with the concept of escalating rewards.

3   Such strategies were occasionally reminiscent of a tightening "iron cage." As Jim (Teacher) explains: "So I went to go talk to the Principal and said like, 'Why is there just a piece of paper that says they're 45 minutes late, and like no reason on it or anything like that?' And she said, 'From now on we're going to use Truant.' See I don't care that…. You're missing the point. I don't care if they use Truant, I don't want a green piece of paper, a white piece of paper, a computer generated piece of paper, I think if a student, and I talk to students too, but if a student is chronically absent and truant and late, and I can't convince them that that's not a good idea um, you know, the Vice Principal needs to […] intervene as to whatever is going on."

as repeat offenders. For others, it is a tool to address those who fail to comply with lower-level consequences, by skipping a detention, for instance. In either case, escalating consequences provides a way to up the *ante* in the face of failed governmental techniques, the third form of power relations considered below, involving "all endeavors to shape, guide, [and] direct the conduct of others" (Rose, 1999, p. 3), wherein 'free subjects' have not made the right personal choices.

Indeed, after repeat offences an infraction becomes *redefined* as "opposition to authority."

> Brian (vice-principal): [A] second offence could be a single or double detention. Persistent opposition to the authority to the school is a suspendable offence.

> Gemini (teacher): If it becomes beyond five or six lates, then[…]they're in opposition to authority, or to rules, and they might get suspended.

Escalating consequences is therefore a way to be 'tough' with students, with suspension the final sanction to reinforce authority. According to these staff, the rules are ultimately reinforced through an attempt at a sovereign display of power enacted on the body of the student through their detention and removal from the school. To most participants, such escalating consequences, when consistent, were logical and fair, yet undermined by frequent inconsistency of surveillance and record keeping. Various researchers caution, however, that certain students, often minority, working class or otherwise marginalized young people are more likely than others to 'become' repeat offenders: their actions are more likely to be interpreted as infractions, their infractions more likely to be noticed and their infractions more likely to be remembered (Bhattacharjee, 2003; Ferguson, 2000; Morris, 2005; Skiba & Rausch, 2006). While this web of sovereign, disciplinary and governmental power relations may seem to equally entrap all, it does not. As I will argue below, tensions among these forms of power are partly massaged through such dividing practices.

Guidance is also embedded in the concept of escalating consequences, or education to shape students into self-governing students who will make "the right" choices (Laws & Davies, 2000; Levinsky, Unpublished paper). Rather than resorting to direct social control, with a focus on absolute obedience, such governance practices conceptualise people "as subjects of responsibility, autonomy and choice, and seek to act upon them through shaping and utilizing their freedom (Rose, 1999, p. 54). This "conduct of conduct" (Gordon, 1991, p. 2) is not simply repressive, or about control, but facilitates a variety of ways of being, including healthy, happy, virtuous and so forth (Rose, 1999). As such, this governmentality may be about control but also good governance of self and others (Besley & Peters, 2007), which is in turn accomplished through processes of ethical self-formation, which I will address below. A number of staff talked about escalating consequences within this governmental discourse, focusing on choice.

> Chicago (vice-principal): And do I always tell the kid…"this is a last ditch option"? Yes. Does it make any sense? No. Um, do I wish we never got here? Sure. Have you changed enough to make sure we didn't get here? No. Um do I hope that you'll see that there's a different way of going about things after this? Yeah [chuckles].

> Dylan (teacher) framed it: "You've had your choice, now you're choosing that you want to go to suspension."

Such comments present consequences as guiding young people towards learning to make different choices. Analysing interviews conducted with Ontario principals, Levinsky (Unpublished paper) similarly foregrounds a governmental approach as students are considered able to make choices, or to be responsible, which means they need to be "ceded a degree of freedom" (p. 16). As such, principals similarly understood that students could choose to be good or bad, or rather to make 'good' or 'bad' choices. On the one hand, as Laws and Davies (2000) contend, such an understanding of students is central to discipline and based on a humanistic discourse of natural reason in which young people make reasoned choices in the face of consequences and accept "responsibility for their actions" (p. 208). On the other, that they need guidance in appropriate dress and choice making is really about practice in making the right choices within a context that is reinforced by top-down consequences.

Ultimately, escalating consequences are deployed to engender obedience while also defining student subjects as both having the freedom and needing the guidance to make the correct choices. Further, in some instances such intervention is presented as a penalty while in others it is presented as an opportunity for education. In part these distinctions are managed through the creation of the repeat offender through surveillance, evaluation and consequent categorization of students.

Suspension

> But if something is really, really serious, then sometimes the first thing you do is really, really serious too. (Jim, teacher)

Suspension is a common automatic consequence used across North American secondary schools in cases such as drug possession, swearing at a teacher, or actions considered endangering others.[4] As I have discussed, except in more rare instances of expulsion, suspension is the common endpoint for a series of escalating consequences. Most suspensions run from one to twenty days and during that time students are not welcome in the school. Currently in Ontario, it is only after five days that schools must provide students with educational materials. A minority of schools have in-school detentions where the time is served on campus, with students separated from their peers but still engaged in schoolwork.

While not entirely happy with the concept of suspension, most staff tended to agree with their use, as an automatic consequence for serious rule violations and as the final endpoint in escalating consequences.[5] In the former, staff were particularly inclined to suspend in order to ensure the safety of other students although overall suspension was alternatively framed as an opportunity to review problem behaviour, to involve parents, to potentially modify future behaviour, to remove problem students, and as a punishment (and therefore deterrent).

---

[4] In some American jurisdictions, zero tolerance requires that even very minor violations receive an automatic, serious consequence such as an immediate suspension (Skiba & Rausch, 2006).

[5] Incidentally, the illogic of suspending a student for missing school was not lost on most respondents and a number favoured the idea of in-school suspensions in those instances.

Four staff members who most enthusiastically embraced suspensions saw them as a deterrent based on separation from peers.

> Jack (vice principal): But ultimately, there is a serious group of kids with attendance problems that come to school, that come for the social part of it. In that regard, when you suspend a kid from school, it's very effective. One day? Maybe not. Two days? Enh. You put those kids at home for three days, five days and in conjunction with that set them up for volunteer work at Community Care, with parents' approval? They miss their friends! They miss lunch hour!

Because of this effect, and its reputed seriousness as a consequence, suspension was considered by various staff to be an important tool that "sends a clear message" to offending students and to others that certain behaviours are not tolerated. Most, however, saw suspensions as an unfortunate consequence of having limited options. They were considered efficient, at least in the short term, and a logical consequence when others had been exhausted, but were also of particular concern. Some argued that suspensions deny the most marginal students their education, a criticism frequently raised in the literature (e.g., Skiba & Rausch, 2006; e.g., Slee, 1995). Others suggested that suspension fails to address the underlying issues, removes the protective buffer school provides for some students, and reflects a lack of logical link to the initial discretion. A number of staff preferred the idea of in-school suspensions but within a climate of perpetual cost-cutting most felt they did not have the resources to support in-school suspensions.

Similar to escalating consequences, suspension reflects an attempt by school staff to both exercise sovereign power over students and at the same time to guide them towards self-discipline through what is considered to be a 'meaningful' consequence. As an exercise in sovereign power, Slee (1995) argues that suspension has simply replaced corporal punishment; in fact, two staff, when talking about suspension, joked that they resort to suspension *because* they can no longer paddle a student.

> Chicago (vice-principal): "So sit at home, eat chips, you know, watch Jerry Springer, uh, nap all day long, play Nintendo, I don't care what you do but you're not allowed here." It doesn't make any sense, you're absolutely right. What it does is it reflects a limitation frankly of the school system. I can't paddle them [laughs] you know.

Slee (1995) finds that merely having replaced corporal punishment with suspension fails to address the underlying issues of authority and control represented in both techniques, as we see in the argument that suspension is unpleasant for students because it denies them the opportunity to be with peers. Suspension is framed as a form of social control attempting to engender obedience while concomitantly defining student subjects as having the freedom and needing to make the correct choices. In some instances such intervention is presented as a penalty while in others it is presented as an opportunity for guidance or education. Again various relations of power intertwine and contradict wherein exclusionary punishment is meant to guide young people toward a governmental form of self-discipline.

Slee (1995) contends that through overuse, particularly for petty issues, repeat offenders are unduly and repeatedly suspended. While escalating consequences rely on record keeping creating the category of repeat offender, suspension escalates it to 'problem student'. As such, suspensions work as dividing practices between the 'bad' student and the 'good' one (Slee, 1995). Reflecting such practices, a few staff suggested that suspensions are really used (by others) to temporarily remove difficult students. Further, two participants felt that such students with behaviour problems should receive suspensions more quickly than others.

> Chicago (vice-principal): Um, there are a handful of kids who are so difficult, who are so, um, behaviourally challenged, maybe emotionally, uh, maybe unbalanced, maybe a whole series of things…that [resolution in the classroom is] going to be very hard to do and then we need to put in place much stricter, much more formal, much more aggressive constraints on their behaviour and say "hey Billy, cross the line a little bit and you're gone."

> Barb (teacher): What I wanted to start to implement—and these were the kids who were chronic problems, like kids who got no credits, you know were just…not doing well at all. Um, that set up some parameters that "ok, so you need to have your work done, you need to come to class on time, these are the rules of the classroom and if you deviate from that, that's one. Do it two, that's your second time, you know third time, you're suspended. That's it."[…]You know so that, it's not…a guessing game for them?[6]

While a number of staff suggested that students who had repeated behaviour problems were sometimes unfairly targeted for rule enforcement, these two cases were unique in advocating differential, more severe treatment. In these instances, "problem" students are considered less able to make good choices and therefore need to have the logic of good and bad choices more directly thrust upon them through harsher consequences. There is a certain irony here in that the students most in need of support due to their marginalisation, family problems, learning difficulties and/or the structure of their schooling are those most likely to receive direct, top-down punishment, perhaps with teachers resorting to authoritarian techniques because they feel that the situation is out of control (Porter, 1996).

Social Responsibility Assessments

The final and contrasting disciplinary technique I will examine is considered preventative. Social responsibility assessments reflect a voluntary initiative introduced in British Columbia (B.C.), Canada, in which students are evaluated and can evaluate themselves for their social skills. In 2001, the B.C. government introduced performance standards for assessing reading, writing, mathematics and 'social responsibility.' The performance standards for social responsibility provide evaluative criteria for students in grades K to 3, 4–5, 6–8 and 8–10 in each of the following four categories: 1) Contributing to the Classroom and School Community; 2) Solving Problems in Peaceful Ways; 3) Valuing Diversity and Defending Human Rights; and 4) Exercising Democratic Rights and Responsibilities (British Columbia, 2001).[7] Each one of these criteria is broken down

---

[6]   This is reminiscent of the American "three strikes you're out" approach to crime that became particularly popular in the late 1990s wherein it did not matter what someone did, if they broke three laws then they would go to jail.

[7]   While British Columbia public education goes up to grade 12, it was originally felt that grades 11 and 12 should be excluded because these students are focused on writing up-coming provincial exams, although now there is some consideration of expanding the social responsibility

into observations that can be categorized as "Not yet within expectations," "Meets expectations," "Fully meets expectations," and "Exceeds expectations." The guidelines also supply teachers with sample classroom exercises for developing and observing students' behaviour.

Only one interviewee mentioned social responsibility assessments because they were being used in her school in Ontario. In response to student bullying, staff developed a "social responsibility report card" based on the B.C. criteria, through which teachers formally evaluate junior students at midterm and finals.[8] These evaluations are intended to indicate: "That it doesn't matter if you're an A student or, you know, a D student. We want to know you are a really good person and you are being commended for that."[9] The respondent felt that these assessments were having a good effect in terms of determining the context of student misbehaviour and using that information to affect interventions. For instance, it allowed staff to identify patterns in behaviour: "maybe they're misbehaving only in the afternoons, no matter what classes they have it's always in the afternoon. Or it's just in the mornings or it's just with... male teachers or just with female teachers." These assessments were also considered handy guides for parents, providing an alternative to a focus only on grades, although a new category of potential failure as well as potential reward.

The B.C. social responsibility performance standards are developmental in that they determine different criteria across ages, but they are also framed in terms of the incremental learning of skills through specific school practices. The assessments are inevitably normative, evaluative and prioritise values such as emotion management, friendliness, leadership and investment. These assessments are therefore disciplinary as, like most assessment documents that outline learning objectives, they examine, categorize and consequently normalize certain behaviours through the language of expectations. The category "Not yet meets expectations" suggests a need for improvement and therefore intervention. New categories of problem student are created. As outlined in Chapter 3, Fendler (2001) argues that developmentally appropriate discipline defines a sequence of capabilities, feelings and/or morals for children at different ages. These processes infiltrate every aspect of young people's selves. These assessment guidelines are similarly broken down into specific, detailed criteria for evaluating students in each of the above categories where "the success of a pedagogy is evaluated according to the degree to which the specified objective is achieved" (Fendler, 2001, p. 133).

Such assessments are, therefore, also governmental as they seek to encourage the self to work on itself (Fendler, 2001). Part of the idea behind the B.C. social responsibility performance standards is that they provide an opportunity for teachers and families to assess students, but also for students to assess themselves. Fendler (2001) describes how education is currently producing a flexible, educated subject through various disciplinary discourses that might look like exercises in freedom but are really about control. Education

---

performance standards to grade 12 (Nancy Walt, personal communication, March 13, 2009).

[8]   Keeping these evaluations to junior grades was considered necessary because of the amount of resources and paperwork it required.

[9]   Because this was a unique intervention among the schools represented in this research, I have omitted the location and pseudonym of the speaker to ensure anonymity.

that focuses on the "whole child," for example, is bringing more features of the self under educational management and ultimately encouraging the self to work on itself to be positive and reflexive. The assessments also reward the belief that people can make change in the world around them. There is, as such, an obligation to join, to invest in school and community, and to have the desire to participate. As Fendler (2001) critiques, certain pedagogical techniques are about 'internal motivation' in that the child should want to learn, to have a positive attitude and here, to participate and make change for the better.

While technologies such as social responsibility assessments aspire to be exercises in democracy, participation and therefore freedom, they can also be considered mechanisms of control that attempt to shape and manage students' freedom and choices (Fendler, 2001) as individuals become responsible for the development of their own moral standards. Such forms of discipline involve a shift from external to internal control, with the latter a "more personal, intensive and insidious regulation that is disguised in discourses of liberation" (Millei, 2007, p. 1). Indeed, these techniques can be considered forms of domination that are hidden, manipulative and profound in that individuals become involuntary co-producers of a process of a form of control that is "rendered anonymous" (Pongratz, 2007, p. 40). I will return to this position shortly.

Student Involvement in Decision-Making

Social responsibility assessments reward student participation in democratic processes and yet such processes are rare in most North American schools. This final section considers staff comments on student input into school codes of conduct, involvement championed by advocates who draw on democratic, participatory citizenship and/or the sovereign discourse of right (Dobozy, 2007; Kohn, 1996; Schimmel, 1997). Yet Pongratz (2007) counters that through such involvement students "can experience themselves as the subject of processes to which they remain completely subjected" (p. 37). Some staff comments on student participation advocate participation based on obedience, self-regulation and responsibilisation, others embrace participation through recourse to democratic engagement and/or rights. Reflecting on such comments, I now explore the problematic between more insidious processes of control (Millei, 2007; Pongratz, 2007) and the mobilization of an ethics for the care of the self (Besley & Peters, 2007; Gore, 1993).

Staff from the semi-rural region spoke of very limited student participation, if any. Despite this, most spoke positively about the idea of some form of student involvement, primarily through student council, creating classroom level rules, or students educating each other about the rules. Some also favoured informal processes that are currently available to students, such as talking to teachers or administrators to address their concerns with a rule. Four staff members were interested in developing a more formal system of student representation. For example, Barb described a potential scenario in which each grade would send several representatives to a separate committee that would include staff representations, although with the following caveat: "so long as, you know, you're not just going to have people in there saying 'oh we want to be able to smoke dope in all our classes' you know but, but logical things." Urban staff also raised possibilities for students to address their concerns informally although half indicated that their students currently have representation on the committee that reviews school rules and the rest argued for the successful possibility of such representation. Two discussed student surveys, which are becoming routinely used to seek student views on issues of safety in their schools, and two others mentioned opportunities for students to draw on peer mediation. Finally, four staff did not support student involvement at all, in part because students need to learn within parameters determined by teachers and administrators. Joe (teacher) combined developmental and authoritarian approaches to argue that students do not understand the broader consequences of their decisions, lack the expertise to create rules, and need clear rules imposed from above in order to learn respect:

> Joe: What's wrong with just walking into a school and there being rules? Really, what's wrong with that? Right? And respect has to be learned. If they define their own rules, they're not thinking about it as respect.

To Joe it is only *through* sovereign attempts at control, through top-down rules, that students learn consequences and respect needed to live in a future, hierarchical society. Similarly, Patrick (teacher) argued that in practice students want and value clear rules and boundaries supplied to them by someone else; two other teachers felt that it is part of teachers' jobs and training to provide and enforce the rules.

Staff who agreed with increasing student involvement and those more resistant to the idea shared concerns over the need for resources, staff and broader legislative support, concerns mentioned elsewhere (Blase & Blase, 1997; Mitra, 2008). Staff members were also worried about students introducing "crazy rules," as we see in the above quote from Barb. She, Chicago and Sarah all felt that there needed to be some kind of regulation to prevent students from introducing inappropriate rules and to ensure certain 'non-negotiables,' providing little recognition that student participation is an integrated component of cooperative rule-making with staff, that includes guidance and skill development.

It is also interesting how staff advocated student involvement for reasons that had little to do with the idea that students should have a legitimate voice or in terms of their preparation for the future; I would like to turn to this more strategic, manipulative discussion of student involvement now. For example, several staff felt students need to *feel* that they are being heard, even if it makes no difference:

> Jack (vice principal): And a lot of times in the end, we will not agree and they know that I've gotta make [inaudible]—but at least I've heard them and I've heard their point of view.

> Bill (teacher): There was a little bit of take from them but not a whole lot. We didn't modify a ton of what we were doing.

In related comments, others felt student involvement to be useful for ensuring their compliance. Three vice principals and one teacher suggested that student involvement is valuable for student 'buy in' and consequent obedience to the rules, a position supported by Porter (1996). Others similarly noted that by having students educate each other about the rules that they would be more likely to be followed. This link between involvement and compliance illustrates an overt, calculated embrace of technologies intended to conflate self-discipline with control. From this perspective we can see how calls for student participation resonate with conscious, arguably manipulative, processes of responsibilisation raising the inevitable observation that similar motivations may remain unacknowledged by others.

The above comments from staff point to the cautions already raised in my discussion of social responsibility assessments, for rather than providing children with the freedom to shape their environments and engage in democratic decision-making, children's participation, along with other techniques aimed to foster self-discipline, can become a deeper form of subjugation (Millei, 2007; Pongratz, 2007 and Chapter 3). Rather than being expected to obey or resist when told what to do and when, student involvement can be understood as a technique for facilitating the internalisation of discipline by cultivating young people's investment in their own discipline and conformity (Stasiulis, 2002). This concern has been significantly developed by Millei (In press) in her examinations of guidance approaches to early childhood, such as those outlined by Porter (2003), Kohn (1996), and Gartrell (1998) that aim to democratically share power with students by giving children choice. Millei (In press) cautions that when young people are thus enlisted to construct themselves towards socially desired ends, deep, on-going relations of domination through the regulation of their very inner worlds are being masked. From this perspective, Millei (In press) wonders if sovereign forms of discipline allow for more genuine freedom and agency as they are more overt and resistance more conceivable.[10] We have seen in these staff comments how such 'soft control' through participatory, governmental relations is overtly, and potentially covertly, embraced.

Discussion

Is student participation through social responsibility, committee involvement, or even "free" or democratically run schools (Pongratz, 2007) inevitably about creating compliant, self-disciplined students? Might sovereign power provide clearer avenues for genuine resistance? Within Foucault's conception of power relations, power is productive, creating certain kinds of subjects (1978b). Here we see the dual nature of governmental processes.

Governmental power relations permeate the very self, exhorting individuals to make the right choices, to engage with the rules and to discipline themselves. As presented above, conduct of conduct is about control, but also about facilitating other ways of being. These processes can also produce people invested in their own ethical self-formation. Ethics and the care of the self involve processes "by which one attempts to develop and transform oneself" (Foucault, 1994, p. 27) through practices found in a person's culture, society, or social group. As such, part of the care of the self is not only self-knowledge, but also knowledge of the principles behind rules of conduct in order to be able to engage with 'games of truth.' Such an ethics requires a degree of freedom from domination and, in turn, ethics themselves are the "considered form that freedom takes when it is informed by reflection" (Foucault, 1994, p. 28). Gore (1993) provides an example of how people "constitute themselves as the moral subjects of their own actions" (p. 53) when she

---

[10]   Those working in critical pedagogy might well add that through student participation, they become disciplined into the specifically middle-class regime of the school.

observes that students "keep themselves and each other in check" (p. 60), through raising their hands before speaking. Self-regulation is therefore a part of student management and teacher control, but as it interweaves with care of the self we can see how there are also opportunities for critique and niches of freedom. Care of the self includes self-invention and self-reflection—as part of self-reflection we can examine "the regimes of truth within which we operate, and which we perpetuate [and therefore] the current ways in which we act on ourselves and hence, point the way toward acting differently" (Gore, 1993, p. 131).

Technologies of the self thus become a part of us, facilitating our control but also providing possibilities (Gore, 1993). Skills in the care of the self, self-mastery, self-reflection and self-invention can support strategies by which to engage in power relations and to resist domination. Skills at self-reflection can conjure critical reflection on regimes of truth and disciplinary practices and insight into possibilities for acting differently, for example. To this end, strategies for student participation and assessments such as the social responsibility performance standards are multifaceted tools, which aim to normalize, guide, control and create self-regulating young people but may also foster capacities that allow for an ethics of the self, including student self-knowledge and reflection that can lead to critique of processes of domination within schools themselves. When young people are invested in ethical self-formation and experience themselves as legitimate participants in the social realm who expect consultation, input, and opportunities to challenge unfairness, fissures open in potential tyrannies of domination.[11] Students may be able to more effectively negotiate relations of power than simply rule-breaking, which is so easily redefined as student dysfunction and irrationality (Raby & Domitrek, 2007).

Finally, young people may not respond as expected. As this chapter has illustrated, discourses of discipline and their agents, which attempt to shape us, are not unified or consistent and attempts at "discursive interpellation or constitution…[are] subject to failure, haunted by contingencies" (Butler, 1993, p. 192), thus creating possibilities for the unexpected (Raby, 2005). Indeed, by opening opportunities for genuine, codified student involvement, quite new possibilities for school organization may arise alongside the creation of new and unpredictable subjectivities.

Conclusion

Through this chapter I have explored discourses around several disciplinary strategies as they emerged in school policy and in interviews with school staff to illustrate how various forms of power relations can interweave. Foucault's work on power is useful here as it presents power as far more complex than simply something that is possessed, applied and fought over. This conceptualisation allows us to explore how school disciplinary strategies are discussed in a variety of ways that produce a complex web of power relations. Staff commentaries and the codes of conduct they reflect indicate a tension between exhortations demanding obedience and the creation of self-governing subjectivities; tensions embedded

---

[11] An example of this was evident in the Albany Free School in which any school member could, at any point that they were feeling an injustice was taking place, say "STOP!", at which point a school council would be immediately convened by everyone to address the issue (Mercogliano, 1998).

within the combined forms of sovereign, disciplinary and governmental power relations. These tensions are managed in part through the normalization of adolescent subjectivities as both being and becoming (see Chapter 3), through the creation of the 'good' and the 'problem' student with the consequent exclusion of specific adolescents and through the regulation of students through 'soft control'. Yet tensions between forms of power relations also suggest that current governmental rationalities are not consistent or unified (O'Malley, Weir & Shearing, 1997), therefore providing fissures, which present avenues for contestation or change. Finally, embedded within certain governmental strategies oriented towards democratic practices is the potential production of self-reflexive, ethical selves who are able to critically negotiate such fissures.

References

Besley, T. A. C., & Peters, M. A. (2007). *Subjectivity and truth: Foucault, education, and the culture of self*. New York: Peter Lang.

Bhattacharjee, K. (2003). *The Ontario Safe Schools Act: School discipline and discrimination*. Toronto: Ontario Human Rights Commission.

Blase, J., & Blase, J. (1997). *The fire is back! Principals sharing school governance*. Thousand Oaks, CA: Corwin Press, Inc.

British Columbia, Ministry of Education (2001). BC Performance Standards: Social responsibility: A framework. Student Assessment and Program Evaluation Branch, Province of British Columbia. Retrieved on 4 November 2009 from http://www.bced.gov.bc.ca/perf_stands/sintro.pdf

Butler, J. (1993). *Bodies that matter*. New York: Routledge.

Dobozy, E. (2007). Effective learning of civic skills: Democratic schools succeed in nurturing the critical capacities of students. *Educational Studies*, 33(2), 115–128.

Fendler, L. (2001). Educating flexible souls: The construction of subjectivity through developmentality and interaction. In K. Hultqvist & G. Dahlberg (Eds.), *Governing the child in the new millennium* (pp. 119–142). New York: RoutledgeFalmer.

Ferguson, A. A. (2000). *Bad boys: Public schools in the making of black masculinity*. Ann Arbor: University of Michigan Press.

Foucault, M. (1977). *Discipline and punish: The birth of the prison*. London: Penguin Books.

Foucault, M. (1978a). Governmentality. In G. Burchell, C. Gordon & P. Miller (Eds.), *The Foucault effect: Studies in governmentality*. Chicago: University of Chicago Press.

Foucault, M. (1978b). *The history of sexuality, volume 1: An introduction*. New York: Vintage Books.

Foucault, M. (1994). The ethics of the concern of the self as a practice of freedom. In P. Rabinow & N. Rose (Eds.), *The essential Foucault: Selections from essential works of Foucault, 1954–1984* (pp. 25–42). New York: The New Press.

Gartrell, D. (1998). *A guidance approach for the encouraging classroom*. Albany, New York: Delmar Publishers.

Gordon, C. (1991). Governmental rationality. In G. Burchell, C. Gordon & P. Miller (Eds.), *The Foucault effect: Studies in governmentality with two lectures by and an interview with Michel Foucault* (pp. 1–52). Chicago: University of Chicago Press.

Gore, J. M. (1993). *The struggle for pedagogies: Critical and feminist discourses as regimes of truth.* New York: Routledge.

Government of Ontario, Ministry of Education (2000). Bill 81: An act to increase respect and responsibility, to set standards for safe learning and safe teaching in schools and to amend the teaching profession act" (Safe Schools Act). Retrieved on 4 November 2009 from http://www.ontla.on.ca/bills/bills-files/37_Parliament/Session1/b081ra.pdf

Government of Ontario (2008). Education Act. R.S.O. 1990, Chapter E.2. Retrieved on 4 November 2009 from http://www.e-laws.gov.on.ca/html/statutes/english/elaws_statutes_90e02_e.htm

Kohn, A. (1996). *Beyond discipline: From compliance to community.* Alexandria, VA: Association for Supervision and Curriculum Development.

Laws, C., & Davies, B. (2000). Poststructuralist theory in practice: Working with 'behaviourally disturbed' children. *Qualitative Studies in Education,* 13(3), 205–221.

Levinsky, Z. (Unpublished paper). 'Not bad kids, just bad choices': Negotiating school safety and (re)posing students under a zero tolerance policy.

Mercogliano, C. (1998). *Making it up as we go along: The story of the Albany Free School.* Portsmouth, NH: Heinemann.

Millei, Z. J. (2007). Controlling or guiding students—what's the difference? A critique of classroom approaches to discipline. Paper presented at the AARE Conference Fremantle, Fremantle, WA, Australia. http://www.aare.edu.au/07pap/mil07410.pdf

Millei, Z. (2008). Thinking differently about the guidance approach to discipline. Paper presented at the Early Childhood Conference Canberra, ACT, Australia.

Mitra, D. L. (2008). *Student voice in school reform.* Albany: State University of New York Press.

Morris, E. W. (2005). "Tuck in that shirt!" race, class, gender and discipline in an urban school. *Sociological Perspectives,* 48(1), 25–48.

O'Malley, P., Weir, L., & Shearing, C. (1997). Governmentality, criticism, politics. *Economy and Society,* 26, 501–517.

Pongratz, L. (2007). Freedom and discipline: Transformations in pedagogic punishment. In M. A. Peters & T. A. C. Besley (Eds.), *Why Foucault? New directions in educational research* (pp. 29–42). New York: Peter Lang.

Porter, L. (1996). *Student behaviour: Theory and practice for teachers.* St. Leonards, NSW: Allen & Unwin.

Porter, L. (2003). *Young children's behaviour: Practical approaches for caregivers and teachers* (3rd ed.). Marrickville, NSW: Elsevier Australia.

Raby, R. (2005). What is resistance? *Journal of Youth Studies,* 8(2), 151–171.

Raby, R., & Domitrek, J. (2007). Slippery as fish. But already caught? Secondary students' engagement with school rules. *Canadian Journal of Education,* 30(3), 931–958.

Rose, N. (1999). *Power of freedom: Reframing political thought.* Cambridge: Cambridge University Press.

Schimmel, D. (1997). Traditional rule-making and the subversion of citizenship education. *Social Education,* 61(2), 70–74.

Skiba, R. J., & Rausch, M. K. (2006). Zero tolerance, suspension, and expulsion: Questions of equity and effectiveness. In C. M. Evertson & C. S. Weinstein (Eds.), *Handbook of classroom management: Research, practice and contemporary issues* (pp. 1063–1089). Mahway, NJ: Lawrence Erlbaum Associates, Publishers.

Slee, R. (1995). *Changing theories and practices of discipline.* London: The Falmer Press.

Stasiulis, D. (2002). The active child citizen: Lessons from Canadian policy and the children's movement. *Citizenship Studies*, 6(4), 507–538.

Chapter V

Discipline, Diversity and Agency: Pedagogic Practice and Dispositions to Learning

Megan Watkins

> What, then, makes discipline good? …is not discipline—all discipline—essentially a
> restraint, a limitation imposed on man's behaviour? If life is good, how can it be good
> to bridle it, to constrain it, to impose limits that it cannot overcome? (Durkheim, 2002,
> pp. 32 & 35.)

These questions posed by Durkheim in his course on moral education at the Sorbonne in
1902–3 get to the crux of the dilemma in understanding the nature and role of discipline,
namely its ability to both constrain and enable.[1] Foucault, likewise, explores this apparent
contradiction most notably in Discipline and Punish. Unlike Durkheim, however, who
places emphasis on the enabling potential of discipline in the formation of individual moral
capacities, Foucault views the utility that discipline can provide as largely a mechanism of
subjection. While his later work around the care of the self gives greater acknowledgment
to its capacitating effects (Foucault, 1990), most application of his work appears to focus on
the negative aspects of disciplinary power. This seems especially the case within education
where theory and practice tend to neglect the agentic potential of discipline and the ways
in which an embodied self-discipline provides the condition of possibility upon which
successful academic engagement depends. Drawing on recent research into the differential
achievement and dispositions to learning of Chinese-, Pasifika- and Anglo-background
primary school students in Sydney, Australia, this chapter examines the contradictory nature
of discipline. It considers how various home and school practices in which these students
engage constitute different modalities of discipline, an enabling and disabling discipline of
control and a discipline that promotes either engagement or disengagement in learning.
With some attention to ethnographic detail the chapter explores how these disciplines
are embodied by students engendering different capacities that, while linked to students'
ethnicity through a process of cultural pathologising, are rather a function of the forms

---

[1] Enabling discipline is also an idea discussed in Chapter 6.

of governance their home and school pedagogies generate with certain forms of discipline proving more conducive to educational labour than others.

The Contradictory Nature of Discipline

Prior to a discussion of the study, however, I want to return to the questions Durkheim poses to think through how the constraints that discipline imposes can have a liberatory function providing the means through which agency is achieved. In his explanation of the bases of a moral education, Durkheim (2002, p. 45) prizes the capacity for self-control viewing it as "one of the chief powers that education should develop". He makes a clear distinction, however, between a kind of individual restraint that smacks of blind conformity to rule and a form of restraint that capacitates the body and mind encouraging reflection and self-examination. As he explains, "…it does not follow from a belief in the need for discipline that discipline must involve blind and slavish submission" (Durkheim, 2002, p. 52). The kind of self-control or 'asceticism' to which he refers is not a good in and of itself, it is simply a means to an end; a way of ensuring the self embodies the necessary resources—in his case a secular morality—for effective social participation. In doing this, he is not promoting a teleology of the self but a state of continual becoming, with an internalised discipline as the resource through which this process is achieved (Durkheim, 2002, p. 51).

While seemingly theoretically disparate, Durkheim's notion of asceticism is not that far removed from what Foucault proposed in his lectures at the College de France in the early 1980s, which underpins his conception of 'the care of the self'. Foucault likens this to the Greek notion of 'askesis' as opposed to a contemporary understanding of ascesis, which, as he explains, is informed by a Christian renunciation of the self (Foucault, 2005, p. 333). Both askesis and Durkheim's perspective on discipline are not so much concerned with denial but enablement and the skills acquired through a disciplining of the self. Drawing on Greek scholars such as Epictetus, Plutarch and Pythagoras, Foucault (2005) considers the role of discipline in acquiring the skill of listening and the importance of developing a 'pedagogical silence' (p. 414). He details how Pythagorean communities insisted on five years of silence from their novices who were inducted into particular ways of listening to encourage, not passivity and acceptance, but an active demeanour and attentive mind; a state predicated on bodily composure to maximise scholarly engagement. It is interesting, however, that this Foucault—one who prizes discipline and, unlike his position in Discipline and Punish does not conceive the utility it engenders as a tool of subjection—is generally neglected within critical and cultural theory. Yet, even with his emphasis on constraint in Discipline and Punish, Foucault does provide ample discussion of the productive, or rather empowering, potential of discipline which can be read as inherently enabling, providing the theoretical trajectory for his later examination of the care of the self.[2] As he says 'Discipline makes individuals' but in a seemingly contradictory way in which increased agency is borne of control (Foucault 1977, p. 170).

---

[2]   When using the term 'productive' in discussion of disciplinary power, Foucault does not intend the positive commonsense usage that I employ here. Rather, he simply means productive as in 'to produce', which can have either positive or negative connotations. The focus in this chapter, however, is on the enabling aspects of discipline, and hence I use the term 'productive' in the former sense.

Butler (1997, p. 10) also acknowledges the constitutive role of discipline but poses the question: "If subordination is the condition of possibility for agency how might agency be thought in opposition to the forces of subordination?" In response to Butler, it is not so much that agency and subordination need to be perceived as opposed but rather, the form subordination takes and the process whereby it proves agentic, a process with pedagogic implications. Agency is not merely resistance, a conflation too often made in education, as is the case with critical pedagogy (Heilman, 2005). Rather agency is the point whereby subordination is harnessed, embodied and channelled for productive purposes, productive of the self, with resistance simply one of many possible uses of the power that ensues.

The individual appropriation of disciplinary power is very much a corporeal process. This is evident in Foucault but lacking in Butler where the material body slips from view, overshadowed by the discursive—a body of words—less amenable to a notion of capacitation. This agentic potential of discipline is realised as techniques in the sense that Mauss (1979) espouses, whereby the body itself becomes an instrument imbued with 'practical reason' or know-how. Techniques, however, are acquired in different ways through a conscious or unconscious mimesis or, alternatively, active intervention, what Mauss (1979, p. 73) terms 'education'. Each involves a particular disciplining of the body but discipline itself, acquired through whatever means, does not necessarily produce technique as it may not prove enabling leading instead to a manipulation or control of the self rather than allowing the self to utilise the skill it has acquired. The utilisation of technique, or indeed its initial acquisition, is premised to a large degree on an originary skill or capacity for composure (Noble and Watkins, 2009). As discussed, Foucault (2005, p. 343) views the skill of listening as being dependent upon a certain physical posture in which the body is 'absolutely calm'. Composure, however, does not necessarily denote stillness; it is more a matter of a readiness to perform a task or being actively receptive. Mauss (1979, p. 86) also discusses the importance of composure for a range of bodily techniques explaining the ways in which it acts as a 'retarding mechanism…inhibiting disorderly movements' and allowing chosen goals to be achieved. Restraint, it seems, is a virtue (Pandian, 2008) but in the very act of inhibition whereby control allows the repetition of desired actions, or even thoughts, technique is acquired, a process built upon the formation of habit. Once again the terminology used here requires clarification. Habit may promote stasis but equally so it can act as a pliable, generative phenomenon, or as Malabou (2005, p. 38) explains, a 'plastic operation, which makes the body into an instrument'. Pedagogy, in its broadest sense as practices of instruction in various contexts, will often determine the nature and utility of discipline and whether or not the formation of habits proves productive as technique or enslaves the body and mind minimizing their utility and so individual agency.

Background to the Study

Such a perspective underpins the following examination of the home and school pedagogies of a group of Chinese-, Pasifika- and Anglo-background students who were part of a larger study investigating the relationship between cultural practices and dispositions to learning (Watkins & Noble, 2008). Students from these particular ethnic groups were chosen for inclusion in the study given common public perceptions about their academic achievement. Chinese students are generally perceived as high achievers, particularly in maths and science, with regular flurries of public anxiety, fuelled by the media, of an apparent overrepresentation in Opportunity Classes and selective high schools (Duffy, 2001, p. 28)[3]. On the other hand, Pasifika students, a term used to denote those of Samoan, Tongan, Cook Islander and Maori backgrounds for example, are viewed as prone to academic underachievement with media attention focused instead on either the sporting prowess or criminality of older students (Francis, 1995; White et al., 1999; Dooley, Exley & Singh, 2000; Singh & Sinclair, 2001). Anglo-background students were also included in the study as a kind of 'control' group given their ethnicity is less marked and so their academic performance is more obviously linked to either individual family experience or other socio-cultural influences such as class and gender. The inclusion of Anglo background students is of importance, therefore, in trying to problematise the simplistic assumptions often made about the relationship between ethnicity and academic performance as with Chinese and Pasifika students. This is not to deny that there is a connection, but it is a complex one that needs to be explored more fully. In the case of students with a language background other than English (LBOTE) it is generally their ethnicity, which is privileged in accounting for either their high or low achievement (Matthews, 2002). But even giving consideration to other macro influences such as class and gender can present their own problems when used as explanations for educational disadvantage or academic achievement. This is not to suggest these structural categories are a fiction, but it's worthwhile to consider Latour's comments when examining their impact on learning. He explains—and I quote him at length here—when:

> …social scientists add the adjective 'social' to some phenomenon, they designate a stabilised state of affairs a bundle of ties, that, later may be mobilised to account for some other phenomenon. There is nothing wrong with this use of the word as long as it designates what is already assembled together without making superfluous assumptions about the nature of what is assembled. Problems arise, however, when 'social' begins to mean a type of material as if the adjective was roughly comparable to other terms like 'wooden', steely', 'biological', 'economical', 'mental', 'organisational' or 'linguistic'. At that point the meaning of the word breaks down since it now designates two entirely different things: first, a movement during a process of assembling and second, a specific type of ingredient that is supposed to differ from other materials. (Latour, 2005, p. 1)

The notion of culture I want to pursue here, is processual, namely culture viewed as an ongoing assemblage of practices. While of course social categories such as class, gender and ethnicity are of crucial importance in relation to this, a microanalysis of practice, as was undertaken in this study, allows for a more nuanced treatment of the ways in which certain capacities are acquired as a result of practices both in the home and school, and the degree to which different modalities of discipline are formative in this process. Emphasis then shifts from what students are to what they do—or perhaps

---

[3]   Opportunity Classes are selective classes offered in some primary schools in NSW. Students sit for entry exams for these classes in Year 4. Entry to selective high schools in NSW is also based on a similar external examination process.

more importantly what they don't do, bearing in mind Holliday's (2005) point that, "If we think of a people's behaviour as defined and constrained by the culture in which they live, agency is transferred away from the individual to the culture itself" (p. 18).

The various practices in which students engage that impact on their academic performance is the focus here, in particular those of four students: Yupeng and Vincent of Chinese background, Finau of Tongan/Pasifika background and Braydon, a student of Anglo background. These four boys were chosen from a group of 35 Year 3 students—11 Chinese and Pasifika students and 13 of Anglo background—as their experiences, especially those observed in their classrooms; exemplify the different modalities of discipline that impacted upon the group as a whole.[4] Each of the 35 students from across six schools was selected for inclusion in the study following their parents firstly completing a survey about practices in the home related to academic performance. The survey included an expression of interest for further involvement in the study including both themselves and their child being interviewed and their child being observed during class time. Together with this, the students' classroom teachers, principals and some community liaison officers (CLO) were also interviewed. The study targeted Year 3 given all students in New South Wales (NSW), and now across Australia, complete external standardised testing for literacy and numeracy at this stage of schooling. This provided useful 'objective' data on each child's academic performance. Together with this, by Year 3 students aged 8/9 years, are in their fourth year of school, which is a useful intermediary stage in a child's primary education to examine the dispositions to learning they have acquired to this point which, by the time they start high school in Year 7, have become firmly engrained. Each of the snapshots of practice that follow is gleaned from an amalgam of this data highlighting instances reflective of the students' experiences at home and school. The snapshots are presented as couplets indicative of two continua of discipline: a continuum of disabling/enabling control and another of disengagement/engagement.

An Enabling/Disabling Discipline of Control

Part 1

The first of the students, Braydon, attended Aston Public School (PS), which had high percentages of Pasifika and Aboriginal students and was located in a low socio-economic status (SES) suburb in the western outskirts of Sydney. Braydon was a good-natured student but thought school was 'a bit boring'. He explained how he did his homework each weeknight for about 30 minutes, but as his Dad pointed out he went to football training twice a week after school so not much got done on these nights. This didn't bother Braydon's father, who was a technical college teacher, as, while he thought his son could be working harder, he didn't think homework was very important. He pointed out that 'there is more than enough time at school to do school work' adding

---

4   Of the 35 students involved in the study 12 were girls and 23 were boys. There was no attempt
     to have equal representation of each gender. Students were selected on the basis of their parents
     expressing an interest for further involvement in the study following completion of a survey.
     The four boys focused on in this chapter were chosen as their experiences best represented the
     modalities of discipline that are discussed.

'it is something that could be left to high school'. When Braydon did do his homework it was generally completed at a table in the lounge room. He didn't have a desk in his room, which he shared with his two older brothers. As such, there was no space within the home designated for academic endeavour. The lounge room, which opened onto the dining room and kitchen, functioned as a multiply-coded space, a site for entertainment, relaxation and, to some extent, work—as it does in many homes—but in Braydon's case a regimen of work associated with this space, at set times during the week, was not evident. While he may have completed his homework in this area, it was a communal space with various functions. It lacked an atmosphere to encourage concentration on academic tasks given the numerous distractions of other family members as they also utilised the space. Together with this, the discipline to complete homework was not instilled by Braydon's parents. Academic labour was more clearly associated with school, and, in particular, high school.

As mentioned, however, Braydon played football and he was good at it. He was in a 1st division local team and as his Dad pointed out 'they are pretty disciplined'. This form of discipline and training of the body was encouraged. It seems the physicality of sport is more clearly understood; the need to develop technique by skilling the muscles and limbs for automatic response and the importance of a coach to guide the process. Academic work, however, is perceived as being quite different; a cognitive exercise with its physicality and the discipline to learn given little emphasis. This was the case with Braydon. It was school that was viewed as the site for academic endeavour where he would receive the requisite skills and knowledge for later years. Sporting discipline was something Braydon and his family invested in; academic discipline was the responsibility of someone else, somewhere else.

Braydon was in a boys-only Year 3/4 composite class at Aston. The gender split with a parallel class was undertaken in an attempt to minimise behaviour problems and lift student performance. The following account draws on one of three lessons that was observed, which was devoted to handwriting. The classroom was quite large with two columns of three rows of desks directed towards a whiteboard at the front. There was also space at the back for floor activities. Braydon was seated at a desk at the back. While class monitors handed out handwriting books, Anita, the teacher, used an overhead projector, to display the day's date and a short saying for students to copy into their books. This exercise simply involved printing, there was no cursive script. Anita also pointed out that when they had finished they could continue practising single letters in the next page of their handwriting booklet. There was no demonstration or discussion of posture, grip and the particular directionality of the letters to be written. There was very little engagement with the class at all, simply an instruction to write and be quiet. The boys opened their books and started work. While the noise level in the class did rise at regular intervals, after reprimands from Anita the boys quietened down and overall they were well behaved. Sitting quite close to Braydon, I was interested to see how long it took him to settle down to work. He fiddled with his pencil case, sorting through pens and pencils. When he did commence writing I noticed he was left-handed. As he was sitting at the last desk on the right-hand side of a row of desks, this made writing difficult. So as not to impinge upon his neighbour, Braydon shifted his book to the right-hand edge of his desk with his elbow directed towards the front of the room. Seated in such a way, writing was an uncomfortable process and Braydon seemed to procrastinate over completing his work.

The writing of the class overall varied considerably. Some boys had quite a good hand, but more often than not their writing was overly large with poorly formed letters. A number of the students had no idea about grip or correct directionality in forming letters, which not only proves a problem when they start to use cursive script and affect ease of writing, it also inhibits students' ability to focus on content. Most troubling, however, was a boy called Kenny, another Anglo student, who had no idea about correct grip. He simply held his pencil with a clenched fist as if he had no familiarity with writing at all. He anguished over each letter and not surprisingly was the last to finish the work on the board and then made little headway with his single letters. Despite these problems Anita only checked the students' work on two occasions during the 50-minute lesson. The rest of the time she was at her desk or talking to an assistant who had entered the room after the lesson had begun providing little assistance to students. It seemed the intention was to maintain quiet and order among students and simply let the boys get on with their work. Yet, without direction and intervention to correct problems, they were not only habituating poor technique but, in the case of Braydon and others, a capacity for work avoidance. While a discipline of control appeared to govern this pedagogic space it proved disabling as it seemed to either foster disinterest or else mask the problems some were experiencing with handwriting.

The function of this, and the other snapshots of practice, is not so much to evaluate the teachers' pedagogy but to consider its ramifications. The schools in the larger study with low-SES Anglo students and those of Pasifika backgrounds tended to perform below average on statewide literacy and numeracy tests. Braydon's test results were a case in point. Practices in the home, rather than just the macro-concepts of class and ethnicity, provide some explanation for this as they may contribute to a form of embodiment unsuited to schooling and academic endeavour, as seemed the case with Braydon. Practices within the classroom, however, can prove equally inhibitory. Braydon had not only failed to acquire capacities of effective literate practice within this classroom, poor habits through inaction were also confirmed. Together with this, Braydon's procrastination over work was indicative of a habituated lack of interest. It would be difficult for him to apply himself and improve these poor skills given the discipline of control that governed this space encouraging the kind of 'slavish submission' to which Durkheim referred. While stillness and quiet were encouraged, these were not forms of composure designed to foster the type of skills Braydon required, such as the appropriate posture and grip to write and a readiness to engage in work. They were simply a mechanism of control with the discipline that was engendered impeding rather than promoting any engagement in learning.

Part 2

Braydon's experiences at home and school contrast considerably with those of Vincent, a Chinese-background student who attended Broughton Heights PS. Vincent, from a low-SES family, liked school saying, 'I like to learn and to talk to my friends' but the best part is learning because 'I like reading and doing work'. He also mentioned that he liked homework, and when I asked "why" he pointed out that it was because with rest time he did nothing at home and "it was important to be doing something". Homework was also important to Vincent's mother, May. She felt it gave parents some insight into what was happening at school. It also allowed parents to help out with work and to repeat what was learnt at school. Repetition and regularity were important to May. She explained how he not only did homework every night but also on Saturday. As with many of the Chinese students we interviewed, Vincent attended coaching college, and it was here that he spent three hours doing extra work on a Saturday morning. He also completed college homework during the week. To Vincent this wasn't a chore. He actually preferred this homework because he said it was harder. Unlike Braydon, Vincent had a well-established homework routine. May explained how he had 'a break after school, until quarter past 4, then he start his homework for one hour, sometimes 45 minutes until 5 or quarter past and then he has a shower and dinner and then he starts another time at 7.30 to 8 o'clock until he finish'.

This was all undertaken in a room 'just for study', which Vincent shared with his older brother and father, each of whom had their own desk. Academic work, therefore, was not something simply associated with school and a site outside the home, a separate space was set aside for scholarly endeavour within the domestic sphere, which, not only Vincent, but also other family members used. As such, scholarly labour—sitting at a desk to complete work and concentrate on a task—assumed a naturalness and familiarity that was quite alien to Braydon. Individuals tend to acquire a degree of familiarity towards a space they inhabit on a regular basis; this marks the distinction between a notion of space and place. This familiarity, or what Seamon (2002) refers to as "at homeness" (p. 425), is an embodied phenomenon that can be experienced in a range of settings: home, work, school and elsewhere. Individuals become comfortable within a particular milieu and the "positive affective relationship" that develops encourages a certain naturalness about activities performed there (Seamon, 2002, p. 425). Such was the case with Vincent who, seemed to be embodying a scholarly habitus (Watkins, 2005) allowing for a kind of 'corporeal congruence' between home and school. Braydon clearly experienced a very different sense of place and 'at homeness' in relation to academic endeavour. Highlighting these differences of space, place, corporeality and habitus is not about valorising a particular experience or denigrating another, it is about rethinking what is meant by home/school congruence and the ways in which some students—as seemed the case with Vincent—maybe more appropriately prepared for school. In addition to this quite rigorous homework routine Vincent was also involved in a number of extracurricular activities. He learnt piano, which he practised on a Sunday morning. He also attended swimming lessons twice a week and soccer on Sunday afternoon. Vincent seemed to lead a highly regulated life with his parents actively cultivating particular dispositions in both their children. As May explained, 'When they are young we have to control them like a tree…a small tree. When they are bigger and grow up like a tree they understand what is right, what is wrong, what they can do, what they can't do'.

Vincent had seemingly embodied a discipline to learn. It is interesting, therefore, to consider the degree of congruence between the disciplinary practices in the home and at school. Vincent was in a 3/4 composite class at Broughton Heights PS. As he had arrived late in the year he was placed in the only class with a vacancy. His teacher Carly referred to it as 'the strangest class I've ever had'. Composite classes are generally comprised of a number of independent workers given the teacher is required to direct their attention to different groups at different times of the day yet Carly's class had very few able children. As 90% of the class had a LBOTE—mainly Arabic and Chinese or Pacific Islander languages—there were a number who required English as a Second Language (ESL) support including two Afghani and two African refugees. There were also two integration deaf children and two students with a mild intellectual (IM) disability. They were a handful to say the least, and Carly was very strict in relation to discipline. When I entered the class to observe a lesson it was half way through the middle session of the day when students tend to get a bit restless. The Year 4 students were sitting at their desks in a group arrangement, quiet and focused. Carly was sitting on the floor with the Year 3 students discussing a comprehension exercise. Questions were written on a board close by and Carly was discussing each with the students. Sitting in a circle on the floor, students seemed excited and engaged, but Carly insisted they sit correctly and didn't call out, though she did encourage orderly discussion. When she felt satisfied that they understood what was required the students moved to their desks to complete the activity. With the exception of one of the IM children, who was distracted but not disturbing others, students settled down quickly to work. Activities seemed fast paced. After 10 minutes of sustained work, students returned to the floor to discuss their work with Carly who then collected books to be marked.

This activity was followed by a maths lesson. Using plastic blocks, Carly engaged the class in a concrete activity about fractions. She then followed this with a number of similar examples where she had individual students, including Vincent, manipulate the blocks to produce different fractions and then suggest an appropriate number sentence to represent what they had done. Carly then moved to an abstract treatment of the same process using textbook examples with numerical notation. She discussed a number of these and then had those who felt confident return to their desks to complete a set of equations. The remainder stayed with Carly and she gave these students some further explanation about the transition from the concrete to abstract formulation. Vincent was one of those who moved to his desk. He quickly completed his work, had Carly check each answer and then moved to one of the computers in the room to complete extension maths work. Some other children who finished their work went on to read books just prior to lunch.

While there were various sites of learning in this classroom most children appeared engaged in their particular activities. The capacities these students demonstrated, such as an application to work, seemed to have a direct relationship to the pedagogy that Carly employed. With Vincent there was a definite correspondence between the disciplinary practices of home and school, which inclined him to academic endeavour, yet this may not have been the case with other students such as the Pasifika children and the Afghanis and Africans, the latter with disrupted schooling. It appears that over a period of time in Carly's class these students had embodied the skills required for independent work. While the disciplinary force generated by Carly's pedagogy tended towards control, it also had an enabling effect. This was not a class where constant docility was the rule—the kind of class as an "efficient machine" that Foucault (1977, pp. 164–67) describes in *Discipline and Punish* in which a 'morality of obedience' based on a prescriptive discipline of absolute silence and a Pavlovian process of 'signalisation' and response is evident. Unlike in Braydon's class, this stillness and quiet was by-and-large a productive stillness and quiet that was appropriate and required. Such composure equipped Vincent and his classmates with a readiness for activity. In contrast to Anita, Carly balanced control with engagement through her discussion and scaffolding of her students' learning. She had worked hard to instil particular capacities in her students through the discipline of control she employed which, rather than inhibiting, seemed to engender capacities of stillness, quiet and sustained application to work. It functioned as an enabling discipline of control reinforcing the discipline Vincent had acquired within the home but which many of his classmates had simply embodied on the basis of the pedagogy Carly employed on a day-to-day basis in her classroom.

Discipline That Disengages/Engages

Part 1

In these next two snapshots of practice a different continua of discipline is evident. While still functioning as a form of control, the experiences of the two students described here are representative of different modalities of discipline with intensity, which is far less apparent. It operates more in the capillary-like fashion that Foucault (1980) describes wherein, rather than an overt form of imposition, it "reaches into the very grain of individuals, touches their bodies and inserts itself into their actions…" (p. 39). Such a process seems insidious, which is Foucault's perspective here, yet as with the more explicit forms of disciplinary power already discussed, it too can prove enabling as well as disabling. Its agentic potential resides in the ways in which it is acquired, the pedagogies that foster technique and determine its utility.

The first of the two students discussed here is Finau, a Tongan boy, who like Vincent, attended Broughton Heights PS. Finau indicated that he liked school but as his mother pointed out "he needs a bit of help with school work". He received extra assistance with reading and appeared to have some difficulty with his written work. While Finau liked school, homework was another matter. He thought it was boring and only managed to do it "sometimes". As Finau was one of nine children, four of whom were attending Broughton Heights, it was difficult to find both time and space at home for work. His mother, however, considered Finau had a problem with homework. She felt he didn't receive much, or at least she didn't see it. When he did complete homework it was with his three younger siblings at the dining room table with Finau helping them. Homework appeared a communal activity in Finau's household though one in which his older siblings and Finau's parents had little or no role. His mother explained that "I just make sure they're doing it". Active supervision and an expectation that work was done and done well was not really the focus. It was more the case that the activity occurred on some days during the week. There clearly was not a routine, regularity about when and how homework was undertaken. There was no specific length of time or a requirement to work quietly in a sustained fashion. If homework happened it was all well and good but often it didn't. As the CLO at Broughton Heights explained, who was herself Tongan and had visited Finau's family a number of times, other activities such as church functions, visits from family and friends and rugby practice often got in the way of homework. Rugby was of key importance in Finau's household. Every Tuesday and Thursday night during the season the whole family would attend training and also the game on Saturday. Like Braydon, Finau was good at sport. In discussing what he excelled in at school his mother had actually referred to "football being his best subject". His 'instinctive' manipulation of the ball—knowing without thinking (Crossley, 2004, p. 45)—was a technique he had acquired through regular practice of skills and set plays. Practices around school work within the home, however, had had little impact on investing his body with the requisite technique for academic success; a discipline to sit and concentrate on a task whereby he could develop an automaticity in processing letters and sounds much in the same way as he had with kicking and passing a ball. The former set of skills was given minimal emphasis in Finau's home. Home and school were separate sites each with a different set of practices.

At Broughton Heights Finau was in a Year 3 class across the hall from Vincent. It was comprised of students from not only a diverse range of cultural and linguistic backgrounds but also a wide range of ability levels. Finau was towards the bottom in reading and maths. During one of the observation sessions I followed the students into class after a short orderly morning assembly. Finau surprisingly sat at the back at a desk with his friends Fred and Eli and a couple of Chinese- and Arabic-speaking boys. The orderliness of the assembly dissipated very quickly on students entering the room. There was quite a bit of noise as students chattered, swung back and forth on their chairs and played with equipment on their desks. Over this clatter and talk Kate, his teacher, said "good morning" but without gaining a suitable response started to count to attract students' attention. Although this managed to quieten the class, silence was not maintained and there seemed a constant hum in the classroom that Kate checked at times with either more counting, reprimands or techniques such as hands-on-heads or fingers on lips. Amid this noise, Finau, whom I was seated behind for most of the morning session, also swung on his chair and fiddled with equipment. Unable to achieve quiet, Kate started the lesson, which involved a discussion of the week's spelling words, a different list for set groups in the class followed by students copying their words into workbooks. Although students had no more than 10 words to write, this activity took 30 minutes. Students worked at various rates. Some finished early and settled down to read or complete other work but many, however, were slow to start, Finau, Fred and Eli especially so. Instead they were enjoying kicking each other under the table, attempting to disrupt other students with various levels of success. Fred and Eli eventually commenced writing, but Finau hadn't even put pen to paper when one of the other students at his table—a Chinese boy—had already finished and started reading. During this time Kate moved around the room checking students' work or having students come to her desk at the other side of the room diagonally across from where Finau was sitting. She seemed somewhat oblivious to the different levels of application within the class. After Finau finally did get down to work and finish he then left the class to put something in his bag. When he returned he roamed around the room until he was finally asked to sit down as the class moved onto one of two other tasks in this two-hour morning session. These were both language-based activities: a comprehension and a writing task, in which students showed limited interest. Finau and Eli demonstrated great difficulty with the writing, and Kate completed the activity with them out the front and then had them copy what they had undertaken together. This, however, also proved difficult for the boys. They were frequently distracted by others at their group of desks and had difficulty concentrating, though by this stage the task they were required to complete lacked any intellectual rigour; it was simply copying—busy work. This was very much the type of work the class as a whole undertook, a series of seemingly unrelated tasks without sustained treatment of a topic and the appropriate scaffolding.

As a result, a kind of discipline of disengagement governed this pedagogic space, which was not simply a function of Kate's structuring of activities and approach to curriculum implementation, it was also generated by the regimen of restlessness that pervaded the room. Some students with an existing habitus inclined towards academic endeavour may have been able to apply themselves to their work, and indeed this seemed to be the case. For many, such as Finau, however, the techniques that Kate employed failed to equip them with the discipline to learn and, left to rely on their existing habitus, they simply floundered and instead appeared to be cultivating a disposition of disinterest towards scholarly pursuits. This was not a mindful unwillingness, a conscious rejection of engaging in schoolwork, as in the resistance of the working-class lads that Willis (1981) documents in *Learning to Labour*, rather, it was an embodied disinterest predicated on the corporeality that Finau and others had acquired.

Part 2

The home and school experiences of the fourth student, Yupeng, are representative of a very different disciplinarity to that impacting upon Finau. Yupeng was of Chinese background and attended Colinville PS, located in an inner-western suburb of Sydney. The school was 55% LBOTE with a significant number of students from Chinese backgrounds. At the time of the study Yupeng had only been in Australia for two years and while his English had improved, he spoke little of the language on his arrival from China. Yupeng explained how he liked school "because it is fun and I like the teachers and my friends". Being an only child and with no other family apart from his parents in Australia, school was where he was able to socialise with other children. Yet while he liked "having free time and playing with his friends", Yupeng put a lot of emphasis on his schoolwork and extracurricular music. He explained that he spent up to two hours a night doing homework. His parents felt it was more like 30 minutes and pointed out this was not every night as he also had music practice to complete. Yupeng played three instruments: the violin, piano and recorder. His main instrument was the violin and at age eight he was in Grade 3 with ambitions to be a professional musician. The homework Yupeng completed, however, was not all provided by his classroom teacher. While he didn't attend an academic coaching college, Yupeng's parents, his father a telephone technician and his mother who had been a high school teacher in China, gave him additional work to complete at home from books they had purchased. Yupeng completed his homework in the lounge room yet this was very different to the lounge and dining rooms where Braydon and Finau completed their work. Yupeng sat at a desk in the lounge room. It was an item of furniture that took pride of place in his family's very sparsely furnished flat and, with no siblings, it was a relatively solitary space where his parents could supervise his homework. As his father pointed out, "I want everything finished". Together with his music, Yupeng played T-ball and chess, the latter during lunchtime at school. He and his parents also regularly borrowed books from their local library. As with Vincent, Yupeng had a busy schedule. With the range of activities in which he engaged there was an emphasis on discipline, which was likewise channelled into his academic work where he similarly performed well.

Yupeng was in 3B at Colinville, a class with a diverse mix of students from Chinese, Anglo, Indian, different Northern European and Pasifika backgrounds. While many students at the school were of a relatively high SES, there were those, such as Yupeng, who were not. As mentioned, considerable emphasis was placed on his schoolwork at home and Yupeng tended to be quiet and focused in class. Tom, his teacher, however, put a strong emphasis on structured class discussion and provided detailed explanation accompanying periods of independent work and, within this environment, Yupeng seemed to thrive. He remained quiet and focused when required but also actively engaged in class discussion. This was the case during the four observation lessons, two of which are described here. These two lessons formed part of work related to the Ronald Dahl novel *Charlie and the Chocolate Factory* that 3B was reading. Following a theme around sweets and cake—the link with the text—the first of these two lessons involved the class making patty cakes and the second using this concrete activity to write a procedural text.

In the first lesson after lunch students forwarded in and sat at their desks. Tom had written the instructions for what to do on the board and asked for a volunteer to read them aloud to the class. Yupeng's hand immediately shot up, and he proceeded to read from the board. Following this, groups were assigned a separate area in which to make their cakes where all the necessary ingredients had been laid out. In Yupeng's group each student had a turn of being involved, with group members negotiating the process. During this time Tom and Jay, the ESL teacher working with the class, checked students' progress and, despite the potential chaos of 32 children completing such an activity in a confined space, they seemed quite orderly with one student from each group taking trays down to the staffroom oven where Tom was loading them to be cooked and the remaining students cleared up. After 45 minutes on this activity, Jay called students to attention on the floor and explained how they were to write a procedure on this activity the next day. This session was conducted as a guided class discussion. Yupeng, as before, was actively engaged, volunteering answers to most questions and Jay carefully scaffolding the text they would write. After 20 minutes of outlining the procedure, students returned to their desks to read in the time prior to the bell.

This lesson continued in the mid-morning session of the next day. Students spent part of the morning icing and decorating their cakes. Jay, who was once again seated on the chair, started to count and students quickly forwarded to the floor. Tom was at the back of the class team-teaching with Jay during the lesson. She proceeded to write a scaffold of the text on the board: ingredients and method, and three columns headed 'nouns', 'verbs' and 'prepositions'. With reference to the previous day's discussion Jay, with assistance from Tom, questioned students about these aspects of the text recapping on key points. Yupeng, sitting close to the front, was again actively involved in answering questions. On completing the scaffold, Jay asked students to return to their desks and to use this to write their own text. The class was given 30 minutes to do this. Yupeng and his classmates worked in a quiet attentive manner with most completing a draft prior to lunch. As they left the class each took one of the iced patty cakes as a lunchtime treat.

Unlike in Finau's class a discipline of engagement seemed to pervade this room. Students were gaining a more sophisticated understanding of text and grammar through the careful scaffolding by the teachers. Both Jay and Tom used students' responses to questions to do this. Being teacher-directed, students were effectively engaged in the process and the concrete and highly motivating cooking activity that preceded this heightened their understanding and willingness to be involved. This was a concrete activity that was appropriately pitched, eliciting a sophisticated treatment of language. This approach was particularly effective for Yupeng who, though clearly studious and work focused, needed support to engage in discussion. Also, the whole class nature of the activity created a sense of corporate involvement that had considerable effect. There was still an appropriate level of control within the class but of a type that encouraged rather than stifled discussion. A discipline of engagement was evident with students actively involved. This activity, however, was predicated on a 'corporate composure' unlike the regimen of restlessness within Finau's class. This had been acquired as a result of the discipline generated by Tom and Jay's pedagogy, which not only promoted much needed skills of oral participation but also provided the time, quiet and space for Yupeng and his classmates to work independently and practise their written language skills.

Conclusion

These accounts of the discipline generated by the home and school practices of four students: Braydon, Vincent, Finau and Yupeng, seem to simply reinforce the stereotypes the study was keen to avoid; yet this research aims to get beneath the ideological function of perceptions of ethnicity by 'unpacking' stereotypes. There are different ways of doing this. The first is to challenge the stereotype by demonstrating its reductiveness, showing examples, which are counter to the 'rule'. The second and ultimately more insightful strategy is to examine the 'truth' or basis of a stereotype, and how it is produced. While each of the boys arrived at school having already embodied particular dispositions either inclined or disinclined towards academic endeavour, they also met vastly different disciplinary regimes in their respective classrooms. In Vincent and Yupeng's classrooms, where positive forms of discipline were generated—an enabling discipline of control and a discipline of engagement— students displayed a greater application to their work and appeared more absorbed in their learning. These forms of discipline appeared enabling for all students, no matter what their ethnicity, but for Vincent and Yupeng, this was especially the case. They had already embodied a discipline to learn from routines established within the home and so the relative congruence between home and school supported their learning and overall academic performance.

In classrooms where negative forms of discipline were the norm, such as a disabling discipline of control and a discipline of disengagement, students were less likely to be actively engaged in learning. This was apparent in Finau's classroom, where a discipline of disengagement prevailed. There were far too many distractions for Finau and, given he lacked the self-discipline to work independently or participate effectively, his classroom experiences simply reinforced the poor habits he already possessed. In Braydon's classroom, characterised by a disabling discipline of control, a different dynamic was evident, yet with similar effect. While some of his classmates completed work, Braydon and others did not. The key issue was they were rarely extended and, left to rely on their existing habitus; they simply reproduced what were familiar patterns of behaviour without acquiring the competencies they really needed.

To some extent this corporeality has a cultural basis, but what does this mean? Culture is not a pre-given category, a thing, or as Latour (2005) argues against in relation to the social, "a type of a material" (p. 1). It is a process that is constantly being remade through the iteration of practice. Analytically, the reification of culture makes no sense, as it fails to capture the processual nature of an individual's identity. A focus on practice, however, gives emphasis to the capacities required for successful academic performance, how these are acquired and why they are unevenly distributed. Agency then shifts from ethnicity and cultural background to the students themselves and the home and school practices that constitute them. This does not reduce achievement to a product of individual performance, downplaying the impact of sociocultural processes. Rather, it allows for a more nuanced analysis of students' cultural background. In such a way, culture is not simply perceived as ethnicity, or as a more sophisticated construct combined with gender and class but, as Wicker (1997) explains, "as a set of dispositions acquired by individuals in the process of living" (p. 40). The differential achievement of these students from Chinese-, Pasifika- and Anglo-backgrounds is not a function of cultural pathology but rather can be attributed to the different practices in which they engaged both inside and outside school, the discipline each engendered, and the ways this then disposed them to learning. While appearing to simply exert control, some forms of discipline are actually embodied and utilised for agentic purposes. In education, and socio-cultural theory more broadly, the enabling potential of discipline receives little attention. Consideration, however, needs to be given to how all students, no matter what their background, require a certain discipline to learn. It is through this that the agency for successful participation in schooling is achieved. To paraphrase Durkheim (2002) it "teaches us to restrain and master ourselves" and in so doing provides "a means of emancipation and of freedom" (p. 49).

Acknowledgment

An Australian Research Council Linkage Project with the NSW Department of Education and Training funded the research upon which this chapter is based. I wish to acknowledge the generous support of each body and also the assistance of my co-investigator Greg Noble from the Centre for Cultural Research, University of Western Sydney.

References

Butler, J. (1997). *The psychic life of power*. Stanford, California: Stanford University Press.

Crossley, N. (2004). The circuit trainer's habitus: Reflexive body techniques and the sociality of the workout. *Body and Society 10* (1): 37–69.

Dooley, K., Exley, B. and Singh, P. (2000). Social justice and curriculum renewal for Samoan students: An Australian case study. *Special Edition of International Journal of Inclusive Education, 4*(1), 23–42.

Duffy, M. (2001, September 29). Improved by Asian work ethic. *Courier Mail*, p. 28.

Durkheim, E. (2002). *Moral education*. (Trans E. K. Wilson and H. Schnurer.). Mineola, New York: Dover Publications.

Foucault, M. (1977). *Discipline and punish: The birth of the prison*. Harmondsworth: Penguin.

Foucault, M. (1980). *Power/knowledge: Selected interviews and other writings 1972–1977*. C. Gordon (Ed.). New York: Pantheon Books.

Foucault, M. (2005) *The Hermeneutics of the Subject: Lectures at the College de France 1981–1982*. (G. Burchell, Trans.). New York: Picador.

Foucault, M. (1990). *The history of sexuality volume 3: The care of the self*. (R. Hurley, Trans.). Harmondsworth: Penguin.

Francis, S. (1995). Pacific Islander young people. In C. Guerra and R. White (Eds.), *Ethnic minority youth in Australia*. (pp. 179–192). Hobart, Tas: National Clearinghouse for Youth Studies.

Heilmann, E. E. (2005). Escaping the bind between utopia and dystopia—eutopic critical pedagogy of identity and embodied practice. In Ilan Gur Ze'ev (Ed.), *Critical theory and critical pedagogy today: Toward a new critical language in education*. (pp. 114–142) Haifa: University of Haifa.

Holliday, A. R. (2005). *The struggle to teach English as an international language*. Oxford: Oxford University Press.

Latour, B. (2005). *Reassembling the social: An introduction to actor-network-theory*. Oxford: Oxford University Press.

Malabou, C. (2005). *The future of Hegel: Plasticity, temporality and dialectic*. London: Routledge.

Matthews, J. (2002). Racialised schooling: Ethnic success and Asian-Australian students. *British Journal of Sociology of Education, 23*(2), 193–207.

Mauss, M. (1979). *Sociology and psychology*. (B. Brewster, Trans.). London: Routledge.

Noble, G. and Watkins, M. (2009). On the arts of stillness: Towards a pedagogy of composure. *M/C Journal. 12*(1), 520–538.

Pandian, A. (2008). Pastoral power in the postcolonial. *Cultural Anthropology, 23*(1), 85–117.

Seamon, D. (2002). Physical comminglings: Body, habit, and space transferred into place. *OTJR: Occupation, Participation and Health. 22*(4), 42–51.

Singh, P. and Sinclair, M. (2001). Diversity, disadvantage and differential outcomes. *Asia-Pacific Journal of Teacher Education, 29*(1), 73–92.

Watkins, M. (2005). Discipline, consciousness and the formation of a scholarly habitus. *Continuum, 19*(4), 545–558.

Watkins, M., and Noble, G. (2008). *Cultural practices and learning: Diversity, discipline and dispositions in schooling.* Penrith South, NSW: University of Western Sydney.

White, R., Perrone, S., Guerra, C., Francis, S., Hunter, F. and Lampugnani, R. (1999). *Ethnic youth gangs in Australia—do they exist? Report no. 3: Pacific Islander young people.* Melbourne: Australian Multicultural Foundation.

Wicker, R. (1997). From complex culture to cultural complexity. In P. Werbner and T. Modood (Eds.), *Debating cultural hybridity: Multicultural identities and the politics of anti-racism* (pp. 32–46). London: Zed Books.

Willis, P. (1981). Learning to labour: How working class kids get working class jobs. Aldershot: Gower.

Chapter VI

Discipline and the *Dojo*

Robert John Parkes

This chapter is concerned with the productive nature of discipline. That is, with what subjection within and to a discipline 'produces'. More specifically, I am concerned with the way a "subject comes into being...comes to mastery, comes into existence and agency, through *subjection*" (Petersen, 2007, p. 477, original emphasis). I use martial arts training as a case study for my investigation because it is so frequently depicted as a site of 'serious' discipline; a somewhat 'inflexible' discipline that practitioners more or less willingly subject themselves to in order to attain mastery of the art under study. My aim is to develop an understanding of the deliberate act of subjection that is implicated in the disciplining process by which the individual is transformed through the martial arts. Resting upon Michel Foucault's (1980, 1982/1994) thesis on the 'double nature' of power, I argue in this chapter for both the constraining and enabling effects of discipline as it manifests in and through the martial arts and investigate the way discipline is central to the act of becoming in the *dojo*.[1] Eric Paras (2006) has argued that we should distinguish Foucault's position in the 1980s, that the individual "had the ability to pursue (or not pursue) techniques that would transform its subjectival modality", from his earlier thesis that "no individual received the choice of whether or not to undergo discipline; and only through discipline did one become an individual" (p. 123). This contrast may however be drawn too sharply. I think it is safe to argue that Foucault never abandoned the notion that Judith Butler (1997) has articulated so well, that power is not simply a force that subordinates from the outside, but must be understood as "what we depend on for

---

[1] In italicising Japanese words drawn from the lexicon of martial tradition, I mean to make the point that each of these terms carries a rich array of meanings that are not easily replaced by a single English word. Thus the word *dojo*, which implies the place where the way is taught, means something more substantial than "training hall"; and *Sensei*, although used in everyday Japanese to mean "teacher", carries within martial arts circles the notion of one who in being born before, as the kanji for *Sensei* imply, is further down the path.

our existence... that, paradoxically, initiates and sustains our agency" (p. 2). However, in exploring the 'voluntary' subjection to discipline that is a feature of martial arts training, I am clearly indebted to the position taken up within the later Foucault (1980, 1982/1994), that remains attached to the notion that agency arises only through subjection (a legacy of his earlier work), but that offers the possibility of deliberate and 'motivated' subjection. I am thus using 'subjection' to mean both "subordinated by power as well as the process of becoming a subject" (Butler, 1997, p. 2); and it is the phenomenon of wilful subjection in order to become a particular kind of subject that makes the martial arts an interesting alternative site to the public school classroom.[2] Certainly there is a reason for returning to Foucault's thesis on the productive nature of power in this chapter, and it is at least partially motivated by a desire to challenge the take up of aspects of his theory.

Foucault (1977) has clearly stated that "[t]he chief function of disciplinary power is to 'train'...it does not link forces together in order to reduce them; it seeks to bind them together in such a way as to multiply and use them" (p. 170). In drawing upon Foucault's conception of self-formation through subjection to or through discipline, I seek to challenge those scholars who over-emphasise the constraining and repressive aspects of power and discipline when drawing upon Foucault's (1977) work. While I am not entirely sure why this particular use and reading of Foucault is so common, despite his claims to articulate the productive nature of power and disciplinarity, I would hazard a guess that it arises from residual commitments to an emancipatory project held by many scholars attracted to the early phases of Foucault's work. According to Dominick LaCapra (2000), Foucault "was forceful in bringing into prominence the ways in which marginalisation, subjection, and abjection could take place even in the seemingly most liberal or enlightened policies and practices" (p. 16), and this has undoubtedly been the attractiveness of his work to many scholars in fields with 'social justice' ambitions, such as Education. I intend to challenge the tendency of viewing discipline as a repressive force—exhibited even within the poststructural literature whenever care is not taken to differentiate 'productive' from its everyday association with things 'positive' or 'good'—by putting forward a case that the constraining effects of discipline may be understood precisely as its enabling or productive aspects (as Megan Watkins has also argued in Chapter 5 of this volume, see also Watkins, 2005). To do so is to reject the problematic association of the constraining effects of power with repression, and its productive aspects with positive outcomes. That is to say, I will argue that there is not one set of 'disciplinary' practices (Foucault, 1977) that is constraining, and another set that is enabling. Instead, I hope to make the case that all disciplinary constraints are precisely enabling forces that operate on and through the individual martial artist as a means of self-formation[3]; and that participation in a disciplinary regime or process results in the 'production' of a particular kind of person, individual, or martial artist. I do not believe that I am presenting a new argument here, but simply using the martial arts as a case study to challenge particular interpretations of Foucault's theory.

---

[2]   I am also following Luke (1996) here, in exploring pedagogies of everyday life that occur outside the confines of the public school education system.

[3]   Although I don't elaborate on this, the idea of self-formation being described here can clearly be understood as depicting disciplines and disciplinarity as the means to engage in what German scholars have called Bildung (see for example, Masschelein & Ricken, 2003).

In crafting my argument, I inevitably follow in the footsteps of Claudia Eppert and Hongyu Wang (2008), initiating a dialogue between Eastern and Western perspectives on pedagogy and curriculum, as I engage with Foucault's (1977, 1982/1994) claim regarding the productive nature of power and discipline. This approach registers the Nietzschean strategy of "estranging one's own by means of the foreign" (Scheiffele, 1991, p. 41); and the selection of the martial arts as an educational enterprise worthy of being cast as an object of analysis, is a manoeuvre expressly designed to expose "deficiencies and weaknesses that are not simply seen within one's own horizon" (Scheiffele, 1991, p. 41) when examining taken-for-granted educational sites such as the public school classroom. I am aware that there is always a danger of romanticising the other when enacting this particular kind of scholarly tactic. However, it is not my intention to make a case for the superiority of an Eastern mode of discipline over Western disciplinary forms. I do not use the concept of 'self-transformation' through martial arts discipline in any utopian sense (where the discipline is expected to lead to some form of final liberation). Nor is this study performed in some uncritical celebration of the martial arts (as my discussion of the effects of different martial arts on self-formation should reveal). In fact, I hope to avoid romanticism altogether—including the enduring educational Romanticism of Rousseau and his legacy that would be at best ambivalent towards discipline as pedagogy, particularly when 'discipline' is viewed only through the lens of restriction or constraint. Rather, I am interested in using the martial arts as a case study to understand the complex ways in which discipline and desire interact to produce particular kinds of subjects, and both make available and limit possible subject positions. My adoption of the Nietzschean strategy of "looking back" from a foreign or counterposition (Scheiffele, 1991, p. 42) is designed to enable us to re-examine our understanding of 'discipline' itself, from the perspective of the foreign, in order to better grasp its often misunderstood productive, and seductive, aspects. Thus, using the martial arts, I hope to be able to better articulate a productive view of disciplinarity that might have purchase beyond martial arts training.

Before I begin the task I have set myself in this chapter, informed by the turn towards transgressive methodologies in poststructural educational research (Davies, 2004), it would seem appropriate to acknowledge that much that finds its way onto the page, even though not always stated explicitly, arises from my twenty years of involvement with the martial arts, as both student and instructor.[4] Further, the main thrust of my argument is more philosophical than empirical, though I do where relevant and necessary, draw upon the published instructional manuals and treatises of martial arts instructors, and supplement this material with comment upon popular representations of the martial arts in commercial film media in a couple of places where I think this will help provide wider access to the point I am attempting to articulate. I confine my terminology to that used in the traditional Japanese martial arts, unless otherwise stated, so this chapter does not

---

[4] I began my martial arts training in Wing Chun Kung-Fu, and was quickly exposed to Kickboxing, and a variety of Wushu forms. I later studied Togakure Ryu Ninjutsu, in which I hold a 5th degree black belt, and which informs many of the incidental references in this chapter. Along the way I also picked up skills in Filipino Arnis (stick and knife fighting). I ran my own martial arts schools from the late eighties through the decade of the 1990s, until the academic life took over.

become too confusing. Similarly, for the most part, I will focus my examples on the traditional Japanese martial arts, in order to provide high contrast via the examination of related traditions, that would be lost if I attempted a more panoptic overview of martial arts from around the world. Finally, I will use the understandings developed through my martial arts case study as a lens for exploring the problem of discipline generally, and 'educational' discipline in particular.

Discipline as the Way: Subjection and Desire

"You must be very disciplined?" is a question I've been asked many times, almost the instant after I've revealed my years of involvement in the martial arts. It rehearses a popular perception of the martial arts (Greenberg, 2000) and is frequently the motivation of many a parent who has brought their child to the *dojo* in order to "become more disciplined". It might be said that the *dojo*, the place where 'the martial Way' is taught and followed, does not exist without discipline (Lovret, 1987). But a desire for discipline is rarely the reason any adult or teenager begins the training. Their desire is usually for what would seem to be something else entirely. The most common reasons for involvement in martial arts, in addition to their perceived benefits as forms of self-defence, have often been found to centre on the 'interesting nature' of the arts, their health benefits, and their effectiveness as a means of personal cultivation, or physical and psychological development (Zaggelidis, Martinidis, & Zaggelidis, 2004). A study of martial artists in the West Midlands region of England found that a sense of affiliation, friendship, and fitness were among the highest ranked motives behind martial arts study (Jones, Mackay, & Peters, 2006). This same study also found that status or reward (what we might describe as 'recognition seeking') might certainly be another factor motivating involvement in the martial arts. However, the martial arts present a contradiction in this regard. The members of a *dojo* are not equal in rank, and their status is often marked out publicly by the donning of different coloured belts that mark their level of attainment. So it may take some time before the desired status is achieved. Certainly, a testamur or coloured belt in a traditional martial art is hard to attain and is only achieved through repeatedly subjecting oneself to the discipline of the *dojo* and its martial traditions.

What is interesting in the example of the martial arts, is the extent to which the desire to attain mastery—or what we might describe after Nietzsche and Foucault as 'the will to martial arts power'—so obviously drives the process of subjection. This stands the martial arts in contrast with many formal educational settings, where students are frequently unwilling or resigned participants in the pedagogical enterprise and have never committed themselves to the system's goals or intended outcomes. The desire motivating a person who subjects him/herself to the training regime of the martial arts, to become someone more confident and capable, is probably not unique to the martial arts. It would undoubtedly be true of many extra-curricular settings, like for example music or dance practice. Further, whereas many students in mandatory public education experience discipline as an imposition, it becomes a key feature of the educational journey in the traditional martial arts. However, the desire for some sense of personal mastery or status attainment comes at a cost, which is not always known to students when they start, but becomes clear as they progress. It can be attained only if the student demonstrates the 'proper attitude' of *nyunanshin* (Lovret, 1987), of surrender to the authority of the *Sensei* and the traditions she or he embodies (Lovret, 1987; Schinc, 1995). In practice this manifests as a willingness and commitment to embodying the techniques and tactics of the *ryu* (or 'family tradition') as accurately as possible. The body operates as a malleable substance during the training, which is shaped through 'self-discipline' (and instructor feedback) into a mirror-image of the tradition, and gains in legitimacy and status as its approximations of the *seitei kata* (standard form) improve. The familiar line of Karate students practicing precise *kata* (patterns) in perfect time (as one sees inside the Cobra Kai *Dojo* in the *Karate Kid*, and in Jim Kelly's 'black power' *dojo* during the introductory scenes of Bruce Lee's Hollywood epic, *Enter the Dragon;* where the syncopated strikes of the students is so welldone that the snap of their uniforms makes the sound of a shotgun loading), is one of a number of disciplinary technologies that reinforces this principle. Thus, typical of disciplinary power as Foucault (1977) has described it, legitimacy and status are obtained only through subjection, through disciplining oneself to (re)produce precise technical forms. Stephen K. Hayes (1983), influenced by his Tantric Buddhist training, describes this process as "taking refuge" in the *ryu* (the path or tradition), the *ichimon* (family or community of practitioners) fellow travellers on the journey, and the *sensei* (the teacher), the one who has already travelled the path (pp. 31–33). Importantly, the self that emerges from this process could hardly be described as a 'docile' body (Foucault, 1977), if we understand that to mean submissive. Rather, subjected to discipline, the docile body achieves "efficiency of movements" (Foucault, 1977, p. 137), and in Foucault's (1977) example of the soldier, drawn from the writings of the general Montgomery, develops "an alert manner, an erect head, a taut stomach, broad shoulders, long arms, strong fingers, a small belly, thick thighs, slender legs and dry feet, because a man of such a figure could not fail to be agile and strong" (p. 135). Thus, through discipline a transformation occurs that produces a subject who is simultaneously more 'capable' and perhaps more 'independent' than they were before (Schine, 1995), but also someone who has been shaped and constrained by the features of the discipline that they have come to embody. I will come back to this point in more detail later.

The curriculum of the classical martial art *ryu* is typically organised into three levels: *Shoden,* or basics that embody general principles and prepare the student for serious training; *Chuden,* or middle-level teachings, that dramatically expand the student's repertoire and give the martial art style its distinctive character; and finally *Hiden,* or so-called secret teachings that are not taught in any regular sense (Lovret, 1987). [5] Certainly,

---

[5]   A somewhat more esoteric model of progression through the stages of martial arts mastery has been provided by Stephen K. Hayes (1984), the first American to be awarded the rank of *Shidoshi* (licensed teacher of the 'warrior ways') in Bujinkan Kobudo. Hayes' scheme consists of five stages, moving from: (1) a basic foundation in which emphasis is placed on learning the *kihongata* or fundamental principles and physical forms of the art; (2) the development of *nagare*, a flowing responsive relationship with an attacker, achieved by learning to apply the fundamental principles and techniques with a live opponent, in order to improve timing, distancing, and spontaneous decision-making; (3) concentration on your ability to control and direct the energy of the conflict; (4) concentration on developing an ability to conceal oneself safely in the very centre of the conflict, through mastering principles of *kyojitsu tenkan ho*—the strategy of altering

no *Sensei* instructs his students directly in the *Hiden*. Rather, the *Hiden*, as sets of strategies and dispositions, are learnt during the conduct of the training, through what the Japanese masters sometimes call *Shinden*, which literally means something like 'divinely transmitted' but might be more comfortably translated as 'heart teaching'. Such heart-to-heart transmission can be understood as an instructional metaphor for modelling oneself on the conduct of an accomplished practitioner. It is one of the reasons students are encouraged to seek out instruction from a recognised master practitioner, and presents an interesting contrast with martial sports like Boxing, where the coach is neither expected nor required to be an accomplished practitioner. Within martial arts training, this process of modelling oneself on the conduct of an accomplished practitioner would seem to be frequently achieved without conscious deliberation, although it is explicitly advocated in many traditions (see for example, Hatsumi & Hayes, 1987). Certainly, the student comes to embody these unspoken heart teachings through a process that couples intense desire and subjection. The desire is for the perceived benefits of martial arts mastery— including self-confidence, greater autonomy, higher self-esteem, emotional stability, and improved physical capability (see the review of the literature conducted by Lakes & Hoyt, 2004)—which drive the student to subject themselves to the rigorous schedule of training offered in the *dojo*. They quickly learn in this process that approximating the movements of their seniors is the surest way to both personal accomplishment and social recognition within the martial arts community.

There are frequent admonishments during traditional martial training that to attain mastery one must be guided not only by the attitude of *nyunanshin* (or surrender, like the bamboo in the wind) described above, but also by an attitude of "*mushotoku*—without any goal or desire for profit" (Nakano, 1995, p. 58). This may seem to contradict the claim I am staking around the interaction of desire and discipline. However, it is important to understand, as Helen Nakano (1995) notes, that it is the "twin demons of obsession and compulsion" (p. 57) that are to be targeted by adopting *mushotoku* as a frame of mind, and getting past these impediments is actually tied to achievement of mastery in most martial arts traditions. Thus, the goal is attained, in part, when the desire that has fuelled the journey is extinguished. There is a Buddhist or Zen logic that is operating here, that challenges dualistic understandings of the education of a martial artist (see Lu, 2003, for a discussion of the non-dualist philosophy that underpins the martial arts). Desire fuels involvement and motivation for the training, but a discipline of 'letting go' aids attainment. This is often taught physically during freeform sessions, where students are instructed to immediately 'let go' of a failed technique and move on with some other technique or tactic. Such a training principle is explicitly advocated in Ninjutsu training for example (Daniel, 1986), and works as a disciplinary technology to instil this particular attitude or mindset in practitioners. Certainly the proposal from many traditional *Sensei* like Nakano is ironically, that the desire motivating the quest for mastery must ultimately be overcome or dissipated as part of the process of attainment. Failing to do so is perceived by martial arts instructors to leave desire as a distraction that operates as

---

the opponent's perception of truth and falsehood; and finally (5) the attainment of a state of freedom and spontaneous self-expression described as the *ku no seikai* or realm devoid of specific recognisable manifestation.

an impediment to spontaneous action in a combative situation. In other words, over-confidence or obsessive commitments produced by an intense desire to attain mastery are to be avoided by the ideal warrior, by acknowledging and letting go of one's desires in the heat of combative exchange. Practitioners who are successful at this process of technical and tactical attainment and are capable of maintaining a calm and relaxed frame of mind are said to have attained *mushin* or 'no mind' (Daniel, 1986). It is this complex relationship between discipline, desire, and subjection that has led many *Sensei* to draw on the Buddhist roots of the martial arts traditions and represent the martial arts as a warrior path to enlightenment (Deng, 1990; Hayes, 1981b; Lovret, 1987; Westbrook & Ratti, 1970). While I make no judgements on the truth-value of such a claim, there is undoubtedly a relationship between the goals of a martial art and the operation and effects of its specific forms of discipline.

Disciplines and Their Disciples: Subjection as Self-Formation

As we explore the effects of discipline on the martial artist, it is important to understand that all martial arts are not the same. Within some martial art circles, the ideal outcome or telos of the training is the scholar warrior (as exemplified by the Samurai ideal of *Bunbu Itchi,* or "pen and sword in accord"). However, one can find a rival conception of the ultimate goal of martial arts training in the autobiography of Dave Lowry, a well-known American Kenjutsu practitioner, where it is described as the attainment of *shibumi,* "the aesthetic quality of severe simplicity... quiet, graceful, and hidden beauty" (Lowry, 1995, p. 172; see also pp. 133–48); and another in the semi-autobiographical instructional manual of Stephen K. Hayes, an American Ninjutsu master, where the goal is expressed as the achievement of a level of "freedom and effortless power experienced as the *ku no seikai* (realm devoid of specific recognizeable manifestation)" (Hayes, 1984, p. 154). Derived from historically and culturally diverse contexts, martial arts forms and traditions have decidedly different goals, practices, rules, and structures (see for example, the overview of different martial traditions in Draeger & Smith, 1974), and it is precisely the distinct teleology and practices of Karate-do and Aikido, for example, that has inspired their selection as examples later in this chapter. Sports scientists engaged in establishing the 'benefits' of martial arts training have often ignored such distinctions. However, they have often used their own measures to contrast contemporary and traditional martial arts, and have made the claim that higher self-esteem, greater autonomy, emotional stability, assertiveness, self-confidence, physical confidence, improved self-perception of physical ability, and enhanced body image (Lakes & Hoyt, 2004), have only been found among individuals who study in a 'traditional' *dojo,* once the 'gravitational effects' of self-selection—particular personality types being attracted to particular types of martial arts training—have been controlled and accounted for (Nosanchuk & MacNeil, 1989; Seig, 2004). That is to say, studies that have been conducted from within an empiricallyoriented 'scientific' research paradigm upon the effects of martial arts training on the development of character and personality traits, have mostly been inconclusive, unable to distinguish whether personality features that correlate with long-term martial arts practice were the result of self-selection and attrition or training effects.[6] In terms of the operational effects of discipline this is not particularly problematic, as I hope to demonstrate later. However, in his examination of this 'scientific' literature, Brandon Seig (2004) has revealed that there are a few benchmark longitudinal studies that suggest that the martial arts can indeed have positive effects on personality development through a training effect, but such an outcome is contingent upon the adoption of particular approaches to teaching found in so-called traditional martial arts.

We should certainly approach Seig's (2004) advice with some caution, given the martial arts are many and varied, and there has been little attention to the effect of studying specific martial arts. Further, determining what constitutes a 'traditional' *dojo* is far from simple. Frederick J. Lovret (1987) has argued, most martial arts schools teach a person new things, whereas "the goal of a [traditional] *dojo* is to transform the person into something new" (p. 14). Certainly a common way of determining which martial arts or *dojo* may be considered 'traditional' has its roots in the distinction often made between *jutsu* and *do* martial forms (i.e., Ju-Jitsu versus Judo).[7] The argument follows that there is a relative emphasis on self-protection in *jutsu* arts versus an explicit emphasis on self-perfection in *do* arts. However, in practice, the *jutsu-do* distinction is probably loosing traction as both forms are increasingly subject to commercial modification.[8] In attempting to find their own way of discriminating between martial arts, Nosanchuk and MacNeil (1989) define 'traditional' not by an arbitrary distinction based on the suffix to its name, or on its documented point of historical emergence, but by its emphasis on *kata* (ritualised forms) over *kumite* (sparring); the teaching of ethics and philosophy *(do)* alongside technique *(jutsu)* rather than technique alone; and the degree of restraint shown by, and respect shown to, the *Sensei* (often manifest through a climate of quiet and respectful etiquette). It is important to note that this definition may in fact represent a reinvention of tradition. However, using a similar set of distinctions, Twemlow and Sacco (1998) have argued that progress within a traditional martial arts program follows four distinct stages, which they define as follows: 1) *Gyo*—an initial stage in which the student

---

[6]   In some martial arts, such as *Bujinkan Kobudo*, attrition is understood to be an important factor in the training, that means "that kind of person, the ones with the wrong motivations, disappear by themselves" (Hatsumi & Hayes, 1987, p. 159). Thus, the training is seen to 'weed out' students with undesirable characters, and the tradition understands this as part of its pedagogy.

[7]   According to prominent martial arts practitioners and scholars it is important to distinguish between *bugei* or *bujutsu* "martial arts" and *budo* "martial ways" (Draeger & Smith, 1974). According to this schema, *jutsu* forms such as *Kenjutsu* (the art of the sword), *Jujutsu* (the art of unarmed combat), *Bojutsu* (the art of staff fighting), and *Ninjutsu* (the art of stealth), emerged from the tenth century onwards as family or clan traditions of armed and unarmed self-protection. The *do* forms, such as *Aikido* (the way of harmonising force), *Kendo* (the way of the sword), and *Karate-do* (the way of the empty hand), developed from these earlier military and fighting arts as methods of self-perfection, commencing their evolution in the eighteenth century with the decline of the Samurai class, but quickening after Japan's defeat in WWII when the nation had to come to terms with its martial past. Stephen K. Hayes (1981b) in one of his early books introducing Ninjutsu to the West, described the Zen-influenced *do* arts as 'ritualised forms', seeking to make a case for the effectiveness and vitality of the ancient *jutsu* combat forms.

[8]   One contemporary conception is that *jutsu* describes self-defence techniques or the art studied, and *do* signifies self-perfection or the lifestyle practiced.

begins identification with the teacher and the art and starts to understand the body as a means of self-expression; 2) *Shugyo*—immersion in, and obsession with, the techniques of the art, in which one's enthusiasm results in intense training and often spills into everyday situations, much to the annoyance of parents, siblings, and friends; 3) *Jutsu*— skill mastery accompanied by a graceful calmness and clarity regarding the underlying principles informing the techniques; and 4) *Do*—the emergence of a centred state of mind, where the opponent is understood to lie within and the task is to continuously work upon one's own *suki* or mental and physical 'weak points' (Daniel, 1986), leading to the perfection of technique and the embodiment of the values of compassion, humility, and self-awareness that are argued to be the ultimate goals of many martial arts traditions.

As noted earlier, disciplining oneself to follow the principles and practices of the *ryu* is the path to the level of embodiment and attainment symbolised by the black belt. The reward of discipline is the attainment of a specific set of capabilities and a particular kind of freedom within the constraints of the specific *ryu* that has been studied. Such constraints provide a signature or character to the martial artist's performance that marks the individual as a practitioner of a particular 'style'. More significantly, it could be argued that these constraints shape the practitioners' mental outlook, as well as their emotional and intellectual dispositions (Brown & Johnson, 2000; Moore & Gillette, 1992); or thought about another way, limit the range of available subject positions. Some scholars have argued that the forms of disciplinary practice operating in competitive martial arts are often associated with an increase in aggression, rather than the 'positive' character traits identified as outcomes of traditional martial arts study (Nosanchuk & MacNeil, 1989). However, there are significant differences present in traditional martial arts, and it might be enough at this point to indicate that while most traditional martial arts may have some common sets of practice, there is often significant variation in the values and philosophies that underpin the training regime and most identifiably in the area of the strategic knowledge that they adopt, which arguably reflect and construct dispositional differences.

This shaping effect of martial arts discipline is an expected outcome of traditional martial arts training (Lovret, 1987). In effect, the martial artist becomes a disciple, a practitioner of a particular discipline, who embodies the dispositional technical and tactical knowledge of their art as a result of subjection to its disciplinary forms. The disciplinary technology underlying this process is sometimes described as *sanmitsu,* or 'the triple secret'—the harmonising or alignment of thought (intention), word (strategy), and action (technique) as a single tool of accomplishment (Hayes, 1981b, pp. 143–59). Such alignment is facilitated by the way the fundamental techniques of a martial art instantiate particular strategic principles. Within martial arts traditions, the *kihon kata* or basic techniques are not simply methods of self-defence, but frequently embody complex strategic knowledge and philosophical principles (Lovret, 1987). This is not always apparent to novices (or the parents of children who are brought to the *dojo* to enhance their self-discipline). However, repeatedly working to model one's performance on the standard form of the basic techniques shapes both the body, and the 'strategic disposition'—or the available tactical repertoire—of the martial artist. Within the Japanese art of Ninjutsu for example, there is a sense that the fundamental fighting postures and techniques are "bodily manifestations of our emotional responses" to danger (Hayes, 1989, p. 30), and that through practicing these postures "best understood as the physical embodiment of mental attitude" (Hayes, 1981a, p. 54), one develops a suite of dispositional responses to conflict. This is akin to the 'forms of composure' Megan Watkins discusses in Chapter 5 of this volume. Martial arts instructors have generated a range of metaphors for describing this process of dispositional development, but by far the most common is the idea that through thousands of repetitions a student will come to "internalize" the desired technical repertoire (Palumbo, 1987, p. 16). Thus, a particular type of person is produced through subjection to this disciplinary regime. The black belt may be a subject who is more 'capable' and 'independent' than they were before, but they are also someone whose technical and tactical repertoire simultaneously enables them to act in specific ways, by both its affordances and its constraints. A couple of contrasting examples might help make this point more apparent.

The Productive Effect of Aikido and Karate

Let us turn to the principles underpinning the art of Aikido. I have selected Aikido because it is a highly popular martial art with a clearly articulated telos. Gaining its name in 1941, but developing its public reputation in earnest after WWII, Morehei Ueyshiba's Aikido reconceptualised a range of armed and unarmed martial arts using the "Principle of Aiki" or 'blending' (Saito, 1975, p. 12). Aikido uses circular footwork and limb-twisting grappling techniques to blend one's own body movement with that of the attacker, redirecting the force of an opponent's grab, blow, stick-strike, or sword-slash, throwing them off-balance, and repelling an attack without necessarily hurting the aggressor. The philosophy of Aikido is centred on the idea that martial arts should focus on the compassionate protection of all beings (including some would argue, the opponent), and its strategy is based on a combination of a strong centeredness, coupled with outward extension of body and perception, and the 'leading' of an opponent's force using circular motions, towards a point at which any attack is neutralised (Westbrook & Ratti, 1970). Aikido training constrains its disciples within a technical and tactical repertoire that aims at evading threats and neutralising attacks without retaliation. Its pedagogy promotes interpersonal relatedness and self-learning (Brawdy, 2001). Through the discipline of Aikido practice practitioners become less likely to initiate an aggressive move. The art literally has no attacking forms, and is silent on offensive tactics (the Aikido of Gozo Shioda, 1968, perhaps being the exception with its retention of *Atemi*, or disruptive counter-offensive striking techniques). The emphasis within the training on becoming a good *uke* (attacker who ultimately 'receives' the Aikido technique), powerfully inscribes reception rather than initiation as the dominant strategic disposition. By virtue of practicing a form of strategic knowledge focused on artful defence, the Aikido disciple develops a disposition whose major constraint—the absence of attacking techniques and tactics—produces an individual who is calm and focused during the whirlwind aggression of a combat situation, but whose strategic principles limit his/her capacity for effective offence. Thus, Aikido practitioners can position themselves to ward off attacks as they arise, but may be unable to initiate a decisive attack if provoked, as they have been denied through the training any tactically offensive subject position. This constraint actually produces the productive effect of Aikido training, the development of a 'peaceful warrior'.

Now let's consider the martial art of Karate-do. I have selected Karate-do as an equally popular, high contrast example to Aikido. Originally from Okinawa, and based on ancient Chinese Kenpo (Kung-Fu), Karate-do developed into its contemporary form during the 1930s. Popularised in movies during the 1960s and 1970s, Karate became a household word throughout the world. As a martial art, Karate-do emphasises striking and kicking techniques against the 'vital points' of the human anatomy, and depending on the 'style' practiced, often involves basic grappling takedown and restraining techniques. Karate training is made up of *Kihon* (basic partnered techniques), *Kata* (pre-set solo forms), and *Kumite* (free sparring). The Karate practitioner aims to develop the kind of focus that would knock an opponent down with a single strike. Styles are typically strong in attack, and may be hard or soft in defence. Whereas the Aikido disciple develops a calm and quiet temperament, the Karate-do disciple will often be demonstrably assertive. The emphasis on striking and kicking techniques undoubtedly produces a practitioner who will be confident in any pugilistic exchange, but who may struggle if a fight goes to the ground and they are caught in a grappling situation. The constraining effect of avoiding mastery of the messiness of close-quarters grappling and ground-fighting, produce the productive effect of Karate training, the development of a warrior who can 'stand firm' when challenged or confronted, who may lack sensitivity in a grappling exchange, but will manifest qualities of strength and endurance in other situations.

What can we draw from these examples? Subjugation is an implicit feature of subjection. Martial artists willingly subject themselves to the discipline of the *dojo* in order to attain the promised benefits of the specific art studied. In gaining the capability to perform in certain ways by training in a particular martial art, you may come to be restricted in other ways. Further, discipline would appear to work in two different ways. Firstly, it shapes and coerces in an active sense, shaping and producing a particular kind of person with specific capabilities. Secondly, it develops and administers criteria for inclusion and exclusion as a disciple. In other words, it legitimates or de-legitimates particular practices and people, based on the extent to which they conform to the norms and standards of the discipline. Importantly, the extent to which a discipline produces through practice in some developmental sense (the training effect), versus the extent to which a discipline produces through exclusions (the selection effect), is not significant. The ultimate result is the same. The discipline produces its disciples, who are productive precisely by operating within the constraints that define the discipline.

Conclusion: Multiple Disciplines and Liquid Subjectivity

Throughout this chapter I have explored the 'serious' disciplinary practice of the martial arts, in an attempt to make the case that the constraining effects of discipline are precisely the forces that provide its means of capacity building. Although I have discussed discipline frequently in terms that emphasise its technical, tactical and dispositional aspects, these features are paralleled by a training aspect that emerges from the rules of etiquette and behaviour that construct the atmosphere of the *dojo* (such as bowing on entering and leaving the training hall; addressing instructors exclusively by their titles; adopting a formal sitting or standing posture while watching a demonstration or receiving instruction and correction). The martial arts student will typically embrace aspects of discipline in a *dojo* that might be unpalatable in the absence of a desire to attain mastery of the art being studied (i.e., standing silently while the *sensei* demonstrates a technique or receiving a full speed demonstration of a technique because you were caught not paying attention). Erica Southgate's chapter in this volume is focused precisely on such a problem. This is a point at which classroom education and *dojo* discipline dramatically diverge. The discipline of the martial arts is 'serious' precisely because it manifests in forms that are impartial, inflexible, and immediate (for those transgressing its limits), and it is understood to lead to somewhere in particular, to an optimal endpoint that involves some sense of self-mastery. Students who come to dislike the *dojo*'s discipline are free not to return. This again places it in contrast with discipline as it operates in the public school, where participation is not in any absolute sense, an outcome of personal motivation. Thus, the discipline of the *dojo* is reproduced as much through self-exclusion as through that which Jennifer Gore (1993) has termed 'self-styling'.

I have, of course, argued that within the martial arts, individuals voluntarily subject themselves to discipline in order to attain its promised goals. It might be argued that the voluntary subjection to disciplinary power that has been a focus in this chapter implies a rational subject who is able to choose the path they wish to follow. I would agree with any critic who suggested it is unlikely that every parent who takes their child to the door of the *dojo* understands that each martial art has its own distinct telos, and will therefore subsequently attempt to mould their child into a particular kind of person. I know in my own trajectory through the martial arts that I was initially attracted by one type of martial art (Pa Kua Chang, one of the so-called Chinese 'internal' traditions with an explicit spiritual orientation) but found myself studying something else entirely (the art of Wing Chun Kung-Fu, with its aggressive in-fighting methods and 'scientific' orientation to self-defence). This happened because the nearest martial arts training hall to my home was a Wing Chun school, and I had not fully registered at that point in my life that a profound difference existed between various Chinese Kung-Fu systems.[9] Much later, when I sought instruction in Togakure Ryu Ninjutsu, I was making a much more informed decision. However, the voluntary subjection that I have been discussing should not be equated unproblematically with some notion of a rational choice. Rather, I have attempted to show that voluntary subjection to discipline, at least in the martial arts, is underpinned and motivated by desire (often for some vague sense of self-worth or self-mastery), whether or not the end-goal is fully understood.

Finally, I believe it is worth addressing the problem of the liquidity of subjectivity that is apparent when switching between disciplines. Using the martial arts as my case study, I have argued that disciplines provide sets of limits that enable thought and action

---

[9]   I should note that it was fortuitous that I attended the particular Wing Chun school that I did. Under the tutelage of both Sifu Bob Spano, and Sifu Glenn Turner, I was exposed to a much richer martial arts education than might have been the case had I attended a more 'exclusive' Kung-Fu school. I have fond memories of my teenage years training in their Meadowbank training hall.

of a particular kind, shaping individuals by applying rules for recognition as a disciple (and thus excluding those who do not meet the standards set); and by providing intellectual and/or strategic resources for thought and action, that work like signatures, shaping a disciple's performance into a recognisable 'style' or form. These resources and practices provide a path for thought and action that may not exist without them, while limiting the possibility of a disciple to think or act otherwise. Thus, disciplinary subjection provides the capacity for agency, while simultaneously shaping that agency in particular ways; and following the argument in this chapter, it is precisely the shaping or sculpting effect of various constraints that provides the basis for forming particular capacities, working like a jelly mould for a much more liquid subjectivity. The liquid metaphor actually has a long legacy in the martial arts and remains popular in certain contemporary martial arts circles, since being powerfully advocated by Bruce Lee (1975) in the late 1960s and early 1970s as an antidote for what he saw as the 'classical mess' perpetuated by subjugation to stylistic convention. Lee implored the martial artist to become like water, which adapts to the shape of any container it finds itself in, but is able to switch containers as the need arises. Underlying Lee's conviction was an image of the self as a free-floating subject, and his (at the time) revolutionary philosophy might be interpreted in retrospect as the beginnings of a postmodern turn in the martial arts (see Bowman, 2009). Despite the appeal of Lee's postmodern appropriation of Taoist imagery, undoubtedly there can be difficulties for a martial artist who attempts to change 'styles', not the least being the residual effects of one's previous discipline. This has not affected the popularity of switching or collecting disciplines that has become a feature of the contemporary martial arts scene since the permission provided by Lee as popular 'cinematic pedagogue' (Morris, 2002) and 'oriental master' almost forty years ago. However, the possibility that a martial artist might be subject to more than one discipline does little to challenge the main thesis of this chapter. If the self is liquid, then its capacities are formed precisely when it is moulded into shape through subjection to discipline. The purpose of subjecting oneself to multiple disciplines is most likely to be a desire to develop new capacities, and the new capabilities one attains and new subjectivities that emerge will be formed in the same crucibles of stylistic constraint.

References

Bowman, P. (2009). *Theorizing Bruce Lee.* Amsterdam: Rodopi.

Brawdy, P. (2001). *Exploring human kindness through the pedagogy of Aikido.* Paper presented at the Annual meeting of the American Educational Research Association, Seattle, WA. April 10–14.

Brown, D., & Johnson, A. (2000). The social practice of self-defense martial arts: Applications for physical education. *Quest, 52*(3), 246–259.

Butler, J. (1997). *The psychic life of power: Theories in subjection.* Stanford, CA: Stanford University Press.

Daniel, C. (1986). *Taijutsu: Ninja art of unarmed combat.* Burbank, CA: Unique Publications.

Davies, B. (2004). Introduction: Poststructuralist lines of flight in Australia. *International Journal of Qualitative Studies in Education, 17*(1), 3–9.

Deng, M. D. (1990). *Scholar warrior: An introduction to the Tao in everyday life.* San Francisco, CA: HarperSanFrancisco.

Draeger, D. F., & Smith, R. W. (1974). *Asian fighting arts.* New York: Berkley Medallion Books.

Eppert, C., & Wang, H. (2008). Preface: Openings into a curriculum of the way. In C. Eppart & H. Wang (Eds.), *Cross-cultural studies in curriculum: Eastern thought, educational insights* (pp. xvii–xxii). New York: Lawrence Erlbaum Associates.

Foucault, M. (1977). *Discipline and punish: The birth of the prison.* New York: Pantheon.

Foucault, M. (1980). *The history of sexuality: Volume I, An introduction.* (R. Hurley, Trans.). New York: Vintage.

Foucault, M. (1982/1994). The subject and power (P. Rabinow & H. Dreyfus, Trans.). In J. D. Faubion (Ed.), *Essential works of Foucault 1954–1984* (Vol. 3: Power, pp. 326–348). London: Penguin Books.

Gore, J. M. (1993). *The struggle for pedagogies: Critical and feminist discourses as regimes of truth.* New York: Routledge.

Greenberg, S. H. (2000, August 28). The Karate generation. *Newsweek,* p. 50.

Hatsumi, M., & Hayes, S. K. (1987). *Ninja secrets from the grandmaster.* Chicago: Contemporary Books.

Hayes, S. K. (1981a). *The ninja and their secret fighting art.* Rutland, VT: Charles E. Tuttle Company.

Hayes, S. K. (1981b). *Ninja vol. II: Warrior ways of enlightenment.* Santa Clarita, CA: Ohara Publications.

Hayes, S. K. (1983). *Ninja vol. III: Warrior path of Togakure.* Santa Clarita, CA: Ohara Publications.

Hayes, S. K. (1984). *Ninja vol. IV: Legacy of the night warrior.* Burbank, CA: Ohara Publications.

Hayes, S. K. (1989). *Ninja vol. V: Lore of the shinobi warrior.* Burbank, CA: Ohara Publications.

Jones, G., Mackay, K., & Peters, D. (2006). Participation motivation in martial artists in the west midlands region of England. *Journal of Sports Science and Medicine, 5,* 28–34.

LaCapra, D. (2000). *History and reading: Tocqueville, Foucault, French studies.* Carlton South, Vic: Melbourne University Press.

Lakes, K. D., & Hoyt, W. T. (2004). Promoting self-regulation through school-based martial arts training. *Applied Developmental Psychology, 25,* 283–302.

Lee, B. (1975). *Tao of Jeet Kune Do.* Burbank, CA: Ohara Publications.

Lovret, F. J. (1987). *The way and the power: Secrets of Japanese strategy.* Boulder, CO: Paladin Press.

Lowry, D. (1995). *Autumn Lightning.* Boston: Shambala.

Lu, C. (2003). An understanding of body-mind relation based on Eastern movement disciplines and its implication in physical education. *Avante, 9*(3), 66–73.

Luke, C. (Ed.). (1996). *Feminisms and pedagogies of everyday life.* Albany: State University of New York Press.

Masschelein, J., & Ricken, N. (2003). Do we still need the concept of Bildung? *Educational Philosophy and Theory, 35*(2), 139–154.

Moore, R., & Gillette, D. (1992). *The warrior within: Accessing the knight in the male psyche*. New York: Avon Books.

Morris, M. (2002). Learning from Bruce Lee: Pedagogy and political correctness in martial arts cinema. In M. Tinkcom & A. Villarejo (Eds.), *Keyframes: Popular cinema and cultural studies* (pp. 171–186). London: Routledge.

Nakano, H. (1995). Ishin Den Shin (From my soul to your soul). In C. A. Wikey (Ed.), *Martial arts teachers on teaching* (pp. 56–59). Berkley, CA: Frog Ltd.

Nosanchuk, T. A., & MacNeil, M. L. C. (1989). Examination of the effects of traditional and modern martial arts training on aggressiveness. *Aggressive Behavior, 15,* 153–159.

Palumbo, D. G. (1987). *The secrets of Hakkoryu Jujutsu: Shodan tactics*. Boulder, CO: Paladin Press.

Paras, E. (2006). *Foucault 2.0: Beyond power and knowledge*. New York: Other Press.

Petersen, E. B. (2007). Negotiating academicity: Postgraduate research supervision as category boundary work. *Studies in Higher Education, 32*(4), 475–487.

Saito, M. (1975). *Aikido: Its heart and appearance*. Tokyo: Minato Research & Publishing Co. Ltd.

Scheiffele, E. (1991). Questioning one's "own" from the perspective of the foreign (G. Parkes, Trans.). In G. Parkes (Ed.), *Nietzsche and Asian thought* (pp. 31–47). Chicago: University of Chicago Press.

Schine, R. (1995). Authoritarianism in martial arts teaching. In C. A. Wikey (Ed.), *Martial arts teachers on teaching* (pp. 113–118). Berkley, CA: Frog Ltd.

Seig, B. (2004). Gravitation versus change: Explaining the relationship between personality traits & martial arts training. *Journal of Asian Martial Arts, 13*(3), 8–23.

Shioda, G. (1968). *Dynamic Aikido* (G. Hamilton, Trans.). Tokyo: Kodansha International.

Twemlow, S. W., & Sacco, F. C. (1998). The application of traditional martial arts practice and theory to the treatment of violent adolescents. *Adolescence, 33*(131), 505–519.

Watkins, M. (2005). The erasure of habit: Tracing the pedagogic body. *Discourse: Studies in the cultural politics of education, 26*(2), 167–181.

Westbrook, A., & Ratti, O. (1970). *Aikido and the dynamic sphere: An illustrated introduction*. Rutland, VT: Charles E. Tuttle Company.

Zaggelidis, G., Martinidis, K., & Zaggelidis, S. (2004). Comparative study of factors— motives in beginning practicing judo and karate. *Physical Training: Fitness for Combatives, May,* 1–8.

Chapter VII

Punishing Powerplays: Emotion, Discipline and Memories of School Life

Erica Southgate

Introduction

> Much of the choreography of authority is expressed through the body. (Connerton, 1989, p. 74)

The chapter reports on (and updates) a large-scale empirical mapping of autobiographical stories about Australian schooling (Southgate, 2003). The study sought to describe continuities and disjunctures in relations of power associated with schooling in Australia from the late 19th to the 21st century (for a similar enterprise on pedagogy see Gore, 1998). The analysis was based on stories of school from 289 people (storytellers) published in a range of sources including interviews, autobiographies, Internet sites, newspapers and school magazines. Stories covered schooling from 1870 to the present. Since the publication of the original study, I have continued to collect stories relating to the main relations of power or powerplays, described in stories of school life. Indeed, the Internet with its blogs and social networking sites has precipitated a publishing boom in school memories, and I draw on the tales of thirty extra storytellers to update the current analysis of experiences of punishment. This chapter merges theoretical interests in emotion, power and embodiment to map how authority and punishment are enacted, and reacted to, in autobiographical stories of school that span generations. Mapping continuities in stories across generations is important because of what they say about school as an institution and the lifelong impacts of punishment on the souls of former students (Herman, Depaepe, Simon & Van Gorp, 2007).

I begin this chapter by describing the theoretical tool of the powerplay. I then discuss the use of this tool to analyse how teacher authority operates to physically and emotionally isolate students. The significance of the teacher's voice and silence—its ability to yell, chastise, and confer sarcasm and insults —is explored in detail. The spatial distribution of student 'offender' in punishing powerplays is also taken up. The stories examined in this chapter illustrate that students are left with only a slight possibility (or no option) of resistance, disobedience or oppositional action (contrary to Foucault, 1984, p. 245). This is not to say resistance to punishment and teacher authority is never remembered (I have documented this elsewhere, see Southgate, 2003, pp. 58–80). It could even be true to say that by recounting these memories, the storytellers are engaged in an act of resistance years after the fact. The point of this chapter is to highlight how authority can create conditions where fear and shame blossom and that this immobilises students, with often lasting effects.

Powerplays and Punishing Techniques

Bodies guard their secrets and divulge them at every turn. (Adelson, 1993, p. 1)

Foucault (1979) suggests that "discipline is a political anatomy of detail" (p. 139), and to this end, a micro-analysis or 'stonecutting' approach is required to understand exactly how power functions in particular socio-historical and institutional contexts. In order to undertake a stone-cutting approach to the memories of school I collected, it was necessary to develop a new theoretical tool; the powerplay. While the notion of plays of power is not new (Foucault, 1980; Miller, 1988; Fiske, 1993; Dwyer, 1995), I use the term to denote a nuanced theoretical and methodological tool designed for empirical analysis. The tool brings together different elements in order to account for the micro functioning of power. It consists of:

- Directionality—tracing the flow of power. Who is exercising power over whom?
- Techniques—What specific disciplinary and other techniques are deployed and how do these come together?
- Space—Where is power being exercised? Are specific school spaces linked to certain types of powerplays?
- Bodies—What are the corporeal or embodied implications of the exercise of power?
- Emotion—Does the storyteller talk about the emotional impact of the exercise of power? What types of emotions are associated with particular powerplays?
- Subjective gloss—Does the storyteller provide interpretation of how the exercise of power affected his or her sense of self (both remembered and current)?
- Institutional structure—Do dynamics of institutional structure come into play, i.e., policies, hierarchy, rules and notions of authority?
- Difference—How do social and cultural differences come into play? How does power work in relation to the Other?

Not all elements of the powerplay tool are equally significant when analysing stories of discipline and punishment. Indeed stories of discipline and punishment tend to focus on uni-directional powerplays where teachers enact their authority over students. Accounts of school life describe a myriad of punishments inflicted *on* students. Leaving aside corporal punishment, which is most frequently remembered, approximately 20% of storytellers in my study describe punishments ranging from being yelled at or ridiculed by the teacher, to getting the "silent treatment" or being made to stand in the corner of the classroom. Being put on detention; being given the "evil eye"; writing lines; doing menial or demeaning tasks such as cleaning desks or "scab duty" (picking up litter during lunchtime) are also mentioned. There are also a few stories about serious punishments such as suspension and expulsion. As with stories about corporal punishment, acts of resistance by students are rarely articulated.

Despite the diverse range of punishing techniques employed, there is an element common to most stories: that of isolation. Isolation as a disciplining technique is present when students are physically separated from their peers by being made to stand in a corridor or corner because they are "naughty". It can also be found in techniques, which put the body of the "offender" on show, such as being told to stand at the front of the classroom or school assembly while everyone else looks on. Isolation is apparent in the emotional effects of verbal comments that teachers direct at students: being labelled as "different"; singling someone out with a "tsk tsk"; or being screamed at with regularity, all produce feelings of isolation. Isolation occurs when the teacher responds to some, while ignoring others. Moreover, there are isolating effects when the teacher's gaze settles upon the 'offender'. Isolation is associated with a specific cluster of emotions: humiliation, anger, fear, shame, and sometimes, hate.

The following analysis concentrates on the two most frequently described punishing powerplays and their emotional effects. The first powerplay is primarily verbal. It involves what teachers say and how they say it. The second consists of the physical separation of students from their peers. This powerplay includes techniques of physical distribution in space, surveillance, and punishment as spectacle. A feature of these stories is the rich descriptions of the emotional impact that isolating power has on the self.

Powerplay 1—The Teacher's Voice

The voice of the teacher holds an important place in stories of school life. There are accounts that describe the pleasure to be had from hearing soft, well-modulated tones. Verbal skill in reading poetry is particularly admired; kind words are long remembered. There are also stories that associate the voices of teachers with punishment. In these stories, teachers either yell or employ quiet, menacing tones. There are teachers' voices, which 'drip with sarcasm', and those whose use of 'quiet rational' arguments that serve to embarrass or humiliate students. What teachers say and how they say it can constitute a type of punishing powerplay.

Just Yelling

The volume and modulation of teachers' voices matters a great deal in accounts of school life. The yelling teacher is a standard figure in many stories about punishment. Sometimes the teacher yells at the student during corporal punishment. At other times students report to being subject to screaming diatribes because an offence has been committed. Sometimes the storyteller does not remember why the teacher is yelling. Instead, the memory revolves around the "terrifying volume" of the teacher's voice:

> Me and Danny was sitting there and it was, it must have been (the first year of school) and we were sitting on the floor out the front and she was yelling. Screaming. Just flying off. I don't know what it was about and I don't remember (the reason for the teacher

yelling), only that we was scared and couldn't move. Nearly pissed me pants. *(Interview with Bernie, born 1935)*

There was one (woman) teacher…. She used to sit in the classroom, you could hear her yelling at everyone outside…. It just sounded really scary; you couldn't do anything about it. (So, she wasn't your actual teacher?) No…. I ended up hearing how other children hated her, I remember being quite terrified. *(Interview with Ailsa, born 1977)*

In these accounts the teacher is remembered for the effect that yelling had on the student. The volume of the teacher's voice is enough to frighten some students into almost complete docility. In the first story the "screaming" is so intense that it immobilises the students, making one so frightened that he reports nearly urinating. In the second story, the yelling teacher is not even in the same classroom as the student, yet the effect is to make the student feel terrified and powerless—she just "couldn't do anything about" the yelling except feel fear. Both accounts evoke a sense of student helplessness and passivity, though the latter also talks of the "hate" children felt towards the teacher.

Terror, hate and helplessness are emotions often associated with the figure of the yelling teacher. Emotional effects are generated not necessarily by a teacher's intent to punish, but by the frightening noise the teacher makes. In fact, it is impossible to know exactly what the teacher's intent was in these stories. While it is not possible to assign punishing intent to the act of yelling, the emotional effect on the student self is that of being targets, even if this not actually the case. The terrifying effects of yelling are evoked in other accounts. In these accounts teachers incorporate yelling into their pedagogical routine as a means to promote learning:

Mrs P. liked to move about the room and shout in your ear as we did times tables. We'd chant them together, in unison, and she would come up behind you and shout in your ear…. You dare not flinch or she'd get you out the front to do it (recite) yourself. Her voice was deafening. I remember times tables even today. *(Interview with Charles, born 1962)*

In this account the teacher has developed a pedagogical routine in which she circulates around the classroom and shouts in the students' ears during mathematics lessons. The teacher combines yelling with other punishing techniques such as the threat of being singled out by a teacher whose position in the room is uncertain. The storyteller describes a strict disciplining of his body not to "flinch". Discipline and docility are linked to the undesirability of "bodily betrayal" (Featherstone and Hepworth, 1991, p. 376). Yelling as a teaching technique is discussed in a different way in the following story. This account exemplifies how teachers who incorporate yelling into teaching practice, remain unaware of the terrible effect that it can have on their students:

In all my years of school I suppose the thing that's always caused me the most angst was my relationship with a fourth grade teacher…. I was positively ill for about six months of the year, vomiting every morning because I was terrified of him. I didn't want to go to school…. I lost about three quarters of a stone…. And every morning I'd be ill, and, you know, didn't want to go to school…. And I don't think he meant to be mean, but he was just trying to…whip us all into gear, you see, because we had all done so badly in mathematics. And he used to sort of fire mental arithmetic questions at you, and you know, bang rulers on desks (and) I just sort of tried to shrivel down so he wouldn't see me, but he always did. And, I mean, the minute he fired it (a question) at me…I just went a total blank with fear….

It was just that he had a very loud and, you know, bombastic way of behaving. And he would have this great long, sort of, three-foot ruler that he'd bang down and fire a...'three sixes' or 'six eights' (question at you). *(Interview with Juliet, born 1950)*

Juliet's story is indicative of how the majority of storytellers speak of yelling as a pedagogical technique. In this account the storyteller suffers "angst" from being subjected to the teacher's "loud" and "bombastic" way of teaching. The physical manifestations of terror are clearly described: the student is physically ill and loses a great deal of weight and she physically shrinks in her seat in an attempt to escape the teacher's gaze and his rapid questioning. The use of military metaphors such as having questions "fired at (you)" like orders and being "whip(ped)...into gear" suggests a unidirectional play of power. A number of techniques combine to create fearful pedagogic practice: shouting; firing questions in rapid succession; surveilling and singling out students; and punctuating the performance with the loud noise of a large ruler banging the desk. These techniques configure to induce terror, not learning (in the conventional sense). Later in the interview, the storyteller states that she has always "hated maths" since attending that class.

Stories of teachers just yelling, with or without punishing intent, depict a unidirectional powerplay. Teachers yell, shout, scream and raise their voices for various purposes and students generally do not resist; their usual reaction is to quietly shrink into their bodies. The image of the inert or shrivelling student contrasts sharply with the expansiveness of the teacher's voice, which travels quickly to occupy the space of their classroom and even neighbouring classrooms. It is a voice that immobilises and isolates. Students in these stories do not move when the teacher yells, nor do they communicate with each other, except in a kind of shared bodily language of fear.

Sarcasm and Insults

Teachers' insults and sarcasm are long remembered as having negative effects. Sarcasm manifests itself in mocking comments, snide jokes told at the student's expense, and the acerbic, offhand remarks. Even the smallest remark can have most profound effects:

> Education, especially during our early, vulnerable years at infants and primary school, was administered through persecution and humiliation, both cruel and damaging forms of punishment. There was little compassion or nurturing. When I was seven our teacher prefaced her remarks with 'Since you're so smart...' and pointed and pounced and ridiculed as she called on us to recite a poem, or spell beetroot. I think we all must have been terribly unhappy. I certainly was. *(Glenda Adams, born 1939, cited in Modjeska, 1989, p. 18)*

In the stories I collected, insults range from offhand remarks to more prolonged sessions of abuse. The use of sarcasm and insults often served to differentiate 'good' teachers from 'bad':

> I had very good teachers. The fifth grade teacher (was) a brilliant teacher. When she left...we got a sort of relief teacher for the rest of the year. And she was an absolute bitch.... Oh, she was dreadful. She used to sit in class and tell us off, and call us morons and numbskulls and all sorts of things and she'd eat in class. And she was pregnant at the time, and so she'd say...'Don't eat in class!' And she'd sit there and just put her legs on the tables and just eat peanuts and stuff. Everyone hated her...because she was just so mean. *(Interview with Kate, born 1974)*

When I would be brave and ask a question (in class) he (the schoolteacher) used to say, real sly-like, 'You're all bloody idiotic and you're not worth two bob'. No wonder we wouldn't ask questions in his class. We all felt like idiots. *(Interview with Glen, born 1957)*

In these accounts the use of insults has the effect of not only differentiating 'good' teachers from 'bad', but of enforcing a binary opposition between the 'knowing' teacher and the 'stupid' student. The teacher embodies the position of talking expert who can stand in front of the class and pronounce judgments on students. In the second story, the students take to heart the teacher's comments that they are 'worthless idiots'—The teacher has the power to pronounce, while the students can only feel stupid. In both accounts it is the teacher who has the power to speak and direct insults, not the student. In most stories students do not speak back or verbally challenge the knowing position of teacher. In these classes, even asking questions is a 'brave' act.

While the stories cited above span half a century of schooling, they describe very similar vocal punishing techniques. Like other techniques of regulation documented by Foucault (1979), they require no overt physical contact (Rousmaniere, Dehli and de Coninck-Smith, 1997), yet at the same time they are profoundly physical. Stories about punishment emphasise the materiality of the teacher's voice and the concrete effects it has on the subjectivity and body of the student. As Poynton (1996) stresses, it is not the metaphorical voice of critical and liberatory theory, but physical vocal practices that play an important part in the everyday interactions of schooling. Material, embodied voices are profoundly implicated in these types of powerplays. These memories illustrate the immobilising and isolating effect that voices can have on students, who themselves do not offer verbal resistance. These stories highlight what Poynton (1996) describes as the "wresting of voice(s) from the bodies of students" (p. 104), who feel they cannot verbally respond, question or speak up.

Powerplay 2—Distributing Offenders

Stories about punishing powerplays often depict the teachers as possessing an almost magical ability to arrange the bodies of students in time and space. Arranging students does not so much involve the physical handling of student bodies, although sometimes this appears to have been the case. Rather, students self-regulate, obeying the commands of teachers to move away from their peers, occupy a designated space and adopt particular postures (Davies and Hunt, 1994; Preston and Symes, 1997). In stories about punishment there are four techniques used to distribute student bodies. The first is detention, a technique in which offenders spend a set amount of time in a room away from other students. During detention offenders occupy their time with schoolwork or repetitive tasks such as "writing lines" or cleaning inkpots or desks. The second is suspension or expulsion, in which serious offenders are forced to leave the grounds of the school altogether. The third is where students are made to stand away from their classmates (the collective student body), either outside the classroom or in the corner of the room. The fourth relies on the notion of 'spectacle' in which students are made to come to the front of the class or assembly. Once students have repositioned themselves away from their peers they are subject to a variety of verbal punishing techniques and/or the prolonged gaze of those who occupy the space. The following analysis concentrates on the third and fourth techniques, which are most frequently mentioned by storytellers in my study. The powerplays involving these techniques are closely associated with intense, lifelong feelings of shame.

Standing Away From

> It is a segmented, immobile, frozen space. Each individual is fixed in his place. And, if he moves, he does so at the risk of…punishment. (Foucault 1979, p. 195)

People remember standing and sitting in corners, hallways, cloakrooms, toilets, and outside offices and staff rooms. Punishment involved being physically isolated in a space specified by the teacher for an exact period of time or at the teacher's discretion. Separation was not only physical but also psychic. Usually the student was given nothing to do; minds as well bodies are left idle and isolated. Former Justice of the High Court of Australia, Michael Kirby, describes (tongue-in-cheek), the "ignominy" of "corridor" punishment:

> A form of severe punishment for boys was to be sent to stand in the corridor of the girls' school for all the girls to see. It never happened to me—but it was regarded as worse than capital punishment by those who had to wear the ignominy. *(Michael Kirby, born 1939, in Kirby, n.d, pp. 7–8)*

The gendered aspect of this punishment serves to exacerbate the humiliation of being sent out of the classroom. While this account is humorous, for some storytellers being sent out of the classroom was a very unpleasant experience. While there are a few tales of the pleasures of escape, most tales are of compliance and a fear of being forgotten. This fear is particularly evident in accounts about being punished in infants' school. Such fears do not appear to be completely ungrounded, as the following story demonstrates:

> I was between five and six (and our) teacher's name was Miss Tottie Hines…. One morning, as we were all crossing the log at the first creek on the way to school, Miss Hines…discovered that she had lost her purse. She thought she must have dropped it in the creek (and so she made a student dive in to find it)…. He couldn't find it, so she became cranky and irritable with all of us. As soon as we reached the schoolhouse she sent me into the spare room and made me stand behind the door with my hands on my head. When it was time to go home she locked the door and left with all the other children. They were halfway back to Renmark before anyone remembered that I was locked in the spare room, and they came back to let me out. *(Dorothy Roysland, born early 20th century, in Roysland, 1977, pp. 36–37)*.

While being physically excluded from the classroom has the advantage of removing the offender from the direct gaze of the teacher, it also carries with it the risk of being "checked up on" at unexpected moments. The uncertainty of never knowing when the teacher might appear is similar to the effect of Bentham's panopticon (convincingly explored as a disciplinary technology by Foucault, 1979). Even though the direct disciplining gaze of the teacher is absent, offenders regulate themselves to behave in the proper manner. The regulating gaze is turned inward on the self to "function ceaselessly" (Foucault, 1979, p. 195). As a technology of power, panopticons work by fixing individuals in their places: if they move, they do so at the risk of further, harsher punishment (Foucault, 1979, p.

195). Punishment can work as a panoptic "laboratory" designed to "alter behaviour" through self-regulation (Foucault, 1979, p. 203). This effect is evident in the following tales, the first related by an interviewee schooled during the 1930s and the second talking about school in the 1980s:

> Jeez, that was tough. When you were bad (in primary school) you had to go to the coatroom, bloody cold in winter too. But I tell you what, you never played up because you always thought you might be checked up on at any time…. Made you behave. (How do you mean?) Well, because you didn't want to get into trouble more than you already were. *(Interview with Wally, born 1930)*

> I got…made to stand in the corner for chucking (throwing) a rubber. It was pretty bad. I felt dumb and I kept thinking that they (her classmates) were laughing at me. I tried to turn and see but was too scared in case the teacher saw me and I got in more trouble. *(Interview with Janice, born 1971)*

In both accounts, being physically isolated produces uncertainty and discomfort. In the first story, the student never knows when he will be checked up on. In the second, the student cannot be sure if the teacher or her classmates are watching. Moreover, the second storyteller has the humiliating feeling that her peers are laughing at her. Not knowing when or whether they will be scrutinised produces a self-disciplining inactivity. The panoptic schema of this type of isolating punishment has a normalising effect on students (Foucault, 1979). They feel "bad" for their offence. They fear getting into more "trouble". They comply exactly with the teacher's instructions to stand where they are told, for as long as the teacher wishes. As Walkerdine (1990) points out, pedagogical discourse posits the "normal child (as) self-regulating": the "normal child" does not display "overt conflict" or "failure of reason" (p. 34). Put simply, "normal" children learn to behave themselves (also see Davies and Hunt, 1994).

Standing Out

Barry Oakley (1985), a writer schooled in Melbourne during the 1930s and early 1940s, captures the peculiar logic of punishment in schools when he writes:

> That was one of the funny things about school. Like the stage, it's an image of life: life accelerated, life concentrated, and life more formidable. Life's a contest, but only at school do they number you 1–40 at the end of each year. Life's hard, but school's worse. Fail and fall at school and it's a public thing, a slow motion nightmare up there in front of the mob, a hundred eyes enjoying each turn of the screw before you can creep back into the safety of the herd. School's the kind of test that belongs at the end of life, not the beginning. (Oakley, 1985, p. 94).

Oakley provides a masterful summation of the intense emotional impact of punishing powerplays enacted in public. Of all the stories about punishment, those, which describe being made a spectacle of, are most likely to convey the "powerful stuff" of shame (Biddle, 1997, p. 227). The "slow motion nightmare" of being singled out, physically distributed, isolated and surveilled, has devastating effects on the self. Storytellers schooled in almost every decade of the 20th and 21st century talk of the humiliating consequences of being made to "stand out", usually because of some relatively minor offence. There are stories about being made to read poems in front of the class despite speech impediments; of being singled out for chatting instead of listening at assembly; and of being sent to the front of the class to do a complicated maths problem because homework was not handed in. These stories rely on a series of "micro-penalties" integral to the disciplinary regime of school:

> The workshop, the school, the army were subject to a whole micro-penalty of time (lateness, absences, interruptions of tasks), of activity (inattention, negligence, lack of zeal), of behaviour (impoliteness, disobedience), of speech (idle chatter, insolence), of the body (incorrect attitudes, irregular gestures, lack of cleanliness), of sexuality (impurity, indecency). At the same time, by way of punishment, a whole series of subtle procedures was used, from light physical punishment to minor deprivations and petty humiliations. (Foucault, 1979, p. 178).

Memories of punishment document a wide range of micro-penalties. What they also record is a range of not-so-subtle procedures. Storytellers speak of harsh rather than light physical punishment and of humiliations that, while "petty" in one sense, are devastating in their emotional impact on the self. In particular, the powerplay of publicly punishing students produces intense, lifelong feelings of shame and humiliation. While the techniques of this type of powerplay are few, they combine to create what Garfinkel (1956) describes as the conditions for a successful degradation ceremony. First the student is singled out and told, verbally or through gesture, to move her body to the front of the public space. The public spaces most commonly mentioned are the classroom and the school assembly area. The student is then either denounced or simply left on display to face the gaze of the entire class or school body. Students are rarely given the chance to explain their offence and when they are, most say they froze under public scrutiny.

While most powerplays involving public spectacle relate to infringements of rules, there are instances where the teacher asks the student to demonstrate his/her knowledge or skill in a pedagogical context. While the original intention may not have been punitive, the effects of failing the test in public are emotionally punishing, as the following story relates:

> I was asked (by the teacher) to stand up and spell a word…and I tried but got it wrong and he (the teacher)…called me a fool and made me stand while other kids spelt words out loud. It was very embarrassing…I went red. *(Interview with Oliver, born 1949)*

In this account being made to stand up and complete a task is not an inherently bad pedagogical practice. Rather, it is the practice of making the student remain standing (and therefore on public show) while others demonstrate their proficiency (in contrast to this student's inadequacy), which is most humiliating. This, combined with the insult "fool", caused deep embarrassment, manifesting itself in the "red" body of the student. Shame is, Biddle (1997, p. 227) suggests, an acknowledgement, which the body volunteers to those that look on. In this story it is not possible for the boy to resist his public humiliation or control the "embarrassing" reaction of his body.

There are accounts about teachers using pedagogical techniques to intentionally punish students; in such accounts students are punished by being made to publicly perform tasks, which the teacher knows they cannot undertake with success. This tale illustrates that approach:

(I remember) in Year 5, where I had (a) teacher who was fairly strict...I had difficulty with maths...I laughed at somebody who had difficulty as well, because it was something I knew, and the teacher singled me out, and put a big complicated maths problem on the board and told me to do it, and I couldn't do it and I felt very humiliated, but in a way I felt it was kind of self-inflicted.... I feel it was justified but not the way he did it. To humiliate me in front of the entire class, but maybe (he could have) take(n) me aside separately and (spoken) to me because I've never really liked maths...and that probably just brought my confidence down even more. *(Interview with Mick, born 1973)*

In this story the teacher turns the tables against the 'offender', using his authority to reverse a powerplay between students. The student who laughed at a classmate's inadequacy is made to display his own inadequacy, but this does not constitute a simple reversal of the flows of power. The teacher creates a spectacle where the 'offender' is "singled out" and put on physical display. The teacher creates a kind of tension as he stages the spectacle: he takes time to create a "complicated maths problem" on the blackboard while the offender and other students watch. He then summons the 'offender' to go to the front of the classroom and in front of everyone, the 'offender' is required to solve the maths problem. The spectacle of the punishment is not only connected with the body of the 'offender' as he is displayed in front of the class, it is also linked to an impossible task designed for the express purpose of humiliation. While the storyteller admits that he should have been punished for the offence, he suggests that the teacher's staging of his public failure far outweighs the magnitude of the "crime". The effects of such a powerplay are significant feelings of humiliation and a considerable lessening of confidence in maths.

Storytellers also describe witnessing the public humiliation of fellow students. While there are accounts of students sniggering and jeering at 'offenders' as they are made a spectacle, there are also stories, which focus on the injustice of the punishment:

I think when I was in first form, there was a girl who was a year above us who was always in a lot of trouble. And she was in one of the lower classes in second form.... (We) used to have this terrible assembly, where we used to have to stand and stand and stand for ages, in lines and be told boring things...I remember the Principal saying 'Isabel'! You are a girl of whom we are not proud." So this girl had to leave her line and go right out to the front to where the Principal was, and there was a microphone, and all this. And as soon...(as) she got there, he said 'Oh go away! I can't stand the sight of you.' That's pretty cruel. *(Interview with Dolly, born 1950)*

The backdrop for this story of public humiliation is the collective disciplining of student bodies in the space and time of school assembly. Students discipline themselves to "stand for ages" in a specific formation and remain silent as they are "told boring things". In this account the Principal staging a punishing spectacle breaks the boredom. Isabel is made to leave the docile yet safe formation of her class line. The Principal, who makes her stand out as the antithesis of pride, castigates her. He uses the collective "we" in the sentence—"of whom we are not proud"—as a technique to isolate the individual from the collective. Isabel is the pathological school subject: she is "trouble"; she is not worthy of "pride"; and ultimately, she is not even deserving of the gaze of the Principal and the rest of the school. The sight of Isabel's shamed body moving through space, combined with the Principal's curt remarks, leads the storyteller to judge the punishing powerplay "cruel". Like the witnessing of corporal punishment, the shaming of others often has a durable emotional impact. Shame is an intensely social emotion:

> Witnessing someone else being shamed and/or the converse, witnessing when somebody ought to be ashamed and they aren't, is likely to induce shame in response. "Contact" shame may be just as painfully experienced, and equally identity delineating, as a direct shame response. Indeed, that the two are so closely related (it seems to me, confused as they are from childhood on), is what makes shame so powerful and so social an emotion. (Biddle, 1997, p. 230)

The link between public spectacle, humiliation and shame plays out on a grand scale such as that described by Dolly, and on a more intimate level. For example, a number of storytellers describe the embarrassing punishment of being shifted, for a specified time, to the "babies' grade" where their sheer physical size made them stand out for all to see.

There is great generational breadth to stories about the "slow motion nightmare" of public punishment. For example, Barry Oakley, whose story opens this section, was schooled in the 1930s. Isabel's tale relates to schooling in the 1960s. The story about the maths problem comes from a narrator schooled in the 1980s. A key feature of all stories about being made to "stand out" is the power of the inspecting gaze. The gaze involves the collective eye of authorities (principals, teachers) and that of peers. In most stories, the gaze pins down offending students (cf. Walkerdine, 1990), curtails their ability to act or speak back, and almost always generates feelings of shame and humiliation. To borrow a phrase from Foucault (1979), these stories imply that "visibility is a trap, a trap that not only immobilises, but also wounds" (p. 200).

Concluding Remarks

Employing Levi-Stauss's rather colourful metaphors of vomiting out and swallowing up, Cohen (1985, p. 219) suggests that social control in the modern West oscillates between practices of inclusion and exclusion. The pathological are "vomited out" by way of "separation, segregation, isolation, banishment and confinement" or they might be "swallowed up" by modes of "incorporation, integration or assimilation." (Cohen, 1985, p. 219). Stories about punishment describe both inclusive and exclusive practices. Most stories describe degrees or combinations of exclusion and inclusion. Detention is a punishing technique that excludes by degrees: it isolates the offenders from the classroom and peers but does not fully exclude them from school life. Making students stand in the corner of classrooms involves a combination of exclusionary and inclusionary practices: it is a physically and psychically isolating act, yet it does not exclude offenders from the gaze of teachers or students. The act of making students come to the front of classrooms and assemblies functions in a similar manner. Students are "vomited" forth from the collective but they are not excluded—they are simultaneously included in and against the collective as the pathological Other (Canguilhem, 1991).

The complexity of techniques in punishing powerplays should not distract from the emotional impact such actions have on those who experience or witness punishment. Feelings of fear, isolation, humiliation and shame are common. Even if teachers may not intend to induce negative emotional impacts, exemplified in some of the stories about the figure of the yelling teacher, the effect is to induce fear. Those storytellers who have felt the effects of isolating practices become both the object and subject of shame, as Lewis (1992) explains:

> In shame, we become the subject as well as the object of shame. The self system is caught in a bond in which the ability to act or continue acting becomes extremely difficult. Shame (results in an) inability to think clearly, inability to talk, and inability to act. (p. 34)

Stories about isolating punishments remind us of shame's impact and legacy. Generally these stories are not about the subtle Foucauldian techniques of discipline. They are similar to stories of corporal punishment (see Southgate, 2003, pp. 24–40) in that they highlight particular dynamics between teachers and students like domination and cruelty. They are, as the storyteller quoted above suggests, about the "slow motion nightmare" of humiliation and subjection, about the kind of tests of character and strength that should belong "at the end of life, not the beginning" (Oakley, 1985, p. 94).

References

Adelson, L.A. (1993). *Making bodies, making history: Feminism and German identity.* Lincoln, NE and London: University of Nebraska Press.

Biddle, J. (1997). Shame. *Australian Feminist Studies*, 12(26), 227–39.

Canguilhem, G. (1991). *The normal and the pathological.* (C. R. Fawcett, Trans.). New York: Zone Books.

Cohen, S. (1985). *Visions of social control: Crime, punishment and classification.* Oxford: Polity Press.

Connerton, P. (1989). *How societies remember.* Cambridge and New York: Cambridge University Press.

Davies, B. and Hunt, R. (1994). Classroom competencies and marginal positionings. *British Journal of Sociology of Education*, 15(3), 389–408.

Dwyer, P. (1995). Foucault, docile bodies and post-compulsory education in Australia. *British Journal of Sociology in Education*, 16(4), 467–77.

Featherstone, M. and Hepworth, M. (1991). The mask of ageing and the postmodern lifecourse. In M. Featherstone, M. Hepworth, and B. Turner (Eds), *The body: Social processes and cultural theory* (pp. 371–389). London: Sage.

Fiske, J. (1993). *Power plays, power works.* London and New York: Verso.

Foucault, M. (1979). *Discipline and punish: The birth of the prison.* (A. Sheridan, Trans.) London: Peregrine.

Foucault, M (1980). The confession in flesh. In C. Gordon, (Ed.), *Power/Knowledge: Selected interviews and other writings by Michel Foucault, 1972–1977* (pp. 194–228). Hemel Hempstead: Harvester Wheatsheaf.

Foucault, M (1984). Space, knowledge, and power. In P. Rabinow, (Ed.), *The Foucault reader: An introduction to Foucault's thought* (pp. 239–256). London: Penguin.

Garfinkel, H. (1956). Conditions of successful degradation ceremonies. *American Journal of Sociology*, 61(5), 420–24.

Gore, J. (1998). Disciplining bodies: On the continuity of power relations in pedagogy.

In T. S. Popkewitz & M. Brennan (Eds), *Foucault's challenge: Discourse, knowledge and power in education* (pp. 231–251). New York and London: Teachers College press.

Herman, F., Depaepe, M. Simon, F. and Van Gorp, A. (2007). Punishment as an educational technology: A form of pedagogical inertia in schools? In P. Smeters and M. Depaepe (Eds), *Educational research: Networks and technologies* (pp. 203–219). Dordrecht, The Netherlands: Springer.

Kirby, M. (n.d.) *The learning of values: Memories of Strathfield North Public School.* Retrieved March, 27, 2009, from http://www.hcourt.gov.au/speeches/kirbyj/kirbyj_snps.pdf

Lewis, M. (1992). *Shame: The exposed self.* New York: Macmillan.

Miller, D.A. (1988). *The novel and the police.* Berkeley, CA: University of Berkeley Press.

Modjeska, D. (1989). (Ed.), *Inner cities: Australian women's memory of place.* Ringwood, Vic: Penguin.

Oakley, B. (1985). *Scribbling in the dark.* Brisbane: Queensland University Press.

Poynton, C. (1996). Giving voice. In E. McWilliam and P.G. Taylor (Eds), *Pedagogy, technology and the body* (pp. 103–112). New York: Peter Lang Publishing.

Preston, N. and Symes, C. (1997). The architecture of schooling: Buildings for building character. In N. Preston and C. Symes (Eds), *Schools and classrooms: A cultural analysis of education* (pp. 172–194). Melbourne: Longman Cheshire.

Rousmaniere, K., Dehli, K., and de Coninck-Smith, N. (1997). Moral regulation and schooling: An introduction. In K. Rousmaniere, K. Dehli, and N. de Coninck-Smith (Eds), *Discipline, moral regulation and schooling: A social history* (pp. 3–18). New York and London: Garland.

Roysland, D. (1977). *A pioneer family on the Murray River.* Melbourne: Rigby.

Southgate, E. (2003). *Remembering school: Mapping continuities in power, subjectivity and emotion in stories of school life.* New York: Peter Lang Publishing.

Walkerdine, V. (1990). *Schoolgirl fictions.* London and New York: Verso.

Chapter VIII

Disciplinary Power and the Production of the Contemporary 'Healthy Citizen' in the Era of the 'Obesity Epidemic'

Ken Cliff

Introduction

In this chapter I examine the process of "making up" (Rose & Miller, 1992, p. 174) the healthy citizen during a time of widespread and sustained concern about the 'obesity epidemic'. With obesity now claimed to be affecting almost all of the world's population (World Health Organization, 2009a), and with dire predictions for health care capacity and costs, the healthy citizen and how it is constituted has taken on renewed importance as a problem for modern government. While the healthy citizen has been a notable part of sociological analyses of health, medicine and schooling for the last two decades (Burrows & Wright, 2007; Fullagar, 2001, 2003, 2009; Lupton, 1995; Petersen & Lupton, 1996), critical sociological work that specifically seeks to rethink the production of the healthy citizen in the discursive context of the obesity epidemic is only just beginning. Furthermore, the work, which does exist, suggests a range of subtle (and not so subtle) changes in health promotion, and health education policy and practice in response to this supposedly unprecedented public health crisis (for example, Gard & Kirk, 2007; Rich & Evans, 2009). In general terms the analysis in this chapter contributes to understanding the production of the 'healthy citizen' in the context of heightened concern around body weight, waning morality and spiralling health care expenditure. More specifically it focuses on Foucault's (1995) concept of disciplinary power and its role as a constitutive and productive force in the process of making up a certain type of healthy citizen. Understanding power as productive "generates questions of how power is exercised in the construction of knowledge about health" (Wright and Burrows, 2004, p. 212) and turns our attention to the processes that position subjects as 'healthy' or 'unhealthy'. As such I consider how we have come to contemporary understandings of obesity and how these understandings work to produce obesity as a problem of government, which in turn requires intervention into people's lives. Using empirical examples from health promotion and school-based intervention, I suggest that disciplinary power remains absolutely essential to the production of the type of healthy citizen articulated in obesity-era health promotion and policy—though clearly in a manner that sees it tightly entwined with regulative power. I finish with a consideration of the limits of disciplinary power as government through ethics.

Background

According to dominant contemporary understandings, the obesity epidemic is a near global public health problem (Seidell & Rissanan, 2004) that threatens mortality, economy and national well-being (Jennings, 2009). As a public health concern its voracity is generated firstly, by the overwhelming volume and scope of (predicted) health and economic effects that are attributed to it. Looking solely at the so-called economic burden of obesity, one recent report estimated that obesity-related health care costs in Australia had increased from $873 million in 2005, to $2.0 billion in 2008—a figure that the report suggested was only a fraction of the $8.238 billion that obesity cost the country overall when productivity losses and carer costs were accounted for (Access Economics, 2008). Complementing the economic costs are the supposed costs in lives. At the turn of the millennium annual US mortality attributable to obesity was estimated by the surgeon general to have reached 300,000 annually (*New York Times*, 2001, cited in Gard & Wright, 2005, p. 17)—a number that far better supports the idea of an 'epidemic' than the 169 Australian deaths directly attributed to obesity in 2007, or the 869 deaths where obesity was mentioned as an "associated cause" of death (Australian Bureau of Statistics, 2009). However, more than the actual mortality rate, the notion that there is an obesity epidemic is fuelled by the 'risk' of future illness or death. The assertion that all population groups are 'at risk' has helped to underpin the widespread acceptance of obesity as a public health concern without par. According to Gard and Wright (2005, p. 26) this "everyone everywhere" version of the obesity epidemic has come to capture the attention of governments, the general public and the popular media in 'developed' or 'industrialized' or core countries like Australia, Canada, New Zealand, Britain and the US. The World Health Organization's Website (2009b) adds, however, that while "once considered a problem only in high-income countries, overweight and obesity are now dramatically on the rise in low- and middle-income countries, particularly in urban settings". The reported spread of obesity into Asian countries of varying urbanization supports this assertion, with countries such as Taiwan, Thailand, Singapore and China all reporting rises in obesity—though still considerably lower than developed countries (Yoon et al., 2006).

Given claims about the changing demographics of obesity it seems somewhat counter-intuitive that affluent contemporary 'Western lifestyles' are still—as they have been for at least the last fifteen years (Bouchard, 1991) and perhaps longer (Epstein, Wing, Koeske, & Valoski, 1984)—argued to be the primary driver of obesity in the vast majority of bio-medical literature and the health policy that flows from it. Despite significant gaps and inconsistency existing in the research (cf. Gard & Wright, 2005), researchers have continued to claim that high-energy diets, in combination with increasingly sedentary lifestyles brought on by advances in technology and a general laziness, have led to widespread energy imbalances and thus, weight increases (Bouchard, 2000; Cameron, Welborn, Zimmet, Dunstan, & Owen, 2003). The apparent simplicity of the causes of obesity, coupled with the fact that these causes are lifestyle based, has worked to produce obesity as issue of personal responsibility. Far from being particular to those with obese bodies, the virtues of personal responsibility for health are exhorted to individuals of all shapes and sizes (Shilling, 1993).

Powerful truth discourses exist, which work to normalize individual responsibility for health. In particular, such ideas have been greatly advanced by the emergence in Western cultures of the body as an outward sign of an individual's morality (Bordo, 2003; Featherstone, 1991; Lupton, 1995). As Gard and Wright (2005) note, "the body's appearance is taken to be evidence of the care taken of the body, that is, the time, effort and money invested in creating particular kinds of bodies" (p. 176). To fail to live up to these assumptions (or reject them in favour of others) is to become the abject and marginalized 'other' (Burrows & Wright, 2007). Within this context the obese body is frequently imagined as a corporeal sign of personal failure, neglect, mis-management and even loathing. Moreover, attaching such understandings to the corporeal appearance of the body adds a moral element to obesity. In her recent work on the anthologising of the fat body, Murray (2009) argues at one point that obese subjects are tacitly assumed to be "immoral subjects"—"moral and ethical failures that are…unwilling to assume a 'proper' responsibility for their health" (p. 80).

Moralizing of the obese body is an entrenched feature of bio-medical research and associated social commentary around obesity, both of which have generally tended to cast the 'solutions' as a matter of returning to a time when individuals had self-control, personal responsibility and made 'better choices'—all of which are presumed to be within the reach of citizens, irrespective of their social and cultural circumstances. This is well illustrated in the example of David Cameron, the leader of Britain's Conservative party, who recently stated:

> We talk about people being 'at risk of obesity' instead of talking about people who eat too much and take too little exercise…. We talk about people being at risk of poverty, or social exclusion: it's as if these things—obesity, alcohol abuse, drug addiction—are purely external events like a plague or bad weather…. Of course, circumstances — where you are born, your neighbourhood, your school and the choices your parents make—have a huge impact. But social problems are often the consequence of the choices people make (cited in Elliot, Riddell, Davidson, & Coates, 2008).

Alongside the striking puritanical overtones in this comment is the implicit idea that obesity is "a consequence of the choices people make". The idea of choice, particularly consumer choice related to lifestyle, is a significant aspect of contemporary obesity discourse. Undoubtedly this can be attributed to the fact that obesity initially emerged and has remained most prevalent in Western capitalist countries in which free-market economic doctrines champion consumer freedom and individual choice over almost all else. In *Powers of Freedom*, Rose (1999) argues that in such contexts 'freedom' manifests as 'choice', and as such "modern individuals are not merely 'free to choose', but *obliged to be free*, to understand and enact their lives in terms of choice" (p. 87). Perhaps most importantly, choices come to represent and "reflect back upon the person who has made them" (p. 87). This discursive construction illustrates the subtle re-imaginings of the healthy citizen that have taken place in societies like Australia, which have shifted from liberal to neo-liberal rationalities of government. While the citizens of liberal government were to "govern themselves, master themselves, care for themselves" (Rose & Miller, 2007, p. 204), the neo-liberal citizens seek to "enterprise themselves" (p. 214). As a 'critical consumer' the neo-liberal citizen is to engage, assess and utilize health information and services in order to maximize their own productivity, consumption, well-being and happiness. Part of this involves "bringing the future into the present" (p. 215) by calculating the consequences of choices and risks related to things such as diet, exercise, vaccination and recreation. Importantly, with the neo-liberal state largely removed from any direct influence over such decisions, a range of technologies "install and support the civilizing project by shaping and governing the capacities, competencies and wills of subjects" (p. 214). As I will argue later, modern health promotion activities can be understood as one such technology, in that they "translate the goals of political, social and economic authorities into the choices and commitments of individuals" by integrating "subjects into a moral nexus of identifications and allegiances in the very processes in which they seem to act out their most personal choices" (p. 215).

To this point I have argued that contemporary obesity discourse produces the 'problem' as one caused and potentially cured or at least overcome by individual conduct. Constructing obesity in this way casts it as a problem related to the type of citizens who make up a population. The concept of the healthy citizen is not a new one; though there is limited sociological literature that is recent enough to have taken up and responded to questions about this type of subjectivity politics and production, against the discursive backdrop of the obesity epidemic. In describing the contemporary healthy citizen and its constitution, Petersen and Lupton (1996) assert that while health is both a right and a responsibility for the modern citizen, the right to health has for the most part been reconfigured as "the duty to stay well" (Greco, 1993, p. 357), in which the individual must take on "personal responsibility for one's health by accepting and adopting the imperatives issuing forth from the state and other health-related agencies" in regards to maintaining health and protecting against risk (Petersen & Lupton, 1996, p. 65). Halse (2009) explains this particular conceptualisation of the healthy citizen through the use of the concept of the "bio-citizen"—a notion in which citizenship involves a "set of relations between the individual and the state" requiring the citizen to actively and continuously contribute to the citizenry through the demonstration of moral virtues (p. 49). For Halse, the bio-citizen's first contribution to the common good is to take personal responsibility for the physical care of oneself. Modern health promotion plays an important role in shaping individuals' capacities and desires to be personal responsible, through work, which encourages the individuals to "self-regulate", "transform" and "maintain" (Petersen & Lupton, 1996, p. 65) their bodies in ways that align "personal satisfaction with the public good" (p. 70). For example, Fullagar (2001) argues that the *Active Australia* policy from the late 1990s portrays the healthy citizen as one who employs a calculative rationality towards physical activity, supposedly drawing pleasure from the discipline and order, aims and routines and the type of lifestyle they represent. Such an example also begins to illustrate the manner in which individuals are governed through their desire to be a particular person or lead a certain lifestyle. For Foucault (1990b) there is pleasure to be derived from the act of self-discipline, as an individual comes to understand him or herself as a morally virtuous citizen. However, while the healthy citizen might derive pleasure from such alignment, Fullagar suggests that such pleasure does not come without costs to the soul. Here the moral imperative to manage oneself that is produced by modern health promotion requires "continuous self-scrutiny, dissatisfaction and critical evaluation, through which the body can become positioned as the object of measured loathing" (p. 79).

There is also a range of research that has examined the production of the healthy citizen (both directly and indirectly) through schools and particularly through Health and Physical Education (HPE). The process of doing health-related subjectivity work in schools is a major focus of Wright and Burrows' (2004) analysis of New Zealand primary school students' notions of health. They point to the efficacy of "technologies of the self", produced and effected in schools, in teaching students how to "engage in the work on their bodies necessary to become healthy citizens and thereby live the good life" (p. 226). And Evans, Rich and colleagues (Evans, Rich, Davies & Allwood, 2008; Rich, Harjunen & Evans, 2006) argue that schools make use of dominant discourses of health to discipline and regulate bodies. Like Wright and Burrows they link pedagogical work in schools to its end results in terms of subjectivities and ways of knowing about health and bodies. Their research provides a striking example of the negative effects that schooling, when directed towards 'normalising' 'disorderly' citizens, can have on young people. In particular, the development of eating disorders and deeply damaged subjectivities seems to be closely related to the mobilization of biopedagogies that shape understandings of health and the body in narrow and highly prescriptive ways. In the following section I turn to the ways in which this construction of the healthy citizen is manifest as a problem of modern government (Rose, 1999).

Disciplinary Power and Obesity as a Biopolitical Concern

For Foucault, disciplinary power is one of two related forms of power that operate to make up certain types of subjects. Describing the emergence of the two forms, he says that a biopolitics of the human race emerged at the end of the eighteenth century as the State began to concern itself with the population as a productive resource (Foucault, 2007), which needed to be governed in such a way so as to "foster life"—to protect, preserve and fortify it and its capacities (Foucault, 1990a, p. 138). This new technology of power—"Biopower" (Foucault, 2003, p. 242) takes as its first objects of knowledge "a set of processes such as the ratio of births to deaths, the rate of reproduction, the fertility of a population and so on" (p. 243), all of which are focused on increasing the population, its longevity and it's productive capacity. Importantly for the argument made in this chapter, biopower is described as being comprised of two related and complementary powers: disciplinary power and regularizing power. Disciplinary power emerged first and involves "techniques of power centered on the body, the individual body" (p. 242). In describing disciplinary power as part of his 1977–78 lecture series, Foucault says that it involves:

all the devices that were used to ensure the spatial distribution of individual bodies (their separation, their alignment, their serialization, and their surveillance) and the organization, around those individuals, of a whole field of visibility. They were also techniques that could be used to take control over bodies. Attempts were made to increase the productive force through exercise, drill and so on. They were also techniques for rationalizing and strictly economizing on a power that had to be used in the least costly way possible, thanks to a whole system of surveillance, hierarchies, inspections, bookkeeping, and reports—all the technology that can be described as the disciplinary technology of labor (2003, p. 242).

In *Discipline and Punish* (1995) Foucault discusses disciplinary power at length. He writes that disciplinary power (like regularizing power) is a productive power, literally operating to "make individuals", using them as both objects and instruments of exercise (p. 170). It produces, according to Foucault, "subjected and practised bodies, docile bodies" by increasing the "forces of the body (in economic terms of utility)" and diminishing "the same forces (in political terms of obedience)" (p. 138). It works by developing in the subject properties that were not previously there, inserting these qualities into individuals by placing them in an environment "that evaluates, corrects, and encourages responses according to a norm" (Ransom, 1997, p. 19). Importantly, while disciplinary power produces docile bodies it does not work through sheer violence. Instead "it is a form of surveillance that is internalized" (Harwood, 2009, p. 19), a type of power in which individuals discipline themselves. Biopower's second form of power, regularizing power, emerged after disciplinary power and "[u]nlike discipline, which is addressed to bodies, the new nondisciplinary power is applied not to man-as-body but to…man-as-species" (Foucault, 2003, p. 242). Elaborating, Foucault (2003) states that "discipline tries to rule a multiplicity of men to the extent that they can be dissolved into individual bodies that can be kept under surveillance, trained, used and if need be, punished" (2003, p. 242). In contrast, regularizing power "is addressed to a multiplicity of men…to the extent that they form…a global mass that is affected by overall processes characteristic of birth, death, production and so on" (pp. 242–43). Whereas disciplinary power may shape the individual in such ways that they adopt a particular health-affirming behaviour, regularizing power works, for example, by establishing a norm through the collection and calculation of information about the population as a whole, and by monitoring alterations to the norm with a view to intervening to increase the capacity of the population collectively. While regularizing power came later than disciplinary power, it did not come to replace it but rather came to "dovetail into it", embedding itself into existing disciplinary techniques (p. 242).

Foucault specifically tells us that biopower marked a break from top-down, coercive strategies of power. If we are to understand the modern mobilization of biopower as primarily taking place through and with the cooperation of individuals, we also require a theoretical resource that connects the biopolitical aspirations of government (for the health, happiness, longevity and productivity of the population) with the individual's own conduct. Here Foucault's notion of governmentality (Foucault, 1991) has proven useful in other investigations of the politics of subjectivity (for example, Rose, 1999; 2007). For Foucault, governmental activities are directed towards shaping the conduct of the population both as individuals and as a collective. One of the strengths of governmentality as an analytical tool in relation to health is that it moves away from monolithic and totalising forms of power, offering a conceptualisation in which government is the "contact point" (Burchell, 1996, p. 20) where "technologies of power" (external forms of government such as policing, surveillance and the enacting of laws carried out by the state and its institutions) intersect with self-governmental processes in the form of "technologies of the self"—practices through which individuals effect changes to their bodies and souls (Dean, 1999, p. 11). This is vital to the usefulness of governmentality in analysing health-related subjectivity work in neo-liberal political climates, where exercising power through government is "not so much a matter of imposing constraints upon citizens as of 'making up' citizens capable of bearing a kind of regulated freedom" (Rose & Miller, 1992, p. 174). Personal autonomy does not necessarily work against political power in this understanding but is instead "a key term in its exercise, the more so because most individuals are not merely the subjects of power but play a part in its operations" (Rose & Miller, 1992, p. 174). It operates by the "forging of alignments between the personal projects of citizens and the images of the social order" (Miller & Rose, 1988, p. x). This alignment functions through certain technologies of government, which link "a multitude of experts in distant sites to the calculations of those at the centre" (Rose, 1999, pp. 50–51). For Nettleton (1997), the proliferation of activities of health-related expertise is directly related to the need to support the "autonomous, enterprising self" (p. 218) in the ongoing project of self-governance. While the modern art of government "requires and develops knowledge of its population" (Nettleton, 1997, p. 211), the ideal neo-liberal healthy citizen requires the knowledge, prescriptions and advice of a range of experts and institutions in order to become the active, entrepreneurial and self-disciplined subject that modern government presupposes.

While biopower and governmentality provide the theoretical resources that frame an analysis of obesity as a significant contemporary health concern, they also leave us with a number of questions in relation to disciplinary power and the obesity-related health activities that are employed in the early twenty-first century. Firstly, a number of authors (for example, Rose, 1999) have suggested that while the 'disciplinary society' may work as a characterization of the eighteenth and nineteenth centuries, we need to rethink its usefulness today, suggesting instead that Deleuze's 'control society' might be more apt. In *Postscript on Societies of Control*, Deleuze (1992) declares that Foucault's "environments of enclosure" have broken down and that "societies of control...are in the process of replacing disciplinary societies" (p. 3). The breaking down of the environments of enclosure may well have consequences for the modern working of disciplinary power in relation to a biopolitical problem such as obesity, given that disciplinary power primarily (though not exclusively) operates through institutions, according to Foucault (1995; 2003). Closely related to the shift to control societies, we might also look to analyse disciplinary power's operations within a biopower configuration, given that so many modern health activities take the regularization of the population as their initial concern.

The role of disciplinary power in making up the healthy citizen of the obesity era might also be interrogated in terms of Gard and Kirk's (2007) argument that we may be seeing a "crisis of faith in disciplinary technology" (p. 17) and a shift from an "internal locus of control" to an "external locus of control" in relation to health-related governmental work as a result of the "obesity epidemic" (p. 17). They suggest the possibility of a fracturing of confidence in regards to "the covert, nuanced, individualized and internalised practices of corporeal regulation and normalization that have increasingly operated in advanced capitalist societies as a means of securing and sustaining a productive and compliant citizenry" (p. 33). In the following section I seek to respond to these questions through two empirical examples. I argue that these examples are illustrative of practices related to the government of individuals and populations in the context of the obesity epidemic, and provide useful insights into the operation and limits of disciplinary power in the early twenty-first century.

Health Promotion: "How do You Measure up?"

How do you measure up? (Commonwealth of Australia, 2008) was a national health promotion initiative in place in Australia at the time of writing and which involved cooperation and funding agreements between the Australian Federal government and the governments of the States and Territories. Part of the *Australian Better Health Initiative*, *Measure Up* was arguably the key obesity-related health promotion initiative in 2008, with advertising in the media and in public areas such as shopping centres. The central feature and concept of the *Measure Up* campaign was a push for both male and female Australian adults to measure their waist circumference—a measurement that the campaign promoted as a means of "see(ing) whether you are at risk of chronic disease". Under the heading "Why measure up?" the campaign website (www.measureup.gov.au) states:

> In 2005, 7.4 million Australian adults or 1 in 2 was overweight or obese, and, irrespective of your height or build, if your waistline is getting bigger it could mean you are at increased risk of developing a chronic disease such as some cancers, heart disease, and type 2 diabetes.

Despite the relatively clear statement of the problem in the previous quote, in different parts of the Website the problem seems to alternate between: waist measurement as a signifier for heightened chronic disease risk, waist measurement as a signifier for an unhealthy lifestyle, or despite the fact that "(i)t is not yet clear exactly what links intra-abdominal fat with chronic disease", overweight and obesity as a sign of (potential) intra-abdominal fat accumulation, which in turn (may) heighten the risk for chronic disease. Similarly, the campaign moves uncritically back and forth between waist measurement, chronic disease and "unhealthy eating and not enough physical activity"—with little regard, at least on the Website, for the complexities of the relationships between these. Though it is shrouded in the language and supposed objectivity of science, such intratextual slippage operates to heighten the sense of risk, which in turn works to "mobilize emotion or affect" and "shape how we conduct ourselves" (Fullagar, 2009, p. 122).

The accompanying television advertisement is even less subdued in its mobilization of risk and fear. As a gradually aging man walks a tape measure, with the numbers increasing to signifying his weight gain, a voiceover tells us that "1 in 2 Australians is overweight" and "unhealthy eating and drinking and not enough physical activity can seriously affect your health". The man becomes visually fatter, first losing his breath and then having to stoop over. His initial lack of concern about weight gain ("You know how it is...you settle down...put on a few kilos...but I'm not worried") is replaced by anxiety, particularly in relation to his young daughter (in the background), who he is no longer fit enough to "play tip" with. Here the explicitly ethical aspects of making up the healthy citizen are apparent. In particular, we can see the mobilisation of government through ethics—the idea that an individual might be governed from a distance through his/her own ethic, or ideas about how one should conduct oneself (Foucault, 1990b). Here government through ethics works by positing one choice, or way of conducting oneself, as morally virtuous. In this case, exercising regularly and adopting healthy eating and drinking behaviours form part of a moral code against which individuals are asked to measure their own actions—a process they can apparently begin by measuring their waist. The next section further illustrates the process of government through ethics, in this case by outlining the self work that individuals are encouraged to practice in order to 'become' the ethical subject.

Under the heading "How do I measure myself?" the Website includes a downloadable tape measure, instructions on how to measure and importantly, norms against which to evaluate oneself. Individuals are told that waist measurements of more than 94 centimetres for men and 80 centimetres for women are associated with "increased risk of chronic disease", while more than 102 centimetres for men and 88 centimetres for women are associated with "greatly increased risk". Given the volume of information on the Website, it is interesting to note that the section on measuring is relatively brief (though there is a lengthy paragraph arguing for the validity of the previously stated waist measurement norms across most of the world's population). Rather than spending time going over the results of the measurement and how they should be interpreted (for example, there is nothing at all about what one should do if they are below, or even greatly below the norms) much of the information contained on the campaign Website is designed to be accessed *after* an individual self-diagnoses his or her 'weight problem'. At this point the Website shifts into pedagogical mode, educating by instructing individuals about how to eat healthy food and stay active (Wright, 2009). Online quizzes are a central feature of both the "Tips for getting active" and "What should I be eating?" sections. Respondents are asked to reflect on their lifestyles (particularly diet and physical activity) through questions such as:

For household chores like vacuuming, mowing the lawn, cleaning the windows, etc., do you:

1. Get someone else to do it for you
2. Do it only when you have to
3. Enjoy doing it because it's a good way to combine chores with a workout.

As this question suggests, there is a markedly disciplinary aspect to the "How physically active are you?" quiz, with individuals who receive a low score told, "if you can't find time to be active, you'll need to make time to be sick!" These quizzes, like the section "Seven golden rules for healthy eating habits", construct 'truths' about healthy living, which individuals choose to take up in order to become a certain ethical subject. In this regard the purpose of the Website is very clear. On the one hand it is regulative in so far as it reports on and is concerned with the population as a whole. Ultimately, however, its aims are disciplinary in that it requires individuals to take up and turn these newly developed capacities (surveillance, comparison, evaluation) on themselves (via technologies of the self), in this way functioning as a biopolitical strategy.

This analysis of the *Measure Up* campaign highlights the mobilization of disciplinary power as part of the biopedagogical strategies of contemporary health promotion. In the first instance it shows the production of understandings of the body in which we are all to understand ourselves as at risk. Alongside this the campaign reproduces particular truths about healthy living and lifestyle. Such truths have salience both because 'experts' and 'science' support them, and because the campaign explicitly links these behaviours with notions of being a happy, healthy, morally virtuous person—the type of citizen many would aspire to. In this way disciplinary power does not work *on* individuals, so much as it works *through* them, shaping their conduct and aspirations. In the next example I shift away from broad-targeted health promotion strategies such as *Measure Up*, to look more specifically at the school as a site for shaping the conduct of young people in response to the obesity epidemic.

Young People, School and Food: "Lunchbox Inspections"

In Australia, much of the focus of preventative health promotion measures related to obesity is currently directed at children and young people. It also seems that the school is one of the key settings of choice for the enactment of these measures. Amongst other reasons, the focus on targeting children through the school can certainly be connected with the fact that historically, schools are pedagogical spaces through which it is expected that certain capacities, skills and knowledges will be developed in young people. This is perhaps particularly important when the capacities, skills and knowledges are health-related because childhood is widely considered "to be the point in the lifecourse at which good habits can be inculcated" (Coveney, 2008, p. 203). Historically the school has also been a key setting for the education, surveillance and evaluation required to shape the individual in order to increase their potential contribution as a citizen (Foucault, 1995; Kirk, 1998). As analyses of school HPE have shown (Leahy & Harrison, 2004; Wright & Burrows, 2004; Wright & Dean, 2007), classrooms and playing fields are frequently used as sites for the production of particular truths about healthy living. Equally importantly they mobilize the pedagogical work required to convince young people that it is socially and morally valuable to align one's conduct with these truths. In order to illustrate the making up of the healthy citizen in relation to schooling, I begin with an example of a kind of "lunchbox inspection". As I will explain in a moment, while lunchbox inspections are not institutionalised in Australian schools, they are becoming more commonplace in primary schools (ages 5–12). The following quote is taken from an interview that was conducted as part of an international research project that sought to examine the impact of obesity-related health imperatives on schools, teachers and students (Burrows et al., 2008). The teacher quoted here is a year five teacher (10–11 year-old students), working in a coeducational school that is in an ethnically diverse urban setting, and which did not seem to have an overt focus on health- and body-related biopedagogies (Harwood, 2009; Wright, 2009).

> ...when I first started they [the girls of the class] were missing recess.... I don't think it was a conscious thing, they just wouldn't eat it and I just don't think there was enough of a routine there instilled in them. So now, well then I had to put procedures in like 'ok, you must show me your recess [food].' So every time I say that they have to walk out the door with their recess above their head. I know it sounds a bit awful, but it would get them into the routine of going to their bags and getting their recess out and actually eating it.... And I've structured lessons around it. 'Ok, if you don't eat properly what's (sic) the effects on you?' [They reply] 'I feel tired, I feel cranky and I don't want to do my work.' 'Ok, tomorrow eat your food and then see what the difference is.' So they do it: 'oh, I've got so much more energy and I can think, I can answer the questions.' So they can do it physically for themselves and that means we don't have to go back and explain everything. And as a result of that, they will then tell me, 'oh, you haven't had breakfast this morning because your sentences aren't making sense and they'll be right because I might have rushed.... It's a good thing, but now it's an automatic thing as well.

And later,

> ...because once again it's getting children into the routine. I've noticed now, in my class, lots of the kids they're not bringing in the (and this is not from my influence it's probably from them writing it on the shopping list or whatever), they're bringing in the fruit... it's not the chips or the cakes, it's the fruit which is coming in more often now, which is a good thing.

In Australia, lunchbox inspections are part of a broader set of obesity-related initiatives targeted at improving the quality of food consumed by students in schools, however, while changes to school canteens have been legislated (in some states) resulting in their adoption across all government and many non-government schools, lunchbox inspections are much less widespread and have encountered at least some public opposition. It is also important to note that in comparison to reports about lunchbox inspections in preschools (Edwards, 2006), the process being detailed above seems much lighter and less draconian. Nevertheless, this recount of the weaving of lunchbox inspection into classroom routine provides a vivid example of disciplinary power operating in conjunction with regularizing power to make up certain types of young people. The teacher describes a process of surveillance, or "hierarchical observation" (Foucault, 1995, p. 170) as the students are asked to "show" her their food and "have to walk out the door with their recess above their head". Through this students, and their food, are individualized and made "clearly visible" (p. 171) to the teacher's authoritative gaze and to surveillance by the other students. While this example of mass surveillance being used to induce self-regulation is clearly disciplinary, following Leahy (2009) I suggest that it does not become a fully assembled biopedagogical device until it is coupled with health education 'knowledge', a process the teacher alludes to when she says "And I've structured lessons around it". We can imagine this as a process where students are taught about healthy foods, the risks associated with consuming unhealthy foods and the skills and capacities required to self-regulate and apply this knowledge to their own conduct. Even the language here is important: "energy" and "effects" give a sense of the science of nutrition being employed to 'produce' better workers, or in the language of the new public health, assist citizens to realize and reach their full potential. Though we do not get to see the "messiness" (p. 177) of how this plays out in the classroom (biopedagogies of course, should not be conceptualised as totalising and as such there are no guarantees as to how students' subjectivities will be effected), the teacher's comments that the students are not bringing the "chips or the cakes, it's the fruit which is coming in more often now", suggests that the "lifestyle" change, which is the desired outcome of this governmental work, may well have been achieved. In the final line we are also referred back to the specific disciplinary work involved in the inspection process as a whole, as the teacher refers to the establishment ("instil") of a pattern of behaviour, or "routine", for the third time.

Discussion

The two examples presented here provide some insight into how disciplinary power currently plays a significant role in the production of the healthy citizen. In the case of the lunchbox inspection example this disciplinary work is highly explicit. It centres on the classroom as a site for mass surveillance and individualized self-regulation and at least some degree of seemingly very public evaluation. Obesity discourse legitimises these practices in the name of health, producing a context in which young people are encouraged to "effect changes to their thoughts, conduct and bodies" in order to become healthier (Wright & Burrows, 2004, p. 212). In the case of *Measure Up* individuals are disciplined in regard to their lifestyles, knowledge and attitudes through the information presented under headings such as "What should I be eating?" and "Tips for getting active" and particularly through the online quizzes. For those readers having trouble conceptualising disciplinary work across the two examples as anything but top-down coercion, it is important to remember that within advanced liberal (Rose, 1999) societies such as Australia, individuals choose to take up exercise and eating practices such as those encouraged in *Measure Up*, often because of the salience of the truths and the work of a whole range of social actors to align these truths with notions of being a 'good' citizen. As noted in the introduction, the examples presented here also illustrate the entwined nature of disciplinary power and regularizing power. For example, the disciplinary work that I just argued was so vital to the *Measure Up* campaign would have far less impact were it not mobilized following regularizing power. Regularizing power's focus on the population *as a whole* provides the epidemiological data that underpins the establishment of a norm: waist measurements of more than 94 centimetres for men and 80 centimetres for women are associated with "increased risk of chronic disease" (Commonwealth of Australia, 2008). This norm thus defines the 'abnormal' and begins the process of disciplining those subjects who threaten the population's overall well-being and productivity.

An analysis of disciplinary power in the lunchbox inspections example also points to the need to consider how biopolitical strategies and disciplinary technologies are likely to figure in responses to the obesity epidemic in the next five to ten years. Following Gard and Kirk (2007), we might ask how long will it be until the relevant Australian authorities decide that biopolitical strategies have failed because they rely on individuals to discipline themselves and that the solution to the obesity problem lies in intervention activities that suspend individual 'choice' in favour of the 'good of the nation'? Such questions ask us to interrogate the limits of disciplinary power in contemporary societies and surely require further empirical investigations across a range of different contexts. However, based on the data here I suggest that disciplinary power is currently tempered by advanced liberal understandings of the citizen as "free to choose" (Rose, 1999, p. 87). In particular, the potential for disciplinary power to operate from an external locus of control is limited in so far as it requires a reconfiguration of the triangular relationship between sovereignty-discipline-government. Such reconfiguration is not only possible, but is already underway in some specific contexts. Here discipline works as a form of power that government through ethics uses to imbue obesity with ethical and moral legitimacy. Because obesity is constituted as an individual problem, the obese subject is seen to have 'failed' in his or her responsibility to self-govern. The government decision to intervene in people's lives is thus legitimated on the grounds that they have made a 'bad choice'. Perhaps the clearest examples of this include threats to remove obese children from their parents' care (Evans, Rich & Davies, 2008), on the grounds that parents have been neglectful in exercising their moral responsibilities, and moves to introduce "fat taxes" and employ purposefully discriminatory job hiring practices in order to force obese individuals to change their behaviours and bodies (Leonhardt, 2009). Such strategies point to current understandings of the limits of disciplinary power as a form of self-government, while reiterating that disciplinary power (in some form) remains crucial to 'making up' the healthy citizen.

Acknowledgments

The "lunchbox inspection" data was collected as part of a project funded by the Australian Research Council. My thanks to colleagues Jan Wright, Valerie Harwood, John Evans, Emma Rich and Lisette Burrows for allowing me to use this data. Thanks also to members of the University of Newcastle School of Education writing group for their helpful comments on an earlier draft of this paper, and to Dylan Cliff and Phil Morgan for their assistance in regards to the Bouchard and Epstein et. al references.

References

Access Economics (2008). *The Growing Cost of Obesity in Australia.* Retrieved August 19, 2009, from http://www.accesseconomics.com.au/publicationsreports/showreport.php?id=172

Australian Bureau of Statistics. (2009). *Causes of Death, Australia, 2007.* Retrieved August 19, 2009, from http://www.abs.gov.au/AUSSTATS/abs@.nsf/DetailsPage/3303.02007?OpenDocument

Bordo, S. (2003). *Unbearable weight: Feminism, Western culture and the body.* (10th ed.). Berkeley, CA: University of California Press.

Bouchard, C. (1991). Current understandings of the etiology of obesity: Genetic and nongenetic factors. *The American Journal of Clinical Nutrition, 53,* 1561S–1565S.

Bouchard, C. (2000). *Physical activity and obesity.* Champaign, IL: Human Kinetics.

Burchell, G. (1996). Liberal government and techniques of the self. In A. Barry, T.

Osbourne & N. Rose (Eds.), *Foucault and political reason* (pp. 19–36). Chicago: University of Chicago Press.

Burrows, L., Cliff, K., Byrom, T., De-Pian, L., Evans, J., Harwood, V., McCormack, J., Rich, E., & Wright, J. (2008). *Researching the new health imperatives in schools: Stories from the field.* Paper presented at the 2008 Australian Association for Research in Education Conference, Brisbane, Qld, Australia.

Burrows, L., & Wright, J. (2007). Prescribing practices: Shaping healthy children in schools. *International Journal of Children's Rights, 15*(6), 83–98.

Cameron, A., Welborn, T., Zimmet, P., Dunstan, D., & Owen, N. (2003). Overweight and obesity in Australia: The 1999–2000 Australian diebetes, obesity and lifestyle study. *Medical Journal of Australia, 1789*(9), 427–432.

Commonwealth of Australia (2008). How do you measure up? Retrieved August 17, 2009, from www.measureup.gov.au

Coveney, J. (2008). The government of girth. *Health Sociology Review, 17*(2), 199–213.

Dean, M. (1999). *Governmentality: Power and rule in modern society.* London: Sage Publications.

Deleuze, G. (1992). Postscript on the societies of control. *October 59, Winter*, 3–7.

Edwards, H. (2006, April 13). Chocolate birthday cake is out, lunch-box checks are in. *Sydney Morning Herald.*

Elliot, F., Riddell, P., Davidson, L., & Coates, S. (2008). David Cameron Tells the Fat and the Poor: Take Responsibility. *The Times*, Retrieved August 19, 2009, from http://www.timesonline.co.uk/tol/news/politics/article4290298.ece

Epstein, L., Wing, R., Koeske, R., & Valoski, A. (1984). Effects of diet plus exercise on weight change in parents and children. *Journal of Consulting Clinical Psychology, 52*(3), 429–437.

Evans, J., Rich, E., and Davies, B. (2008). *The rise and rise of the child saving movement. Resisting class and cultural rehabilitation?* Paper presented at the 2008 Australian Association for Research in Education Conference, Fremantle, WA, Australia.

Evans, J., Rich, E., Davies, B., & Allwood, R. (2008). *Education, disordered eating and obesity discourse: Fat fabrications.* Abingdon, Oxon: Routledge.

Featherstone, M. (1991). The body in consumer culture. In M. Featherstone, M. Hepworth & I. Turner (Eds.), *The Body* (pp. 170–196). London: Sage.

Foucault, M. (1990a). *The history of sexuality volume I: An introduction.* New York: Vintage Books.

Foucault, M. (1990b). *The history of sexuality volume II: The use of pleasure.* New York: Vintage Books.

Foucault, M. (1991). Governmentality. In G. Burchell, C. Gordon & P. Miller (Eds.), *The Foucault effect: Studies in governmental rationality* (pp. 87–104). Harvester Wheatsheaf: Hertfordshire.

Foucault, M. (1995). *Discipline and punish: The birth of the prison.* New York: Vintage Books.

Foucault, M. (2003). *Society must be defended: Lectures at the College De France 1975–1976.* New York: Picador.

Foucault, M. (2007). *Security, territory, population: Lectures at the College De France 1977–1978.* Basingstoke and New York: Palgrave Macmillan.

Fullagar, S. (2001). Governing the healthy body: Discourses of leisure and lifestyle within Australian health policy. *Health, 6*(1), 69–84.

Fullagar, S. (2003). Governing women's active leisure: The gendered effects of calculative rationalities within Australian health policy. *Critical Public Health, 13*(1), 47–60.

Fullagar, S. (2009). Governing healthy family lifestyles through discourses of risk and responsibility. In J. Wright & V. Harwood (Eds.), *Biopolitics and the obesity epidemic: Governing bodies* (pp. 108–126). New York and London: Routledge.

Gard, M., & Kirk, D. (2007). Obesity discourse and the crisis of faith in disciplinary technology. *Education and Democracy, 16*(2), 17–36.

Gard, M., & Wright, J. (2005). *The obesity epidemic: Science, morality and ideology.* London: Routledge.

Greco, M. (1993). Psychosomatic subjects and the "duty to stay well": Personal agency within medical rationality. *Economy & Society, 22*(3), 357–372.

Halse, C. (2009). Bio-citizenship: Virtue discourses and the birth of the bio-citizen. In J. Wright & V. Harwood (Eds.), *Biopolitics and the obesity epidemic: Governing bodies* (pp. 45–59). New York and London: Routledge.

Harwood, V. (2009). Theorizing biopedagogies. In J. Wright & V. Harwood (Eds.), *Biopolitics and the obesity epidemic: Governing bodies* (pp. 15–30). New York and London: Routledge.

Jennings, G. (2009) Whether or not obesity is increasing, too many people are too overweight for good health. In *Baker IDI Perspectives Volume 1.* Retrieved 2 September 2009, from http://www.bakeridi.edu.au/Assets/Files/127871_BakerPerspectives_HR_singles.pdf

Kirk, D. (1998). *Schooling bodies: School practices and public discourses.* London: Leicester University Press.

Leahy, D., & Harrison, L. (2004). Health and physical education and the production of the 'at risk self'. In J. Wright, D. Macdonald & L. Burrows (Eds.), *Critical inquiry and problem-solving in physical education* (pp. 130–139). London: Routledge.

Leahy, D. (2009). Disgusting pedagogies. In J. Wright & V. Harwood (Eds.), *Biopolitics and the 'obesity epidemic': Governing bodies* (pp. 172–182). New York: Routledge.

Leonhardt, D. (2009). The way we live now—should fat people pay more for health care? *The New York Times.* Retrieved September 13, 2009, from http://www.nytimes.com/2009/08/16/magazine/16FOB-wwln-t.html

Lupton, D. (1995). *The imperative of health: Public health and the regulated body.* London: Sage Publications.

Miller, P., & Rose, N. (1988). The Tavistock program: The government of subjectivity and social life. *Sociology, 22*(2), 171–192.

Murray, S. (2009). Marked as 'pathological': Fat bodies as virtual confessors. In J. Wright & V. Harwood (Eds.), *Biopolitics and the obesity epidemic: Governing bodies* (pp. 78–90). New York and London: Routledge.

Nettleton, S. (1997). Governing the risky self: How to be healthy, wealthy and wise. In A.

Petersen & R. Bunton (Eds.), *Foucault, health and medicine* (pp. 208–222). London: Routledge.

Petersen, A., & Lupton, D. (1996). *The new public health—health and the self in the age of risk.* St Leonards, NSW: Allen and Unwin.

Ransom, J. S. (1997). *Foucault's discipline.* Durham and London: Duke University Press.

Rich, E., & Evans, J. (2009). Performative health in schools. In J. Wright & V. Harwood (Eds.), *Biopower, biopolitics and the obesity epidemic: Governing bodies* (pp. 157–172). London and New York: Routledge.

Rich, E., Harjunen, H., & Evans, J. (2006). 'Normal gone bad': Health discourses, schools and the female body. In V. Kalitzkus & P. Twohig (Eds.), *Bordering biomedicine* (pp. 177–194). Amsterdam and New York: Rodophi, B. V.

Rose, N. (1999). *Powers of freedom: Reframing political thought.* Cambridge: Cambridge University Press.

Rose, N. (2008). *The politics of life itself: Biomedicine, power and subjectivity in the twenty-first century.* Princeton, NJ: Princeton University Press.

Rose, N., & Miller, P. (1992). Political power beyond the state: Problematics of government. *British Journal of Sociology, 43*(2), 173–205.

Seidell, J., & Risannan, A. (2004) Prevalence of obesity in adults: The global epidemic. In G. Bray & C. Bouchard (Eds.), *Handbook of obesity: Etiology and pathophysiology, volume 2* (pp. 93–108). New York: Informa Health Care.

Shilling, C. (1993). *The body and social theory.* London: Sage.

World Health Organization. (2009a). Controlling the global obesity epidemic. Retrieved September 2, 2009, from www.who.int/nutrition/topics/obesity/en/index.html

World Health Organization. (2009b). Obesity. Retrieved August 17, 2009, from www.who.int/topics/obesity/en/

Wright, J. (2009). Biopower, biopedagogies and the obesity epidemic. In J. Wright & V. Harwood (Eds.), *Biopolitics and the obesity epidemic: Governing bodies* (pp. 1–13). New York and London: Routledge.

Wright, J., & Burrows, L. (2004). 'Being healthy': The discursive construction of health in New Zealand children's responses to the national education monitoring project. *Discourse: Studies in the Cultural Politics of Education, 25*(2), 211–230.

Wright, J., & Dean, R. (2007). A balancing act: Problematising prescriptions about food and weight in school health texts. *Education and Democracy, 16*(2), 75–94.

Yoon, K., Lee, J., Kim, J., Cho, J., Ko, S., Zimmet, P., & Son, H. (2006). Epidemic obesity and type 2 diabetes in Asia. *The Lancet, 368*(9548), 1681–1688.

Chapter IX

Disciplining Desire: Young Children, Schools and the Media

Affrica Taylor

> Desire is spoken into existence, it is shaped through discursive and interactive processes, through the symbolic and the semiotic. Desires are constituted through the narratives and storylines, the metaphors, the very language and patterns of existence through which we are 'interpellated' into the social world…(Davies, 1990, p. 501).

It is now some twenty years since Bronwyn Davies contemplated 'the problem of desire' as part of the paradoxical process of sex/gender subjectification. Taking the sex/gender ordering of desire as axiomatic, she argued that our desires and hence our subjectivities are neither rational nor essential, but are constructed (by ourselves and others) from a multitude of contradictory discursive positions and practices (Davies, 1990).

Picking up and extending Davies' musings on 'the problem of desire' in the ordering of sex/gender as a troubling concept for educators, I offer a commentary on the disciplining of children's desires by focusing upon two key discursive sites across which young children are very differently interpellated: early childhood education and children's popular culture. Despite the radically disparate ways that schools and the media constitute children's desires, I argue that both these discursive sites have disciplinary effects upon their sex/gender and their sexual subjectivities. Across these sites, I tease out some of the paradoxical ways in which young children are codeterminously disciplined to become desiring, denying, regulated and self-regulating gendered and sexual subjects. I also explore how schools and popular culture moderate young children's multiple sexual subjectivities through regulating their desires in quite contradictory yet equally problematic ways. Into this Foucauldian inflected discussion of the disciplining of young children's desires I inject an additional psychoanalytic perspective. I do this in order to illuminate the complex adult anxieties and ambivalences that underpin the disciplinary regimes of schools and the media.

Competing Pedagogues: The School and the Media

Although schools are mandated to educate young children, the media also performs a significant pedagogical role. In addition to the programs produced by children's educational media, children's popular culture, produced by the corporate media, is centrally implicated in this pedagogical process. Children's learning about the world and their own place in it is facilitated across the diversity of media that children consume on a routine, usually daily, basis.

As well as sharing a pedagogical role in relation to the same captured audience of young children as students and media consumers, schools and media are simultaneously engaged in generating, reinforcing and disseminating various understandings of childhood. They are key discursive as well as pedagogical sites. Although their ways of knowing about and representing childhood can be highly contradictory, both these discursive sites contour and shape adults' and children's thinking about childhood and thus frame the ways that children can embody and perform being a child (Butler, 1990; 1993). In other words, through producing and disseminating discourses of childhood and interpellating children as learners, both schools and the media contribute towards the construction and disciplining of children's subjectivities, including their gendered and sexual subjectivities.

A number of scholars have noted that in media-saturated consumer societies there is an increasing sense of tension and rivalry between schools and popular culture for the hearts and minds of young children (Buckingham, 2000, 2005; Cannella & Kincheloe, 2002; Kenway & Bullen, 2001; Postman, 1994; Walkerdine, 1997, 2001, 2009). United States childhood studies scholar Joseph Kincheloe (2002) claims that: 'corporate-produced kinderculture is the primary source of knowledge in the new childhood' and suggests that educators of young children are still in denial about the fact that the media has now eclipsed their pedagogical role (p. 116). Regardless of their opinions about the corporate media's ascendance and influence over young children, most academic commentators agree that the media is fundamentally changing the landscape of childhood. To put this in Michel Foucault's terms—by shifting the relations of knowledge-power that cohere around both constructions of childhood and the education of young children, the media is decentring the school's hegemonic position. This clearly poses new sets of challenges for early childhood educators. Moreover, if Kincheloe is correct, these are challenges that early childhood educators are not necessarily well prepared to address.

Contrary to Kincheloe's assertion that educators do not fully appreciate the pedagogical sway of 'kinderculture', Jane Kenway & Elizabeth Bullen (2001) report that many of the high school teachers in their Australian study explicitly complain of: "having to 'compete with' the media as a source of knowledge and values" (p. 2). The overt sense of opposition and rivalry that they identify between high school and adolescent consumer culture cuts both ways. They discuss the ways in which schools moralistically construct the corporate media as "unworthy" and "non-educational" and the corporate media constructs the schools as "anti-pleasure", boring and regulatory (p. 77). This simultaneous negative positioning of one by the other exacerbates the sense of difference and reinforces the enmity between these two key pedagogical and discursive sites. It sets up young people to feel they have to choose between popular culture and the schools, and it sets up teachers to feel that they have to match the entertainment appeal of the media if they are going to maintain their students' loyalty and attention. Kenway & Bullen (2001) surmise that because schools increasingly lack a "sense of enchantment" for students (p.

151) and young people are increasingly interpellated by consumer culture to negatively view the school as "other" to their pleasures (p. 77) "…many young people now relegate school education to the margins of their identities" (p. 151).

So how is the relationship between the school and the corporate media worked out in the early years? Although it might not be articulated in such clearly rebellious, oppositional and identity-related terms, some of the same trends can be discerned. For instance, early childhood educators frequently regard popular culture toys and texts produced for young children as non-educational and they are often banned in early childhood school settings. As in the later years of secondary education, popular culture tends to be regarded as 'low culture' as opposed to the 'high culture' of the official curriculum. This predetermines children's popular culture artifacts and texts as lacking in quality and substance, and disposes them to be regarded as either an impediment or a threat to the serious and proper education of young children (Walkerdine, 2001; Kincheloe, 2001).

Although much commercial children's popular culture is discounted as being of little or no educational value, not all children's popular culture is seen as a direct threat. It is those popular culture texts that are positioned at the representational nexus of childhood, desire and sexuality, which are most likely to be regarded as significant threat to young children. This brings us back to the 'problem of desire' (Davies, 1990) and the issues that are raised by the radically different constitutions and interpellations of children's desires across the media and the schools.

To say that desire is done differently in some quarters of children' popular culture and in the early years of schooling is an understatement. In the desire-driven environment of contemporary consumer societies there is a palpable and growing gap between the increasingly sexual-desire-producing corporate media domain, which targets young children, and the sexual-desire-denying domain of early childhood schooling. This growing gap is significant because it constitutes a problematic schism between the two key pedagogical and discursive domains, which vie to construct children's desires and interpellate them as sexed/gendered and thereby sexual subjects.

Sexual-Desire-Denying Domain of Early Childhood Schooling

It is the particular combination of hegemonic discourses that prevail within the early years of schooling that ensure that school functions as a sexual-desire-denying domain. These discourses shape and contour the ways that childhood and children's sexuality can be known about and regulate the ways that early childhood educators can respond to children.

To begin with, the field is dominated by the orthodoxies of Developmentally Appropriate Practice, or DAP (Bredekamp, 1986). Within DAP, the well-entrenched and defended belief that 'exposure' to sexual knowledge per se and sexual desire in particular is age inappropriate for young children, positions early childhood educators, a priori, as the gatekeepers of children's sexual innocence. As a result, very few early childhood educators dare to engage with children's pleasure-based desires or their sexuality (Jones, 2004, 2006). Guided by Froebel's natural play theories and Piaget's cognitive theories of child development (James, Jenks & Prout, 1998; Jenks 2005), most early childhood professionals regard childhood as a naturally pure, simple and asexual life stage.

The developmental educational theories that determine sexuality to be age inappropriate for young children are reinforced by the overarching, pervasive and persistent Western discourse of childhood sexual innocence (Kehily & Montgomery, 2009; Robinson, 2005; Renold, 2006; Taylor & Richardson, 2007) and increasingly underscored in more recent years by society-wide efforts to protect young children from sexual abuse. Nowhere are the anxieties over child sexual abuse more acutely felt than in the world of early childhood education, where the politics of sex and gender (including controversies over the role of men in early childhood education, children from same sex families and children's sex/gender knowledges and behaviours) are played out against the powerful twin regulating discourses of childhood sexual innocence and child protection (Robinson, 2008; Taylor, 2007).

As Joseph Tobin (1997) surmises, the disciplinary effects of these discourses are evident in a myriad of regulatory practices, architectures and legal requirements, which monitor the behaviours and bodies of children and adults in early childhood centres and classrooms. Some examples of these are the constant surveillance of children and teachers, the spatial design of early childhood centres and classrooms to ensure unobstructed lines of sight, police checks on all new staff, no-touch rules for early childhood teachers and the mandatory reporting of children who display behaviour that might indicate sexual abuse.

Not surprisingly, all this regulation and anxiety inhibits positive discourses about children's sexuality and sexual desire. Tobin (1997) identifies children's sexual desire as a conspicuously "missing discourse" within contemporary early childhood education, and reminds us that this has not always been the case (p. 4). Up until the 1970s (and predating the discourse of child sexual abuse), Freud's early twentieth-century infantile sexuality theory was a standard component of child development studies within teacher education programs. While not advocating for a wholesale resurrection of Freud's prescriptive theory, which overdetermines children's desires as fixed, staged and essentialised indicators of their 'innate sexuality', Tobin (1997) points out that young children's sexual desires are not so much "undiscovered" by early childhood educators today, as anxiously "forgotten" (p. 5).

Not only are the everyday practices of early childhood educators and children subject to the disciplinary regimes, which disavow children's sexual desires, but the production of knowledge about children and sexuality is also highly regulated. Another of the disciplinary effects of these powerful discourses can be observed in the kind of research that is funded and pursued around children and sexuality. It is not surprising that the vast majority of this research is concerned with the identification and prevention of child sexual abuse. In a world preoccupied with the dangers of child sexual abuse and beset by the anxieties that this possibility produces, very few early childhood scholars or educators are prepared to discuss children's desires in sexual terms (Jones, 2004, 2006).

There is one group of scholars that is an exception. With an enduring interest in the relationship between sex and gender, and in the orderings, which produce sexual subjectivities, feminist and queer scholars point to the role that schools play in 'silencing children's sexualities' (Epstein, O'Flynn & Telford, 2003). In addressing the early childhood context of sex/gender politics, Kerry Robinson (2005) and Emma Renold (2006) theorise the connections between adult constructions of children's sexual innocence, the normalising assumptions of heterosexuality (or heteronormativity) and the silencing of children's sexualities. These theorisations are confirmed by a number of empirical studies (such as those conducted by Maria Pallotta-Chiarolli in Australia, Emma Renold in the UK and Deevia Bhana in South Africa), which look at the ways in which children's sexuality is regulated and performed in primary school settings (cited in Epstein et al., 2003). Similar findings from these studies confirm the paradox that even while schools maintain the official discourse of childhood sexual innocence: "… sexuality pervades primary school playgrounds and classrooms and children draw on it as a resource for constructing themselves as boys and as girls" (Epstein et al., 2003, p. 19). This conclusion is based upon repeated observations that teachers do not regard young children's play—such as that involving reenactments of heterosexual family life, or even the girl friend/boy friend, kiss and chase, getting married and date and dump games—as sexual play.

A closer look at the dynamics of one of these common games, kiss and chase, helps us to appreciate how the discourses of heteronormativity and childhood innocence combine to discipline children's sexual desires and to discipline teachers' thinking about them. To begin with, this game is very embodied and characterised by a high level of affect and desire: it is characterised by tension, excitement, squealing, laughter, physical struggle etc. The game is also very gendered. It is common for boys to chase girls and vice versa within the ordering of heterosexual attraction. The discourse of heteronormativity positions these children to perform their gender/sex identities in predictable ways, and for the most part they comply. From the teachers' point of view, this game is simply a lively expression of the normal and natural ways that boys and girls learn how to relate to one another. Because the discourse of childhood innocence presupposes that children are asexual beings, and because heteronormative discourses normalise the 'hetero'-ness of the behaviour while obscuring its 'sexual'-ness, teachers are predisposed to see this play as innocent good fun, rather than as a sexual game driven by children's desires. With further recourse to developmental theory, they are most likely to see play such as this as the children's way of "'practicing", "trying on", or "mimicking" older sexualities', and thus as a natural and inevitable 'induction' into their correctly gendered heterosexual roles (Renold, 2006, p. 495).

Through such Foucauldian-inflected analyses we can see how discursive silences around children's sexuality in schools have paradoxical disciplinary effects. These discursive silences create disciplinary regimes that simultaneously deny the sexual agency of young children and normalise and de-sexualise their (hetero)sexual identity performances. These studies also show us that the contradictory interpellations of young children as both sexually desirous and asexual subjects occurs within the schools, as children are implicitly positioned as heteronormative sexual subjects within the 'hidden curriculum' even as their sexual subjectivies are 'silenced' in the official DAP-based curriculum.

Sexual-Desire-Producing Media Domain

At the same time that most educationalists hesitate to acknowledge, let alone address young children's sexualities and desires, the corporate media is preoccupied with comprehending and thus exploiting young children's desires in order to attract younger and younger audiences to broaden their consumer market base. As Kenway & Bullen (2001) point out: "Children's commercial culture appeals so much to children because it takes children's play, pleasure and desire seriously" (p. 46). Clearly the corporate media is actively producing children's culture, not just tapping into it, but their success in engaging young children is dependent upon their ability to understand, harness and cultivate children's desires. This requires the promotion of cultural products that will please and delight children.

It is well known that market researchers segment and target children's desires in terms of age and gender in order to create niche markets that appeal directly to their different demographics (for a more detailed discussion see Kenway & Bullen, pp. 47–55). For young children, this means appealing to their aspirations to be older, to be in control, and to identify with distinctively gendered attributes: such as action, conflict and heroicism for boys; and relationships and physical beauty for girls. Such predictable formulas result in the manufacturing of hyper-gendered popular culture products: like Spiderman for young boys, who are encouraged to identify with the physically powerful and active macho heroes; and Bratz for girls, whose aspiration to be older and more powerful are tapped through identification with the 'sexy' teenager personas with 'girl power' attitude. Both products are sexually suggestive through their hyper-gendering, but it is the brazen seductiveness of the adolescent Bratz figures, rather than the implied prowess of the adult Spiderman, which is immediately read as sexual and often condemned as inappropriately sexualising children (SBS, 2007). When sexuality is apprehended within children's popular culture, it commonly ignites controversies about the power of such representations to distort the natural innocence of childhood, to render children vulnerable to adult sexual exploitation and to prematurely escalate children's nascent sexual development.

Media-driven controversies about the increase in sexual representations of young children (usually those 'sexy' girls) in corporate advertising and popular culture are as commonplace as the sexual representations of the children themselves. Public debates are often fuelled by outraged and concerned-citizen media 'watchdog' activities (Kf2bk, 2009). In the most recent Australian round, they also involved the publication of a couple of highly publicised Australian Institute discussion papers (Rush & La Nauze, 2006a, 2006b), which accused advertising and marketing corporations of 'corporate paedophilia' and in turn triggered an Australian Government Senate inquiry into the *Sexualisation of Children in the Contemporary Media* (Commonwealth of Australia Senate Standing Committee on the Environment, Communications and the Arts, 2008). While there were plenty of media commentators, child psychologists, advertising industry defendants, and concerned citizens driving these Australian debates (see SBS, 2007; ABC, 2007; Channel Nine, 2008), there was a noticeable absence of engagement from the early childhood education sector.

This lack of early childhood education voices within the public debate over the sexualisation of childhood in the media echoes the avoidance of children's desires and sexuality within the early childhood classroom. Moreover, in stark contrast to the emotional charge that fuels public reactions to the presence of children's sexuality in the media, and to the corporate media's opportunistic commercial exploitation of children's sexuality, there is barely a whisper of concern about the absence of a professional discourse about children's desires and sexualities in early childhood education. This is further indication of the curious disconnection between these two domains.

In spite of an appreciation of the powerful disciplinary framings that regulate and silence early childhood educators, it still seems ironic that early childhood educators proceed with the business-as-usual of educating the asexual child, even as these very heated wider social debates about the 'inappropriate' acceleration of young children's sexual knowledges rage around them. What happens to these same public concerns about young children's prematurely escalated sexual knowledge that many teachers presumably share, when they enter the classroom and teach their 'asexual' pupils? The disconnections, the disassociations and the displacement of children's sexualities within early childhood require more deliberation. In order to do this, I return to thinking more about why desire is such a troubling concept for educators of young children.

Troubling Desire

Desire is a troubling notion for all educators because it blurs a number of boundaries, which structure and secure the business of education. To start with, desire moves beyond the known and knowable cognitive and rational ground on which education traditionally takes place. If educators were to fully acknowledge the pedagogical implications of desire (let alone explicitly trade in them as does the corporate media) this could potentially disrupt the notion of the autonomous rational individual—the bedrock assumption of dominant educational theory. For desire is enigmatic and clearly exceeds the domain of the mind. As Megan Watkins (2008) points out, desire implies that the unconscious and the body play a significant role in the teaching/learning process.

As well as this, desire is a slippery concept. It connotes sexuality even though it is not synonymous with sexuality and cannot be reduced to sexuality. It is this very relationship that advertisers so well understand and exploit and educators so anxiously avoid. One of desire's alluring complexities is the way in which it is so often shadowed by sexuality and for many educators, this remains troublesome and inhibits an exploration of desire's pedagogical potential.

In calling for a more productive understanding of desire, Watkins (2008) argues that there is a need to look beyond what she describes as psychoanalytic theory's tendency "to simply sexualise desire" (p. 113). However, by refusing the simplistic conflation of desire with sexuality, Watkins excludes sexuality from her considerations of the corporeal and affective dimensions of desire. This displacement of sexuality not only limits the consideration of the affective and embodied nature of pedagogical desire, but also ignores the significance of the disavowal of children's sexuality within educational discourses. While I agree with Watkins that desire troubles educators because it disturbs the premise of the rational individual learner, I also believe that desire troubles educators because it connotes sexuality.

Desire also causes trouble for educators because it blurs the boundaries between self and others, between teachers and students. Once again, Watkins (2008) provokes us to consider desire in productive terms. She suggests that rather than considering students' and teachers' desires in separate and narrow terms (such as students' innate desires to learn and teachers' innate desires to teach), we need to pay more attention to the: "intersubjective nature of desire; namely the ways in which what teachers do in the classroom is fundamental to the cultivation of student desire and resultant achievement" (p. 117). Watkins is drawing other educators' attention to the pedagogical possibilities of students' and teachers' generative and interdependent desires.

Any appreciation of the intersubjective nature of desire involves an understanding that all desires are constructed through boundary-crossings, a kind of imaging of self beyond the boundaries of the (existing) self. Coupled with the educational context of adult/child relations and the persistent connotation of sexuality, this makes desire a very transgressive consideration for educators of young children. It implies that we can no longer consider children's desires and sexualities without simultaneously considering how our own adult desires are co-implicated with theirs.

A Final Troubling

I conclude my discussion about the schools' and the media's disciplining of desire by picking up on some of the insights and challenges raised by Valerie Walkerdine (1997, 2001, 2009) and Deborah Britzman (1998). Both of these feminist scholars further trouble the notion of desire by combining Foucault's understandings of the discursive production of our sexual subjectivities with some additional insights from psychoanalytic theory.

For Walkerdine, it is the uncomfortable contradictions, paradoxes and ambivalences that infuse (adult) representations of young girls in popular culture that provide the clue for understanding the complex relationship between adults' and children's desires and sexual subjectivities. Focusing upon popular culture's uptake of the Lolita figure (of which Bratz dolls could well be regarded as the latest incarnation), she reworks Freud's Oedipus complex as a cultural manifestation of not only young girls' desires for their fathers, but co-determinously, of adults' projected desires for children (1997). She reflects upon this as a productive circuit of exchange: "…in which cultural fantasies, fantasies of the parents, and little girls' Oedipal fantasies mix and are given a cultural form that shapes them" (Walkerdine, 2001, p. 30).

Underpinning Walkerdine's understanding of this complex and constitutive adult/child and desire-driven relationship is the significance she places on adults' anxious denial of children's sexual desire and insistence upon the protection of childhood innocence. She believes that adults' obsession with childhood innocence is ubiquitous, a deeply anxious defence and a projection. According to Walkerdine (2001), it is the "desire of adults for children" (p. 15) that fuels these commonly held adult anxieties and drives calls for child protection,

> the little seductress is a complex phenomenon that carries adult sexual desire but also hooks in to the equally complex fantasies carried by the little girl herself. The ideas of

a sanitized natural childhood in which such things are kept at bay, having no place in childhood, becomes not the guarantor of the safety of children from the perversities of adult desires for them but a huge defense against the acknowledgement of dangerous desires on the part of adults. In this analysis, 'child protection' begins to look more like 'adult protection' (Walkerdine, 2001, p. 29).

Walkerdine is not the only scholar to note that adults' desires for childhood innocence are fraught. In his elaborations in *Erotic Innocence*, James Kincaid (1998) also argues that the (adult) construction of the pure, innocent and asexual child is an erotic fantasy, as it is always shadowed by its constitutive other—the lurking possibility of this same child as sexually knowing and potentially seductive. In other words, the very insistence upon innocence always suggests otherwise, and this is what makes it so desirable. David Archard (1993) also expresses his concern about perpetuating notions of childhood innocence in a world in which this same innocence constitutes adults' desire. He points out that "innocence…connotes a purity, virginity, freshness and immaculateness which excites by the possibilities of possession and defilement" (Archard, 1993, p. 40).

It would seem that these insights into the psychology of adults' desires might be useful in considering the contradictory positioning of young girls as compliant sexual innocents (as in the disciplinary regimes of the classroom) and as seductive little Lolitas (as in the disciplinary regimes of popular culture). Both discursive positionings can be read as projected adult fantasies about children—and both require a considerable amount of honest reappraisal. This kind of reconceptualising work is especially incumbent upon those who work with young children.

Britzman (1998) is one educational theorist who directly challenges teachers to consider the ways in which adult desire "structures educational imperatives and the construct of child development" (p. 72), and to consider the costs of denying children's sexuality. For her, as for me, one of the greatest challenges is to imagine a new kind of knowledge about children and adults' desires, which will create the space for "new practices of the self" (Britzman, 1998, p. 73). According to Britzman (1998), such a space will only be possible when we somehow move beyond the dominant sexuality discourses of "moral panic, protection of innocent children, the eugenics of normalcy, and the dangers of explicit representations of sexuality" (p. 73).

Thinking about the imbroglio of adults' and children's mutually constituting desires outside of a framework that is propelled by disavowals, defences, projections, disassociations and denials is a difficult task. But it is another kind of desire well worth pursuing.

References

Archard, D. (1993). *Children: Rights and Childhood*. New York and London: Routledge.

Australian Broadcasting Corporation (2007). Sex sells—but at what cost to our kids? Difference of Opinion. Broadcast 27 September 2007. Transcript retrieved 2 September 2008, from http://www.abc.net.au/tv/differenceofopinion/content/2007/s2042109.htm

Bredekamp, S. (1986) (Ed.) *Developmentally Appropriate Practice*. Washington: NAEYC.

Britzman, D.P. (1998). *Lost Subjects, Contested Objects: Toward a Psychoanalytic Inquiry into Learning.* Albany: State University of New York Press.

Buckingham, D. (2000). *After the Death of Childhood: Growing Up in the Age of Electronic Media.* Oxford and Malden, MA: Polity Press.

Buckingham, D. (2005). A special audience? Children and television. In J. Wasko (Ed.) *A Companion to Television* (pp. 468–488) Malden, MA, Oxford, UK and Carlton, Vic.: Blackwell Publishing.

Butler, J. (1990). *Gender Trouble: Feminism and the Subversion of Identity.* New York and London: Routledge.

Butler, J. (1993). *Bodies that Matter: On the Discursive Limits of "Sex".* New York and London: Routledge.

Canella, G.S. & J.K. Kincheloe (2002) (Eds.) *Kidworld: Childhood Studies, Global Perspectives and Education.* New York: Peter Lang.

Commonwealth of Australia Senate Standing Committee on the Environment, Communications and the Arts. (2008). *Sexualisation of Children in the Contemporary Media.* Retrieved 30 September 2008, from http://www.aph.gov.au/senate/committee/eca_ctte/sexualisation_of_children/report/report/pdf

Davies, B. (1990). The problem of desire. *Social Problems,* 37(4), 501–16.

Channel Nine. (2008). Sexualisation of children. *Sunday.* Transcript retrieved 19 September 2008, from http://sunday.ninemsn.com.au/sunday/cover_stories/article_2483.asp

Epstein, D., O'Flynn, S. & Telford, D. (2003). *Silenced Sexualities in Schools and Universities.* Stoke on Trent, UK, Sterling, USA: Trentham Books.

Kenway, J. & Bullen, E. (2001). *Consuming Children: Education, Entertainment, Advertising.* Berkshire, Philadelphia: Open University Press.

Kids Free 2B Kids (Kf2bk), (2008). *Kids Free 2B Kids.* Retrieved 30 September 2008, from http://www.kf2bk.com/

Kincaid, J. (1998). *Erotic Innocence.* Durham, NC and London: Duke University Press.

Kincheloe, J.K. (2002). The complex politics of McDonald's and the new childhood: Colonizing kidworld. In G. Cannella and J.K. Kincheloe (Eds.) *Kidworld: Childhood Studies, Global Perspectives and Education* (pp. 75–121). New York: Peter Lang.

James, A., Jenks, C. & Prout, A. (1998). *Theorising Childhood.* Cambridge: Polity Press.

Jenks, C. (2005). *Childhood.* (2nd edition). New York and London: Routledge.

Jones, A. (2004). Risk, anxiety, policy and the spectre of sexual abuse in early childhood education. *Discourse* 25(3), 321–334.

Jones, A. (2006). Sex, fear and pedagogy: Sylvia Ashton-Warner's infant room. In J.P. Robertson and C. McConaghy (Eds.) *Provocations: Sylvia Ashton-Warner and Excitability in Education* (pp. 15–32). New York: Peter Lang Publishing.

Kehily, M. J. & Montgomery, H. (2009). Innocence and experience: A historical approach to childhood and sexuality. In M. J. Kehily (Ed.) *An Introduction to Childhood Studies* (Second Edition) (pp. 70–92). Maidenhead, New York: Open University Press McGraw-Hill Education.

Kenway, J. & Bullen, E. (2001). *Consuming Children: Education, Entertainment, Advertising.* Berkshire, Philadelphia: Open University Press.

Postman, N. (1982). *The Disappearance of Childhood.* New York: Delacourt Press.

Renold, E. (2006). They won't let us play … Unless you're going out with one of them: Girls, boys and Butler's 'heterosexual matrix' in the primary years. *British Journal of Sociology of Education,* 27(4), 4489–509.

Robinson, K.H. (2005). Childhood and sexuality: Adult constructions and silenced children. In J. Mason, and T. Fattore (Eds.) *Children Taken Seriously in Theory, Policy and Practice* (pp. 66–78). London and Philadelphia: Jessica Kingley.

Robinson, K.H. (2008). In the name of 'childhood innocence': A discursive exploration of the moral panic associated with childhood and sexuality. *Cultural Studies Review,* 14 (2), 113–129.

Rush, E. & La Nauze, A. (2006a). *Corporate Paedophilia: Sexualisation of Children in Australia,* Discussion paper no.90, The Australia Institute. Retrieved 30 September 2008, from https://www.tai.org.au/?q=node/8&offset=2

Rush, E. & La Nauze, A. (2006b). *Letting Children Be Children: Stopping the Sexualisation of Children in Australia,* Discussion paper no.93, The Australia Institute. Retrieved 30 September 2008, from https://www.tai.org.au/?q=node/8&offset=1

SBS (2007). Bratz, bras and tweens. *Insight.* Broadcast17 April. Podcast retrieved 20 May 2008, from htttp://www20.sbs.com.au/podcasting/index.php?action=feeddetails&feedid=53&id=4695

Taylor, A. (2007). Innocent children, dangerous families and homophobic panic. In G. Morgan and S. Poynting (Eds.) *Outrageous: Moral Panics in Australia* (pp. 210–22). Hobart, Tas: Australian Clearinghouse for Youth Studies.

Taylor, A. & Richardson, C. (2005) 'Queering Home Corner'. *Contemporary Issues in Early Childhood,* 6 (2), 163–174.

Tobin, J. (1997). The missing discourse of pleasure and desire. In J. Tobin (Ed.) *Making a Place for Pleasure in Early Childhood Education,* (pp. 1–37). New Haven, CN and London: Yale University Press.

Walkerdine, V. (1997). *Daddy's Girl: Young Girls and Popular Culture.* London, Harvard University Press, Cambridge, MA: Macmillan.

Walkerdine, V. (2001). Safety and danger: Childhood, sexuality, and space at the end of the millennium. In K. Hultqvist and G. Dahlberg (Eds.) *Governing the Child in the New Millennium* (pp. 15–34). New York and London: RoutledgeFalmer.

Walkerdine, V. (2009). Developmental psychology and the study of childhood. In M.J. Kehily (Ed.) *Introduction to Childhood Studies* (Second Edition) (pp. 112–123) Maidenhead and New York: McGraw Hill, Open University Press.

Watkins, M. (2008). Teaching bodies/learning desire: Rethinking the role of desire in the pedagogic process. *Pedagogy, Culture & Society,* 16(2), 113–124.

Chapter X

Citizenship? What Citizenship? Using Political Science Terminology in New Discipline Approaches

Rob Imre & Zsuzsa Millei

Introduction

The political concepts of 'democracy' and 'citizenship', in the broad field of education and more particularly in theories of classroom discipline and associated welfare policies, are widely utilized. While these powerful concepts are used as taken-for-granted ideas, there is no singularly agreed-upon answer to the question of what 'citizenship' and 'democracy' mean when used in schools and in relation to students, and what practical considerations they carry both for pedagogy and discipline. Moreover, depending on how the concepts of democracy and citizenship are used, they can be both (dis)empowering for their subjects and simultaneously regulate them in terms of directing their activities in some form or another, be it in positive or negative directions. These concepts pre/proscribe behaviour, values and morals for schooled subjects including students, teachers and administrators, such that they simultaneously discipline their behaviour and create practices for their empowerment.

This chapter focuses on ideas of 'citizenship' from the field of political theory in order to begin a discussion about how we might imagine students as citizens. It also examines the possibility of students' citizenship from a particular perspective, that is, students' 'interests'. Political 'interest' is a particularly complex idea that was brought into thinking about the relation of the individual and society by 19th-century political theorists. From Adam Smith to contemporary neo-liberalism and the different variations of Marxism, 'interest' was made into a historical agent of 'human nature'. Political 'interest' is not something that is inherently there for educators to bring out from children, for example through civic education, but rather is a social construct. Usually when we refer to the idea of 'interest' it is in reference to the original liberal concept, which developed in terms of individuals 'mixing their labour with the land' literally, grounding them with the concern for the well-being of that particular parcel of land. Adam Smith discussed the 'unseen hand' in terms of a philosophical anthropological position, the physical marketplace in terms of a natural human endeavour that all modern individuals aspire to participate in, and from this stems the liberal concept (among other things) of interest. In many ways it can be similar to the civic republican idea of the 'interested citizen' who is embedded in the city-state through participation in the daily political, economic, and social life of the republic, thus having a stake in the daily affairs. This idea of citizenship does not rest on blood ties, nor does it rest on having been some kind of original inhabitant of the political territory. Political interest stems from the idea that this 'stake' in daily affairs guarantees that people who participate in society, regardless of origin, have this 'interest'. We still use the terminology in contemporary discourse dealing with 'stakeholders', or people who make use of various resources that governments have the capacity to make decisions about. There is a disjuncture here with children since they can be seen to be stakeholders, yet their legal-political positions are proscribed, and someone must always act *in* their interest, thus gaining possession of their interests. It is this disjuncture we are exploring. In this chapter, the examination of students' citizenship through the perspective of 'interest' delivers some insights into the ways in which children's citizenship is understood in education. Further, this chapter provides some questions and starting points to consider with regards to the use of the notion of 'students as citizens' in discipline theories and practices.

Students as 'Citizens'

The recent use of the concept of 'citizenship' generally in education and more particularly in relation to children appeared concurrently in public and policy discourses with varied discussions concerning the democratic prospects in wide-ranging fields (Kivisto and Faist, 2007). As a specific field that focuses more intensely on citizenship, 'citizenship education' is currently enjoying its own renaissance facilitated by neo-conservative nation building programs in government policies (Kenway, 2008). The term is used frequently in discourses of student empowerment and participation with the aims to create fairness and justice towards and between students, and an equitable environment in which all are considered as members of different kinds of communities, and different kinds of civic groups. 'Citizenship', as a concept utilised in discourses of schooling, is neither a new idea, nor a new strategy. The turn of the twentieth century saw its use in engaging children and education in the nation-building exercises worldwide (Ailwood, 2004; Brennan, 1994; James & James, 2004; Millei, 2007). The United Nations' (1989) *Convention of Children's Rights* and its appropriation in social policy also fuelled the use of this concept in education policies and operated on the assumption that there was a legal-political link between citizenship and rights. The assumption that one could not exist without the other propagated the use of the concept of 'citizenship' as it pertained to children.

Here we identify a few major points that we encountered with the use of the concept of 'citizen' for children in schooling. First, while discourses related to children's citizenship have the potential to empower children, they simultaneously regulate children by prescribing acceptable actions and avenues for their self-discipline. Another point of critique is that if the concept of 'citizenship' is employed without the explication of its purposes, rather than fulfilling its intended emancipatory purposes, it remains a discourse that has no relation to the social reality of children in which their views and desires are only occasionally listened to and acted upon in the public and political sphere, and in their everyday lives. In other words, the use of the concept of 'citizen' to describe children, invokes the idea that they have already gained the status of a particular kind of citizenship and hence further work to translate into practices, the points of the *Convention of Children's Rights*, is not necessary. Moreover, 'citizenship' and 'democracy' are lived practices rather than ethereal rules, therefore it is important to keep asking: what *kind* of democracy and *who* are the citizens and how do the two interact. Third, there is only a limited research literature, including the growing field of citizenship and values education that substantially conceptualises 'citizenship' as a political concept and its take-up in education (for a good start read the 2009 special issue of the journal of *Citizenship Studies* titled: 'Citizenship, Learning and Education'). In policies, theory and practical teaching, and public discourses surrounding issues to do with education, the concept of 'citizenship', if it remains under theorised, can only be used as a tokenistic word. The lack of exploration of the ways in which the concept of 'citizenship' constitutes understandings and practices has the potential to create mismatches between any intended applications of the concept and the potential outcomes of its utilization. Fourth, the use of the concept of children's 'citizenship' appears generally to be unproblematic, however its use is not neutral at all. The concept itself is rarely questioned or explained, and the assumption of its neutrality serves to cover up a number of problems.

This chapter, therefore, begins the task of outlining some of the understandings of 'citizenship' in political theory. It also considers its use in relation to public and educational discourses on discipline in order to highlight the complex discourses and power relations this concept constitutes. Further, the chapter problematises the concept of discipline and the way in which political theory terminology is deployed. We argue that political terminology is taken up in discipline theories and practices with a particular aim to ensure that children are made subjects of institutions rather than authentic participants in those institutions in which they find themselves. This is an important work since the concept of 'citizenship' and its related ideas such as citizen, a citizen's 'rights', 'interests', and so on, all have a history and an intellectual baggage that shape how they are used and received in current discourses. It is only by unpacking that baggage that we can outline the uses of these ideas that are presented unproblematically as benefiting children.

Liberal Ideas of Citizenship

There are a multiplicity of interpretations and problematisations of the idea of 'citizen' and its related concepts such as 'citizenship' (Kivisto & Faist, 2007). For the purposes of brevity, we discuss only a few in order to illustrate that for schooling, and more particularly for disciplining, there is hardly any discussion at all in terms of the range that exists. As such, we are not positing liberal views of citizenship against cosmopolitan, as against multicultural and so on. Neither is this a comprehensive treatment of the political problem of what constitutes the contested concept of 'citizenship' since the problem is bound by a number of factors such as knowledge disciplines (sociologists might view citizenship differently from political scientists, from historians, and so on), political instrumentality (in some countries with established rules of law around *jus sanguinis* (literally, right of blood—the principle that establishes citizenship through heredity regardless of the actual place of birth) instead of *jus soli* (literally, law of the ground—the principle that makes the actual place of birth the primary rule for citizenship rather than heredity), for example it might be difficult to bring in public policy that encourages in-migration), and the various histories of nation-states and how citizenship might be interpreted. Some good works that deal with the idea of citizenship in a broad way include most of Will Kymlicka's writing on liberal pluralism, Kivisto and Faist (2007) *Citizenship: Discourse, Theory, and Transnational Prospects*, Vertovec and Cohen (2002) *Conceiving Cosmopolitanism* and Soysal (1994) *Limits of Citizenship*. Our purpose here is to outline some of these main strands in order to demonstrate the great diversity in interpretation, which is not typically articulated or questioned when talking about children as citizens in education.

During the Enlightenment, European concepts of 'citizens' as individuals and the 'citizenry' as a political body constituting groups of people, was a way in which to take the classical Greco-Roman idea further than the right to vote and observe the senate being composed of representative political leaders. In the Enlightenment version of republicanism, citizenship was premised on the idea of property ownership within a defined territory that naturally delivered rights to individuals. These rights were primarily the right to self-governance and to further one's interests (generally defined as immediate political and/or economic), 'naturally' tied to the property ownership, within a given city-state. This view developed into early modern versions of rights-based citizenships during revolutionary England, France and the United States. Here, the development of liberal concepts of citizens and citizenship were tied to more sophisticated versions of natural rights theory that assumed that all 'men' were imbued with an equal moral worth upon their birth and that this liberty from external corruption was to be maintained. Thus, using this classical liberal notion of 'citizens' and 'citizenship' in regards to children is problematic, since children of any 'type' or 'kind' cannot own property and cannot cast a vote on how the prevailing authorities will deal with the circumstances surrounding their private property. This problem is ignored within citizenship education discourse, and usually will only surface during a 'moral panic' of one kind or another involving searching for drugs or weapons carried by students in schools. Questions may then arise as to whether or not school authorities can act in the name of the state, like police, in order to ensure a particular kind of 'civil order' within their schools and classrooms, and to what extent these de facto police are limited by the rule of law. Since children's rights are not guaranteed in the classroom in the same way as citizen's rights are guaranteed by the nation-state, we are dealing with a separate set of problems and circumstances.

Negative and Positive Liberty and Citizenship

A helpful distinction, when discussing types or kinds of liberal ideas, is to use Isiah Berlin's (1969) division of negative and positive liberty. For Berlin, 'negative' liberty was based on the idea of freedom from coercion of any kind. This means that individual members of a given society were seeking guarantees that would deliver *freedom from* external authorities of all kinds and as such Berlin engages in a particular reading of liberalism and ideas about liberal citizenship. Ideas about 'free markets' from Adam Smith (1776/1982), free men and sometimes women from the French Libertines, and free propertied individuals in England and the newly formed United States, all rested on this negative liberty concept in which the powers of absolute monarchs were challenged successfully so that men were able to exercise power on their own property. There was some significant debate about what might constitute 'their own property'. For example, whether this might include other people such as wives, children, slaves, and servants.

It is here that the 'rights agenda' was attached to citizenship so that the guarantees expanded to suffrage, property ownership, and a universalised capacity to run for public office and to participate fully in the institutions developed in a given society. The emerging rights agenda in the immediate aftermath of the Second World War encompassed both of these aspects, and there continues to be some significant debate about rights, duties, obligations, entitlements, and how this may or may not fit in to the liberal and/ or communitarian traditions/positions. For our purposes, we use the UN conventions as touchstones in our discourse here as they still appear as core components of debates around rights, and when nation-states debate these concepts and ideas among themselves internationally, as well as domestically within their own various political debates, these documents are used as things that frame debates about rights. Article 26 in the *Universal Declaration of Human Rights* (1948), *The Convention on the Rights of the Child* (United Nations, 1989), or Article 13 of the UN International Covenant on Economic, Social and Cultural Rights (United Nations, 1976) that states "Education is both a human right in itself and an indispensable means of realising other human rights", can all be understood as a form of guarantee for students that enables their full participation as citizens through their rights to education. Another way to understand this idea as embedded in discipline approaches is the objective to keep children *free from* teachers or other children's acts that limit their freedom. For example, the third value statement of the Western Australian Curriculum Council's Curriculum Framework states that "each person has the right to a friendly learning environment free of coercive ... elements" (Curriculum Council, Western Australia, 1998, Value Three). This objective cleverly justifies the use of externally imposed discipline in the interests of children, as Levin & Nolan (1991) explain: "the interactionalist teacher promotes individual student control over behaviour when possible but sometimes must subordinate this goal to the right of all students to learn" (p. 95).

Berlin's idea of 'negative liberty' is also contrasted to his idea of 'positive liberty' that can position opportunity in the hands of citizens by delivering on a kind of *freedom to* enact their goals. Berlin's (1969) original distinction was careful to make the point that often totalitarian states would try to justify harsh interventionist tactics and policies by claiming that positive liberty was a position in which activities were done for 'their own good'. This is an apt distinction for us since we cannot escape the problem of having to advocate for children. For Berlin, positive liberty does not escape the moral imperative of non-coercion. Positive liberty must adhere to the non-coercive position and can only intervene to create the conditions for enacting a kind of freedom that is part of a 'self-mastery'. This means that Berlin sought to ensure that the argument about liberty was not to be used for totalitarian purposes. For us, it is quite difficult to imagine a completely non-coercive situation for children in which they are able to act on their in-born freedoms. Berlin's distinction is a useful one since it shows us the limits of where we can take the concept and how we might think about the politics of liberal citizenship.

Most commonly linked with Keynes and his version of redistributive capitalism and the welfare state, citizens enjoying this form of participation, that is, a form of participation in which political power might be redistributed through evening out opportunity, making class distinctions less obvious, and through social services that even out economic (dis) advantages, would see a situation in which their status as a citizen would be enacted by not only a redistribution of monies in an individual economic sense through taxation and the like, but also a situation in which some forms of positive discrimination were to be brought in to common use. For example, beyond the guarantee that external powers did not have the capacity to infringe on the liberty of the individual, Keynesian economics sought to change the conditions under which individuals experienced the inequities of a liberal capitalist system.

This type of liberalism was also referred to as 'wet' liberalism in that it was opposed to the 'dry' liberalism of the classical liberals such as John Stuart Mill and John Locke. 'Wet' liberals then, advocated a 'watered down' version of a liberal democracy and the capitalist system that it was naturally assumed to be attached to, by promoting various schemes to bring in 'desired' levels of activity among various types of citizens. For example, if a defined group was not participating in property ownership, then a 'wet' liberal might advocate certain kinds of financial incentives for that specific group in order to encourage more full participation in that particular marketplace. This is the way in which 'positive' discrimination began to operate in the post-World War II era in order to open up opportunity of employment and education for women, quotas of various categories of people in workplaces and in educational institutions, and so on.

If we look at this particular distinction, positive and negative liberty, wet and dry liberalisms, then it is difficult to see how the use of 'child-citizen' terminology can be employed unproblematically. Children, by being citizens, are supposed to be autonomous and participating members of communities; in other words, children should be free from certain constraints on their liberty, and free to do other things. In reality, however, they are left with little choice. Even though Article 3 of *The Convention on the Rights of the Child* (United Nations, 1989) guarantees children's rights, it does not guarantee their citizenship. The Convention outlines that the child's best interest should be the primary consideration in matters relating to them, however, as a report further discusses this idea:

> [by] virtue of their relative immaturity, young children are reliant on responsible authorities to represent their rights and best interests in relation to decisions and actions that affect their well-being, while taking account of their views and evolving capacities (Committee on the Rights of the Child, 2005, p. 1).

It is interesting to note that there is almost no mention of the place of children in the 'good life' of the polis in contemporary political theory. Indeed, there are some reasonably well-known references in the classical reference points that the discipline uses, but nothing that systematically treats the role of children in democracy in a serious way in political theory as a discipline. This would be a very interesting project to embark upon for some further investigation. A liberal-democrat of any kind would argue that it is individual choice, not the capacity to have an authority figure choose for you, that defines the actions of liberal citizens. Children do not have the capacity to avoid participation in institutions, and the 'positive discrimination' tolerated by some versions of liberalism, still does not bring children in to participate fully as citizens in the world around them. They cannot drive cars, buy houses, use credit cards, vote for a parliamentary representative, run for public office, and so on, since none of these are considered to be part of their natural rights as 'liberal citizens' in a liberal democracy. Children are not co-equal with adults in liberal democracies, nor do they enjoy the same freedoms as adults. Policies regarding the early years and children's day-to-day realities in institutions preclude any notion of this and merely gloss over the problem that 'rights' do not equal a guarantee of citizenship and conversely, simply claiming that children have rights by enacting a policy that suggests this, does not equal a guarantee of citizenship with all of its possibilities.

Communitarian Ideas

Communitarian concepts of 'citizenship' emphasise duties and obligations above and beyond notions of liberty. MacIntyre's (1984) work on communitarianism is a well-known touchstone for this kind of thinking about citizenship. His analysis was one that, among other things, was an attempt to discuss citizenship outside of the traditional divide within liberalism, between liberty and equality, together with the traditional divide between liberal individualism and socialist collectivism. From this perspective, communitarian ideas meant that citizens were to participate in a somewhat different way in terms of enacting their citizenship in a given community. MacIntyre developed ideas about duty and obligation much more fully than modern liberal versions that sought to clarify the distinction between 'wet' and 'dry', 'positive' and 'negative' liberty, and a false dichotomy between freedom and equality.

MacIntyre claimed that citizens could realise all of these aspects of their lives through reciprocal arrangements in the form of duties they must perform in order to be considered citizens as well as particular kinds of obligations that were assumed as a result of being members of a given social, political and economic community. These duties and obligations would then outweigh liberal ideas of individualism, accumulation of capital without participation in the community, and freedom without consequences for the collectivity of the community.

MacIntyre's work and subsequent communitarian approaches are similar to early versions of republicanism that developed in the Enlightenment and are attempts at bringing together the needs of collectivities, or to paraphrase Polanyi's (1957) work on political economy, a 're-embedding' of the economic into the social so that collective use of a capitalist system of exchange exists simultaneously with democracy within a social framework. This is still not the same as socialism but might be akin to a kind of social democracy, the distinction being that socialism as a political ideology eschews competitive political parties and parliamentary democracy and seeks to dismantle capitalism as a system of production, whereas social democracy is an ideology that seeks to reform capitalism and can accept competing political parties within parliamentary democracy.

Both socialism and social democracy, like communitarianism, will place emphasis on collective problems and solutions as opposed to liberalism, which is grounded in the fundamental principle of freedom of the individual. References to children as citizens, indeed citizens in general in contemporary education texts, typically frame people as living in 'communities' of all kinds without defining what those communities might constitute. For example, the *Melbourne Declaration on Educational Goals for Young Australians* (2008) states that

> partnerships between students, parents, carers and families, the broader community, business, schools and other education and training providers bring mutual benefits and maximise student engagement and achievement. Partnerships engender support for the development and wellbeing of young people and their families and can provide opportunities for young Australians to connect with their communities, participate in civic life and develop a sense of responsible citizenship (p. 10).

Simply attaching a label to the word 'community' is not a definition. Referring to the community where children live, a learning community, the community of a school or child care, an Aboriginal community, the migrant community, the community of a profession, and the like, does not constitute a collectivity with duties and obligations until they can be demonstrated to function as such. Consequently, the idea that children can act as citizens in a communitarian version of the notion of 'citizenship' is idealistic to say the least and is conditional on a whole lot of practices already being in place.

One of the key points that MacIntyre and subsequent communitarians have made is that this 'system' of duties and obligations is meant to be part of a demonstrable civic empowerment. For communitarians, there is a virtue in 'good life' and an essential part of that good life is the political life. This is, of course, MacIntyre's revisiting of the Aristotelian view that participation in politics, and here he means the politics of the community, is the normatively correct path. Even if we accept this normative position, the question remains as to how we actually go about empowering and developing the political lives of children when they are not able to participate fully in political life in the same ways as adults in any given community apparatus.

Children are excluded from arenas of political discourse and practice that form an important platform for participation as citizens in communities. Political discourse can have two arenas as described by Lister (1996): "'strong' and 'weak publics' according to whether or not they encompass decision-making as well as opinion-forming" (p. 171). Children are rarely involved in political processes, consequently they have minimal opportunities to express their opinions or make their input into how institutions, policies and laws are shaped in relation to their interests. There are discussions and initiatives that attempt to engage children in 'weak publics', such as the establishment of the position and offices of ombudsman for children or research aiming to delineate their views on certain issues that matter to them. Hence, children are included in 'weak publics' but still lack representation in 'strong publics' or decision-making and planning. Accordingly, an essential question we must ask when using the concept of 'citizenship' is whether it encourages children's participation in decision-making and planning or remains as a kind of tokenism (Hart, 1992).

Children have no legal status and only limited administrative capacity to engage in politics, as we established above. The fundamentals of a good political life, so essential to communitarian theory, are mostly inaccessible to children, especially in institutional settings. As we previously noted, one of the core ideas of communitarianism is the virtue of the political life as equated with good life. This is a key normative aspect of the good communitarian citizen, but is notably absent from the discourse on children as citizens at the present since children are rarely politicised citizens with the capacity to act politically. This capacity and belonging to a community, however, is discussed widely in the citizenship education literature. Even for young adults, however, as Evans & Prillelrensky (2005) argue, "opportunities that develop political competence, power and self-determination are...limited" (p. 4). Ironically, even when the Australian governments commit to offer these opportunities to students, they express this assumed intention in an ambiguous way. For example, the *Melbourne Declaration on Educational Goals for Young Australians* (2008) states that they work with "school sectors to ensure that schools engage young Australians...with rich learning, personal development and citizenship opportunities" (p. 10). Students' citizenship in this document thus appears as conditional on engaging in these opportunities despite that they were explicitly named Australian (thus assumedly citizens) at the beginning of the sentence.

Moving Beyond the Nation-State

There is at least one other fundamental definitional component to the concept of 'citizenship', the nation-state. Liberals, social-democrats, socialists, and communitarians, have all developed their ideas from within the confines of the nation-state. Citizens are members of political communities that might not begin nationally, but they must necessarily end there. In the modern period, the status of citizenship allows individuals to access their rights and to actively complete their duties and obligations. In many cases, concepts of globalised citizens, global citizens, or cosmopolitan citizens, have included a discussion about moving beyond the nation-state reinforced by a kind of Kantian world-view (Bauböck, 2002) emphasising universal normative concepts. In this context, we are referring to a particular kind of German Idealism, as delineated by Kant, in which there is a kind of 'world government' brought together by morality and reason. (We deal with this in a different way in Chapter 11.)

Broadly speaking, a Kantian citizen is a world citizen, a cosmopolitan who has the capacity to enact their rights anywhere in the world, or at the very least in a plurality of spaces beyond the nation-state of their birth. Here, one of the most important points is that there are concerns that touch all human beings, and that these concerns are not bound by national borders. Global citizens would share concerns, perhaps about the environment, poverty, freedom from violence, and so on, but not in a Marxian sense in which a shared class antagonism develops and there is a revolution desired in order to overthrow world capitalism. In the case of this Kantian approach, and what later became versions of liberal-institutionalism, individuals form associations that go beyond their nation-state and seek to develop cooperative initiatives based on this voluntary association. In some cases, these associations are based on working through the nation-state to go beyond it: for example, representing one's own national identity through an inter-governmental organization like the United Nations. In other cases, individuals might form associations that involve organizations subverting their own nation-state and working for some kind of socio-political change. Non-Governmental Organizations (NGOs) delivering food aid, medical care, disaster relief, and so on, might well involve an ethical stance that goes beyond a national citizen identity and instead focuses on global civil society.

But again, where are the children? The rights-based approach has some merit in that a charter for the rights of the child is part of precisely this approach. It is a move towards a global citizenry of children, a kind of cosmopolitan civic culture of childhood. Unlike adult versions of this, however, children cannot activate these rights on their own. Furthermore, they do not choose to become global citizens acting upon a shared issue, shared problem, shared area of concern other than that they are disciplined to act as and think of themselves as 'global citizens' in prescribed ways.

Global citizenship in relation to children appears to be related to the increasing effects of globalisation rather than the moral position of a Kantian worldview, as the following quote from the *Melbourne Declaration on Educational Goals for Young Australians* (2008) illustrates:

> Global integration and international mobility have increased rapidly in the past decade. As a consequence, new and exciting opportunities for Australians are emerging. This heightens the need to nurture an appreciation of and respect for social, cultural and religious diversity, and a sense of global citizenship (p. 4).

'Global citizenship' in this context is understood as a particular extension on being an Australian citizen, and is predicated upon Australia and Australians becoming 'more' involved in a particular process of globalisation. This is not a normative demand for children to be 'global citizens' but rather as the *Melbourne Declaration on Educational Goals for Young Australians* (2008) demonstrates, Australian policymakers see this as an extension of global capitalism and Australia's successful performance within the global economy.

There is much more to this in terms of the extensions of communitarian ideas into cosmopolitanism (Vertovec & Cohen, 2002) in which individuals can conceive of themselves as citizens of the world rather than of a nation-state with borders and limitations on daily practices. For example, while adults might have the capacity to think of themselves as cosmopolitan, they can only do so with the material conditions and the administrative/legal capacity that is manipulable that children cannot possibly have. Children cannot obtain passports on their own, they cannot obtain work permits for a variety of countries, and cannot travel around the world at their own discretion. Global citizenry means that some people can do all of these things and have the capacity to move beyond their national borders. By definition then, children cannot be global citizens.

Disciplining the 'Interests' of the Child

The political 'interests of children' as citizens is a complex idea and is often overshadowed by another understanding that is linked to child-centred pedagogy and motivation theory that takes as its central concept the need to cater for the 'interests of children'. The latter interests are related to intellectual curiosity, while the earlier ones are associated with individual children's interests in relation to issues they consider important or good for themselves as agents in society. The notion of the child's 'best interests' is further complicated by the concept of 'childhood', which is a "*structural* site that is occupied by 'children', as a *collectivity"* (James & Prout, 1997, p. 14, original emphasis). As James and Prout (1997) argue further, in political discourses the issues related to all children or the child as an individual are often conflated so that "principles such as 'best interests'—which are, in fact, structural and culturally specific and refer to the collectivity of children—can be applied, unproblematically and always, to *the* (individual) *child*" (p. 15, emphasis original). Consequently, the idea of 'best interests of children' stands for children collectively (James & Prout, 1997) and disregards what the child, as an individual considers advantageous for himself or herself. This idea is even further complicated with a particular understanding of 'the child' as dependent on adults to know and advocate for what is good for him or her. These discourses legitimate and prescribe actions on behalf of children because adults know better what is good for children in general and because children are considered reliant on them.

Policies and institutions for the care and education of children are formed with the notion, among others, to serve the 'best interests' of children. The 'child's interests', however, occupy a place at the intersection of the interests of other children, parents, the state and preschool teachers and most of the time are in tension (Halldén, 2005). Using the concept of 'citizen' in regards to children, in which the 'child citizen' is considered to have an equal worth equal with 'adult citizen', has the potential to negate sources of social tension or overlook the power relations that can either facilitate or constrain children in exercising their rights and making known their interests. The 'child' is understood as bearing rights and having capabilities to form and express her or his interests, but the question remains, what if they go against what other children, the carers, the families, the state or policies construct as children's best interests? Do these tensions work in ways that discipline thinking about what we can consider as children's interests?

Discipline Through Learning

Children are only recently being thought about as political members of nations, societies or communities. As Qvortrup (1994) argues, children were regarded as part of families rather than individuals on their own rights, whose lives were strongly entangled with families. Since *The Convention on the Rights of the Child* (1989) and the emergence of the new sociology of childhood (James & Prout, 1997; Mayall, 2002), this notion started to change slowly. Thinking about children as agentic individuals and ratifying their rights, contributed to understandings of children as autonomous, strong and capable individuals and also through a legal-political link between rights and citizenship to the conceptualisation of children as citizens. In recent policy discourses in confluence with other discourses around childhood and teaching children are more frequently conceptualised as 'citizens', as more capable and akin to adults. A good example of this discourse in relation to very young children is the Australian federal government's *A national quality framework for early childhood education and care: A discussion paper* (Early Childhood Development Sub-group, 2008) in which young children are portrayed as "competent and strong" with "unique capabilities" who "represent their thinking and learning in many ways" (p. 39). The document further develops this position with the following statement: "children are able to form opinions and express and respect ideas. They are also able to develop a connection to their country and a sense of place within it and a sense of agency" (p. 36). This discourse constructs children as citizen members of communities and the country and as partners or human capital in the international economic competition (Millei & Imre, 2009; Millei & Lee, 2007). Consequently, on the one hand this thinking if translated into practices has the potential to empower children and create spaces where their voices are heard and acted upon. On the other hand, this discourse also prescribes for children to act in certain ways and therefore regulates them through their own self-government.

Moreover, recent education policy frameworks understand education as children's right and, with a slippage between education and learning, construct learning as the duty and responsibility of the 'child citizen' (Millei, 2008, 2007). Learning is also presented as something that is required to become an "active and informed citizen" (Second goal in *Melbourne Declaration on Educational Goals for Young Australians,* 2008). Consequently the question might be asked: are those children who show less required ability or difficulties in learning considered as citizens who are unable to fulfil their civic duties and therefore considered as 'second-class citizens', or are these children excluded from citizenship entirely? Moreover, are those children who are disengaged from curriculum and pedagogy and therefore are unable to learn or do not wish to learn what is taught, considered as citizens? Even more provoking, should those children who do not desire or who are unable to participate in 'learning citizenship', be labelled as having learning difficulties? Which causes the other and why? Does the discourse of citizenship discipline children to learn? What is the role of school discipline in ensuring that children are learning as good citizens? If children do not fulfil their citizenship duties should the punishment or consequence be the suspension of their rights?

The General Question and Some Suggestions

The concepts of the 'citizen' and of 'citizenship' are highly contested terms in social and political theory and have manifold interpretations (Kivisto & Faist, 2007). The subsequent critiques of these definitions also offer a broad variety of understandings. Therefore, to employ these terms in education without their conceptualisations is highly problematic. If we are asking children to act as citizens, are they to be liberal citizens with minimal participation limited to voting on some key issues as per a representative parliamentary democracy; social democratic citizens participating in the governing of the institutions in which they spend their days; socialist citizens striving for a collective emancipation from capitalism; communitarians working on duties and obligations to and for someone or something termed as a community, preferably something close to a classical civic republic, in which they dwell? Are children limited to specific possibilities because of their phenotypic appearance as children, their acculturated gender, or their current earning capacity or social status? Can children form labour unions, press governments to change political and social conditions, demand changes from the institutions in which they find themselves, self-organise representative political parties, organise armies for defence of property and territory? All of these are at least possibilities for citizens in all sorts of situations and governments, and some of these we have dealt with and some are to be explored in further research on the topic. We also discussed some ways in which the interpretations of the concepts of 'citizenship' and 'rights' discipline our ways of thinking about children. The understandings formed through these discourses make possible or impossible practices with and of children that both empower and regulate children. Further, 'citizenship' of any kind is a political practice rather than solely an administrative status. Children are not yet, or only in limited ways, part of this everyday political practice. We think the question still remains as to whether or not, and through what avenues children can be part of this everyday political practice, and there is much work to be done in this area. Another general set of questions that we might ask is what kind of agency the concept of 'citizenship' may constitute for children and to what extent children's assumed and 'real' interests are aligned with these forms of agencies. What is 'good life' for children? What is 'good life' for them in the future and what is it at present? A liberal answer might be the pursuit of productivity and entrepreneurship through learning. Another way to conceptualise the problem is to claim that by focusing on their future, children are shut out from citizenship in the present.

References

Ailwood, J. (2004). Genealogies of governmentality: Producing and managing young children and their education. *The Australian Educational Researcher, 31*(3), 19–33.

Bauböck, R. (2002). Political community beyond the sovereign state, supranational federalism, and transnational minorities. In S. Vertovec & R. Cohen (Eds.), *Conceiving cosmopolitanism: Theory, context and practice* (pp. 110–136). Oxford: Oxford University Press.

Berlin, I. (1969). *Four essays on liberty.* Oxford: Clarendon Press.

Brennan, D. (1994). *The politics of Australian child care: From philanthropy to feminism.* Cambridge: Cambridge University Press.

Committee on the Rights of the Child. (2005). *General comment no. 7 (2005): Implementing child rights in early childhood.* Geneva: United Nations.

Curriculum Council, W. A. (1998, March 2003). Curriculum framework for kindergarten to year 12 education in Western Australia/curriculum council. Retrieved December 21, 2003, from http://www.curriculum.wa.edu.au/pages/framework/framework13.htm#value3

Early Childhood Development Sub-group. (2008). A national quality framework for early childhood education and care: A discussion paper. Retrieved October 15, 2008, from www.dest.gov.au/sectors/early_childhood/policy_initiatives_reviews/coag/discussion.htm

Evans, S., & Prilleltensky, I. (2005). Youth civic engagement: Promise and peril. In M. Ungar (Ed.), *Handbook for working with children and youth: Pathways to resilience across cultures.* Thousand Oaks, CA: Sage Publications.

Halldén, G. (2005, 27 November–December). *The metaphors of childhood in a preschool context.* Paper presented at the Australian Association for Research in Education

Conference, Sydney.

Hart, R. A. (1992). *Children's participation: From tokenism to citizenship.* Genf: UNICEF.

James, A., & James, A. L. (2004). *Constructing childhood: Theory, policy and social practice.* Basingstoke and New York: Palgrave Macmillan.

James, A., & Prout, A. (Eds.). (1997). *Constructing and reconstructing childhood: Contemporary issues in the sociological study of childhood.* London and Philadelphia: The Falmer Press.

Kenway, J. (2008). The ghosts of the school curriculum: Past, present and future. *Australian Educational Researcher, 35*(2), 1–13.

Kivisto, P., & Faist, T. (2007). *Citizenship: Discourse, theory, and transnational prospects.* Malden, MA: Blackwell Publishing.

Levin, J., & Nolan, J. (1991). *Principles of classroom management: A hierarchical approach.* Englewood Cliffs, NJ: Prentice Hall.

Lister, R. (1996). Citizenship engendered. In D. Taylor (Ed.), *Critical social policy* (pp. 168–174). London: Sage Publications.

MacIntyre, A. (1984). *After virtue.* South Bend, IN: University of Notre Dame Press.

Mayall, B. (2002). *Towards a sociology of childhood.* Buckingham and Philadelphia: Open University Press.

Millei, Z. (2007). *A genealogical study of 'the child' as the subject of pre-compulsory education in Western Australia.* Unpublished PhD. Murdoch University, Murdoch. http://wwwlib.murdoch.edu.au/adt/browse/view/adt-MU20081002.80627

Millei, Z. (2008). Problematising the concepts of 'citizenship' and 'participation' in early years discourses: Are they so empowering? *International Journal of Equity and Innovation in Early Childhood, 6(2), 41–56.*

Millei, Z. J., & Imre, R. (2009). The problems with using the concept of 'citizenship' in early years policy. *Contemporary Issues in Early Childhood, 10*(3), 279–290.

Millei, Z., & Lee, L. (2007). 'Smarten up the parents': Whose agendas are we serving? Governing parents and children through the smart population foundation initiative in Australia. *Contemporary Issues in Early Childhood, 8*(3), 208–221.

Ministerial Council on Education, Employment, Training and Youth Affairs (2008) Melbourne Declaration on Educational Goals for Young Australians. Retrieved October 15, 2008, from http://www.mceecdya.edu.au/mceecdya/melbourne_declaration,25979.html

Polanyi, K. (1957). *The great transformation: The political and economic origins of our time.* Boston: Beacon Press.

Qvortrup, J. (1994). Childhood matters: An introduction. In J. Qvortrup, M. Bardy, G. Sgritta & H. Wintersberger (Eds.), *Childhood matters: Social theory, practice and politics* (Vol. 14). European Centre Vienna: Avebury.

Smith, A. ([1776] 1982). *The wealth of nations: I–III.* Harmondsworth: Penguin.

Soysal, Y. N. (1994). *Limits of citizenship.* Chicago: University of Chicago Press.

United Nations. (1948). The universal declaration of human rights [Electronic Version]. Retrieved April 16, 2008, from http://www.un.org/en/documents/udhr/

United Nations High Commissioner for Human Rights. (1976). International covenant on economic, social and cultural rights [Electronic Version]. Retrieved August 16, 2009, from http://www2.ohchr.org/english/law/cescr.htm

United Nations (1989). Convention on the rights of the child. New York: United Nations. Retrieved August 16, 2009, from http://www.un.org/en/documents/udhr/

Vertovec, S. and Cohen, R. (2002). *Conceiving cosmopolitanism.* Oxford: Oxford University Press.

Chapter XI

Classroom Discipline: A Local Kantian?

Tom G. Griffiths and Rob Imre

How did classroom discipline become a global 'problem'? Educators are often struck by the use of ideas that are claimed to be derived from their particular contexts and yet have so many similarities to other contexts as to make the question of locally driven education initiatives, independent of wider influences, seem almost farcical. In our collective experience as educators we see the same sorts of cultural frameworks, if not always the same cultural references, as well as the same kinds of policy initiatives in terms of education. Rap and hip-hop stars are everywhere, wearing the same clothes and saying the same things in South Korea, Hungary, Venezuela, as they are in the United States. While the global reach of an individual pop star may not penetrate all localities, the genre seems to be able to do this. The same could be said of various types of television programs in terms of game-show trends, reality television, and so on. The actors change, but the structure remains, often part of a global franchise, and everyone watches the same kind of program the world over. Can the same be said for education policies that appear to be concerned with 'global competitiveness', 'management of school climate', 'whole school discipline approach', 'zero tolerance policies', 'raising test scores', creating 'global citizens', ensuring 'quality' and so on? Statements like these appear to be just as universal as the cultural genre references. More worrying is the fact that they also appear to be beyond dispute. We interrogate this concept here through the lens of international relations theory which, as a sub-discipline of political science, has a number of contested ideas about what constitutes the global political world, and then through the lens of world-systems level comparative theory.

In this chapter we examine the problem of classroom discipline through a political science lens. For us, this means that we are looking at international relations theory, and how specific world views are presented using those theories. This is important because international relations theories compete for particular views of the world, often marshalling the same facts to prove quite different things. Political economy looks fundamentally different to a realist, a liberal institutionalist, a world-systems theorist, and so on. Our central point is one in which we look at the difficulty of bringing together what is considered as 'universal' and what is considered as 'particular' in the way in which we view the world. Global citizens cannot be global if their values are determined by particular cultural considerations, and yet global concerns can arise from, and frequently be invoked by, particular cultural manifestations. Since classroom discipline hinges on our understanding of the world, we begin with some competing views of the world and postulate how this might affect ideas about classroom discipline.

Some postmodern theorists of globalisation have examined the problematics of internationalisation through a re-examination of Kantian positions on global values. RBJ Walker's (1988) work, *One World Many Worlds*, for example, is an attempt to grapple with the universal Hegelian 'right politics' and a Kantian universal ethical position that delivers freedom from oppression. Others, such as Ulrich Beck (2006), have suggested that a cosmopolitanist position will deliver such advances while other kinds of cosmopolitanists, most notably Habermas (1984, 1987), have placed their faith in universalising a kind of communicative action. Habermas goes further in his later work and starts to emphasise a kind of 'constitutional nationalism' in which loyalties are created beyond nation-states and towards a kind of rule of law that transcends national loyalties and rests on pan-national values. Some world-systems theorists see globalisation as the intensification of trends driven by the emergence and development of a single world-economy encompassing multiple polities, and thus reinforcing (even reifying) previous distinctions manifest in empires and modern industrial societies. These distinctions, most commonly based on social class, race, and gender, persist alongside the growth of universal doctrines of meritocracy and the overt rejection of racism and sexism (Balibar & Wallerstein, 1988).

Global Perspectives and the Modern Nation-State

Typically, the position adopted by Immanuel Kant (1983) in his work on the *Perpetual Peace* is taken for granted as a type of world view in which nation-states, as free republics, join their political systems in a mutually agreed upon set of rules. These rules are designed to stop war, limit conflict, and enhance negotiation by political means as much as possible. This is to be contrasted with the understanding that nation-states are always in preparation for war, and that military competition is the norm of international politics (the realist position that we outline briefly below). In the post-World War Two world, political theorists concerned with the relationships between states sought to understand how to possibly bring about a version of cooperation rather than conflict. In brief, most theorists agreed that international relations was about the management of anarchy, this term understood in this context as nation-states existing in constant competition with each other, resulting in conflict at times as a point of resolution. There was no presumed 'order' to the international system. Indeed, the very idea of a 'system' of international relations is in some question here.

Taking from Thomas Hobbes (1668 orig.; 1968 edition with CB Macpherson edition), this anarchic condition, rather than 'system', might be seen to be a deadly form of competition, such that the international norm ought to be a unification under the sovereign in order to be ready for war. Later 'Hobbesians' developed an extant 'realist' position that claimed the 'timeless wisdom' of realism was about just such a preparation for war. This 'kill-or-be-killed' view could not be mitigated by alliances or by friends and allies, as all of these were considered by realists to be temporary categories. Realists typically hark back to Thucydides and the Melian dialogue and cite Machiavelli as the first 'modern' realist. Machiavelli's innovation was to claim, at the expense of his own freedom for he was jailed, that it was neither the good of the ruling families, nor the good of 'universal' Church-led values, that ought to be the driving set of norms for political leaders. It should instead reflect a good that can be enjoyed in some form of collectivity: the 'people', the masses, a voting populace and so on. Machiavelli's innovation then, as claimed by realists in international relations, was one in which overarching ethical norms could not supersede the interest of the republic. This is what contemporary realists would call the 'national interest'.

Early liberals, such as John Locke, disagreed with this normative stance and sought to develop a cooperative normative position based on the idea that international politics could be about non-interference, a strong adherence to the principles of the Treaty of Westphalia, which insisted on the principle of non-intervention in sovereign nation-states. Thus the liberal position, agreeing with realists that nation-states were the primary (and sovereign) actor in international relations, and an anarchic international relations pervaded actions among states, sought to develop a norm of 'live and let live' as the fundamental liberal principle. The non-interference principle is thus aligned with self-interested nation-states. This position begins to change in the inter-war years with Wilsonian approaches to the international world in that Kant's (1983) version of the *Perpetual Peace* was thought to be a development on international relations. Liberal-institutionalism developed as an idea in which a kind of legal-political architecture would permanently mitigate conflict and ensure that war did not become the accepted norm for dispute settlements.

Kant was seen as the founder of the 'cosmopolitanist' position in international relations theory. Kant's idea that there was a way in which to ensure peace among nations, and the notion that a set of international norms could be developed was innovative enough to build an actual institution around it and call it the League of Nations, and subsequently the United Nations. Advocates of this position came to be known as 'liberal-institutionalists', and some realists were also adherents in that regimes of peace could demonstrably stop conflicts, even if it was in a limited way. Some (global) political sociologists developed the cosmopolitanist position further. Both Ulrich Beck (2006) and Jurgen Habermas (1984, 1987) argued for a set of international norms that sought to extend the liberal principle of 'equal moral worth' for all individuals beyond their own citizenships. Here the cosmopolitanist idea, especially as espoused by Beck in *Cosmopolitan Vision* (2006), was one in which global human rights and a series of intrinsic values would tie people together as individuals and groups demanding a recognition of diversity that does not rely on nation-states and is not contained within their borders.

Jurgen Habermas has a somewhat different view than that of Beck, although they have a number of points of similarity. One major difference is that Habermas is grounded in critical theory. For our purposes here, critical theory is the late stage of Marxist thought, generally espoused by the Frankfurt School, and in many ways Habermas' work can be counted as being post-Marxist in character. Critical theory of the kind developed by Horkheimer, Adorno, Marcuse, and others is a type of late-Marxist critique of modern industrial society that sees capitalism merging 'high' and 'low' cultures to create a kind of uniform 'pop' culture. For the Frankfurt School this was a negative development of capitalism since it meant that pop culture, to be equated with a capitalist system of values, was made ubiquitous. Habermas has made some significant innovations on this view. Further, critical theory can only be 'critical' if it actively engages in critique that seeks to liberate human beings from the oppressive conditions in which they find themselves. Theory that does not create the conditions for human freedom is not 'critical' in the sense that the Frankfurt School and Habermas intend.

For Habermas, human beings have a need to work and create, much the same as Marx claimed in his original philosophical anthropological position. Habermas suggests that creativity is socially mediated, and that human beings communicate their creativity as a process, as an activity, rather than as the mere moulding of an object. This social mediation creates a kind of communicative action, and this communicative action is always both rational and productive. Habermas continued to see this as part of the 'radical democracy' approach in which the 'lifeworld' of human beings, that is the sum total of the institutions and practices in which they live their everyday lives, needs to be made more democratic and responsive to human needs. Resistance was to be accomplished through this continuing rational process of engagement rather than dramatic revolutions. As such, Habermas' view is still universalist, not as negative as Adorno and Horkheimer in describing global capitalism, and not always anti-liberal, as many Marxists might claim. His description of global capitalism continues to see possibilities for the dynamic creation of 'lifeworlds' that promote human freedom.

Furthermore, as mentioned above, Habermas increasingly sought to locate this possibility, or set of possibilities, in the 'European project' of the realised politics of the European Union (EU). In the EU Habermas saw a capacity for uniting modern nation-states under the same umbrella of cooperative law. Here, rather than social, political and economic upheaval throughout the sub-continent, the EU would deliver a set of cooperative institutions based on a constitution that brought together nation-states under an agreed-upon set of values, upon which real and practical laws were based (or some might say, derived). This is the 'constitutional nationalism' that Habermas sought to entrench in European thinking. And since constitutions are living, breathing, political animals, the human creative process could be harnessed in this process.

As an alternative supra-national approach, Immanuel Wallerstein's world-systems theorising elaborates the historical development of a single, capitalist world-economy, with a single division of labour across core, peripheral and semi-peripheral states, themselves constituting multiple polities interacting via an inter-state system, with this historical world-system underpinned by a dominant 'geoculture of liberalism' (e.g., Wallerstein, 1994; 1995). Distinctively, Wallerstein's (1995) world-systems perspective identifies key features of a universal ideology of liberalism that encompassed both capitalist and real existing socialist states, including things like a belief in the universal validity of scientific knowledge underpinning endless linear progress everywhere, led by rational policy makers in strong states. As Wallerstein (1995) notes:

> The possibility of the (economic) development of all countries came to be a universal faith, shared alike by conservatives, liberals, and Marxists. The formulas each put forward to achieve such development were fiercely debated, but the possibility itself was not. In this sense, the concept of development became a basic element of the geocultural underpinning of the world-system (p. 163).

From this point of view Wallerstein's theorising provides a case against globalisation accounts of contemporary world conditions that cite unprecedented declines in national sovereignty and autonomy. Such accounts, he argues, are a "gigantic misreading of current reality" (Wallerstein, 2003, p. 45), positing that the processes ascribed to the phenomenon of globalisation are not at all new.

For Wallerstein and other world-systems theorists (e.g., Chase-Dunn, 1989; Chase-Dunn & Hall, 1997), the important timeline in a world-systems account is not the rise of globalisation in the late twentieth century (particularly in the post-Soviet period), but rather what Wallerstein describes as the "world revolution of 1968" which involved both opposition to the United States and Soviet hegemony (e.g., popular movements and uprisings in France, Mexico and Czechoslovakia), and "disillusionment with the Old Left in all its forms" (Wallerstein, 2003, p. 50). This marked a crisis in the ideological underpinning of the world-system, the end of the communisms in 1989–91 being another marker of this secular trend, and so further evidence of the crisis of capitalism as a world-system, rather than its triumph. It is made clear in his work that:

> The year 1989 represented the agonizing end of an era. The so called defeat of antisystemic forces was in fact a great liberation. It removed the liberal-socialist justification of the capitalist world-economy and thus represented the collapse of the dominant liberal ideology (Wallerstein, 1995, pp. 250–51).

Thus Wallerstein argues that the 1968–1989 period has seen the decline of liberalism as the common ideological or 'geocultural' underpinning of the capitalist world-system, both reflecting and contributing to the intensification of three secular trends within the system that he argues cannot be resolved without its substantive transformation (Wallerstein, 1998, 2003). These three trends, approaching their limits, are identified as: 1) the tension between historical rises in real wages over the long durée, placing pressure on profits while sites for the potential relocation of capital to secure cheap wage labour diminish; 2) pressure on States to simultaneously reduce taxes and increase spending on social spending and on infrastructure; and 3) the pressures associated with environmental costs of production, traditionally externalised by industry, the tension here linked to the potential exhaustion of the capacity of the globe to support human activity, and the increasing move to internalise environmental costs of production back to capital, adding to pressures on the State in taxation, and the profits of capital.

One major implication of Wallerstein's scholarship relates to the role of knowledge within educational systems, contained within syllabi and curricula, in both reproducing and legitimising social inequalities within and between nations. Substantial work has systematically documented global trends in national curricula (e.g., Benavot & Braslavsky,

2006), and elaborated the mechanisms by which such common frameworks have been promoted and adopted across the world (e.g., Valverde, 2004). Meyer (2006) has set out some major trends in what might be called a world curriculum that: empowers individuals; provides choice for individuals and is increasingly decentralised; prepares citizens for an imagined "supra-national society"; and constructs the nation-state as a good citizen in world society (pp. 265–70). Wallerstein's work would not necessarily be at odds with these claims, but would emphasise the political dimension and function of such curricula across multiple contexts, in different locations within a single capitalist world-economy. Historically, this involves recognition of the dominant status given to particular forms of scientific knowledge and a nomothetic epistemology, across the curriculum, a result being that:

> The search for the good was now excluded from the realm of superior knowledge, which meant that there was no ground on which to criticize the logic of these inferences, since one was thereby being anti-intellectual. The structural social constraints that prevented people from entering the higher realms of the meritocracy were basically eliminated from the analysis or allowed to enter it only on the terms of accepting the assumptions of the two cultures in the investigation. (Wallerstein, 2006, p. 78).

For Wallerstein then, this historical dominance of scientific universalism, constructed as being 'outside culture', both facilitated the structural dominance of particular zones of the capitalist world-economy, and supported the myth of meritocracy that has functioned across and within political, social, and educational systems to justify class, race and gender based inequalities.

This introduction and overview of a number of theoretical positions employed in international relations and international political science is crucial for any understanding of global educational phenomena, since they are at the crux of what the terms 'global' and/or 'international' mean in a social science context. It is important to at least begin to think about what this distinction between the global and local might mean, what it means for education in a comparative sense, and what it means for the concept of 'discipline' in contemporary education settings around the world. It is precisely this problem: what exactly is this 'world' that these various theoretical approaches are concerned with as a foundational epistemological position that we want to foreground as we consider the 'problem of discipline' as a global and local educational phenomenon?

World-Systems Level Educational Phenomena: A Comparative Perspective

In the broad field of comparative and international education a major line of research developed from the 1970s that, in its comparative analyses, focuses on explanatory accounts of educational phenomena beyond the local/national level. Broadly described as world-systems approaches to comparative education, this research has been dominated by empirical and theoretical work describing a universal or 'world culture' of education, recently articulated by Jones (2007) as the "global architecture of education" (p. 325), whereby educational structures and ideas are diffused, adopted, transferred to nation-states across a single world-system. Baker and LeTendre (2005) stress that the concept of a world culture is inherently and unavoidably dynamic, bound up in the concept of schooling as a global institution across multiple contexts, such that while local, regional and national factors will almost inevitably shape its manifestation, "the basic image of a school—what it is and what it should do—is commonly defined in the same way globally" (p. 9).

The research of the so-called neo-institutionalists associated with Stanford University document a convergence of mass education systems over time, in which universal systems and approaches to the organization of schooling, curriculum design and content, and teaching, learning and assessment, become more or less standardised (for a recent overview see Baker and LeTendre, 2005; see also Boli, Ramirez and Meyer, 1985, for a foundational piece). This approach locates causation for the spread of "homogenous mass education [systems]" (Boli et al., 1985, p. 151) across national boundaries, within vastly different socio-economic and political contexts, in the realms of a world culture that is diffused, in part, through nation-states' participation in international governmental and non-governmental organizations. For example, focusing on the general process and aspects of modern state formation within the world-system, Meyer, Boli, Thomas and Ramirez (1997) argue that "functional justifications of schooling are rarely questioned" (p. 149), regardless of evidence contradicting them. A world culture perspective views the spread of mass school education as a part of the global spread of modern state forms and state institutions, based on globally shared cultural assumptions about these institutions, including a core function of creating members of the modern state.

Contemporary research focusing on the further spread of mass education globally, particularly that which was either achieved, or aspired to, under the banner of Education for All (EFA), linked to the United Nations' Millennium Development Goals, has drawn heavily on this broad comparative approach. Chabbott (2003) for example documents the emergence and spread of the EFA agenda itself via international organizations and sponsored EFA conferences. Critical work like that of King (2007) has examined the nature and content of what is envisaged as 'education for all', its development through various international bodies and conferences, and the resultant ways in which its achievement is to be measured. In both cases the focus is on how a world-level or world-systems approach to the phenomenon of mass education can account for its take up by diverse nation-states across the globe, via their participation in a range of international organizations.

Ginsburg, Cooper, Raghu and Zegarra (1990) advanced an alternative world-systems approach that underscored the importance of the location of the nation-state within the hierarchy of the capitalist world-economy. This approach highlighted the conflicts between and within states associated with the unequal forms of capitalist socio-economic organization, as a conditioning or constraining, and sometimes direct, influence on the content and enactment of educational reform. For example, conflict emerges from peripheral states' exploitation by the centre or core, with direct implications for a state's economic national production and economic development, which in turn has consequences for internal or national conflict and struggle. The point of distinction with respect to the issue of conflict is closely tied to the role given to world economic conditions, processes and constraints. While the world culture and world-system conflict approaches both see international non-governmental organizations and other international agencies as world-system level influences shaping national systems and reforms, a conflict approach is more likely to focus on the political and economic interests represented by international organizations like the World Bank, IMF, multinational corporations and other United Nations bodies (see for example Brock-Utne, 2007; Robertson, 2005; Boli & Thomas, 1997; and Ginsburg et al., 1990, pp. 486–89).

A key point of distinction between these broad approaches then is on the question of causation at the global level. This is well illustrated in the assertion of Boli and Thomas (1997) that the world culture perpetuates the idea that "Mass schooling is necessary for national [social and economic] development; therefore, Malaysia and Paraguay must have schools" (p. 173). Work like this cites the impact of a shared concept of mass schooling as a prerequisite for national development, linked to the dominance of human capital theory globally, and its influence on a range of social policies. The spread and take up of such concepts, however, is attributed primarily to a world culture, rather than the economic interests implicit within such conceptions. Ginsburg et al. (1990), on the other hand, affirm that such institutions carry "economic, political, and military power", and that while educational reform is not simply an automatic, "functional response to the needs of economic elites or of the world capitalist system" as they might be expressed through these institutions, these interests do condition and shape national reform in a dialectical fashion (p. 488).

The economic and cultural character of world-systems approaches to education is evident across the comparative education literature. For example, thirty-years ago Ramirez and Rubinson (1979) argued that national educational expansion was explained by world cultural ideas of schooling as an aspect of intended notions of citizenship and creating members of the nation-state, while simultaneously "legitimating the economic and political allocation of individuals in society" (p. 79). Many world cultural accounts indirectly include world and national economic factors in their explanations of the expansion of school education, highlighting the shared cultural belief or conception across the world-system that education would contribute to national economic development. Meyer et al. (1997), for example, cite the prevalence of this belief as a factor behind the expansion of national systems, despite the fact that "careful studies of, for example, education's effects on economic growth suggest that this functional relationship is at best weak and highly conditional" (p. 149). More recently, Klees (2008) highlights the long-standing critique of human capital theory and its application to education via calculations of the economic rate of return and how despite the critique, the application of human capital theory to educational policy rhetoric and practice has prevailed presumably as part of a world culture of education.

Debate over causation and determination of policy and practice, whether locating this primarily in a world culture, world-economic structure, or their combination, has arguably produced a broad consensus across much of the comparative educational literature on the notion of relative autonomy for national systems, schools, and actors within them (e.g., Arnove & Torres, 2003). Writing at the time from a neo-Marxist position, citing world capitalist economic pressures as shaping national educational responses, Dale

(1994), for example, argued that these world-system level influences were a "matter of constraints and limits rather than determination" (p. 19). Indeed, he cited Green's (1990) work in support of a perspective with an "emphasis on national specificities (within constraining and limiting parameters over which individual nation-states have little control)" (Dale, 1994, p. 22). The point made by Ginsburg et al. (1990) and Dale (1994), was that explanations of national education reform require a world-system level approach that accommodates relatively autonomous local or national level determinants of policy and/or action, situating these specific responses of the nation-state as conditioned or constrained by, and so mediating, the processes and influences of the world-system. For example, Griffiths' (2009) examination of the spread of mass education in contemporary Venezuela argues that this is influenced by global conceptualisations of education for all, but in a way that is mediated by the domestic political project advancing twenty-first-century socialism as a counter to neo-liberalism. Tharp and Dalton (2007) encapsulate this in their conclusion that "the central aspect of universalism is that the best education is culturally realized and thus to a degree localized" (p 65).

We have suggested here that a major line of research within the comparative education field clearly falls into the broad paradigm of a global–local dialectic, through which phenomena like classroom discipline may be examined and understood. Whether focused on the impact on national systems and structures from a world culture of education, promoted by states' participation in international organizations, or from states' participation in the capitalist world-economy, such approaches highlight global or world-system level convergence in policy, structure and practice. Space for local variation is not precluded in these approaches, as particular contexts and polities mediate the impact of world-level influences, but an impact of global constraints or conditioning influences on local policy making and practice is central to such approaches.

Discipline and Global–Local Education

Comparative research that directly addresses, or acknowledges, global convergence in pedagogical practices abounds in the field of comparative education. In particular, the seemingly global move to student-centred pedagogy, with a full spectrum of accounts of this phenomenon, has received much attention. Tabulawa (2003) for example positions this global policy as a disguised form of Westernisation of education imposed on developing countries, connecting with Tikly (2004), whose study makes the case for universal approaches to classroom discipline as part of a 'new imperialism', replacing formerly imposed and 'illiberal' forms of control over colonial populations with Western knowledge and discipline. Tikly (2004) draws on the Foucauldian concept of governmentality to argue that universal concepts of 'development' and associated knowledge and practices of education to support national development work against nations' capacity to authentically set their own educational agenda. Along these lines of Western imposition of policy and practice, Grigorenko (2007) attempts to set out a typology for the adoption and adaptation of Western approaches to education by non-Western cultures, describing the take up of Western educational paradigms through "triggering by the west" and "reinforcing by the west" (p. 168). Grigorenko's work is premised on the claim that "it is difficult to find a widespread educational practice that is radically different from the dominant secular educational paradigm of the west" (p. 165).

A recent study by Carney (2008), on the other hand, makes a fine-grained analysis of the enactment of learner-centred practice in Chinese-governed Tibet, highlighting the ways in which the "Chinese policy-makers and their partners responsible for implementing reforms in regions, counties and classrooms, utilise the international language of progressive pedagogy in ways that fit their particular, localised, culturally-grounded circumstances" (p. 41). Simola (2005) offers an alternative critique of so-called democratic approaches to pedagogical practice, citing the conservatism of Finnish teachers and their authoritarian approach to "pedagogical discipline and order" (p. 462) as a potential contributing factor to Finland's leading performance on international comparative testing regimes like PISA and TIMSS.

On the specific question of classroom discipline, some recent critical work has reasserted the culturally specific character of instruction and assessment practices generally, acting to discipline students in ways that work against non-dominant cultures (Sternberg, 2007). Irwin, Anamuah-Mensah, Aboagye and Addison (2005) similarly argue through a study of policy in Ghana, that official and enacted classroom discipline policies are culturally biased. They make the case then that local variations to the dominant universal Western approach are needed under the banner of social justice and equity. Studies of educational reform and practice in the former Soviet Union and allied Eastern Bloc countries offer some interesting insight with respect to the question of a global or world-system level approach to classroom discipline. Mintrop's (1996) examination of the transition from authoritarian socialism to liberal-democratic capitalism in 8 schools within the former German Democratic Republic (East Germany) finds predictable perceptions amongst educators of declining authority through this transition, citing increased parental and student authority and associated deterioration of student behaviour and discipline. His study shows that teachers did not fully acknowledge their enhanced authority and autonomy as central State directives and prescriptions were reduced. Perhaps most critically, Mintrop (1996) suggests that despite the democratic transition of society, an official move to student-centred pedagogy, and the associated greater freedoms for students within and outside school, much like their counterparts in West German schools, the teachers demonstrated a consistent concern about students' (mis)behaviour, their perceived lack of self-discipline and an associated decline in teacher control. Moreover, a common perception of former GDR teachers was that students had "misunderstood the new freedom" (Mintrop, 1996, p. 373) in ways that undermined teachers' former authority and students' learning.

A more recent study by Elliott and Tudge (2007), focused on Russian teachers' practices in the post-Soviet period, similarly identifies the persistence of their established pedagogical practices in the context of the social and economic transition following the collapse of the Soviet Union. They also document similar concerns amongst teachers about declining social values in the post-Soviet context, with increased individualism, competition, and "the erosion of young people's morality" (Elliott & Tudge, 2007, p. 106). Studies like these document the widely acknowledged difficulty of changing teachers' everyday practices in contexts undergoing substantial social, economic and political change, regardless of the political or ideological direction of that change. More critically, they also highlight common concerns about students, and perceptions about student behaviour, morality, social responsibility, individualism, etcetera, that have their direct parallel in non-transitional contexts, and in so doing support a perspective that identifies some fundamental convergence in policy and practice globally. Indeed, the relative ease in which Soviet and GDR teachers continued in their roles, albeit with increasingly frequent references to a nostalgic past and/or a concern about the associated loss of particular values and standards, says much about what Baker and LaTendre (2005) call the basic image of the school globally, and with it generalised conceptions of and concerns about classroom discipline.

A Universal Discipline?

A central question implicit throughout this chapter is whether and to what extent distinctively national and local approaches to classroom discipline are possible within a single world-system, or twenty-first-century globalisation, that is characterized by convergence in educational phenomena. To put this another way, are we seeing the rise of universalism in a different form, and/or the continuation/intensification of a universal understanding linked to the effective functioning of a world-system? Is it a universally accepted fact that children in classroom settings will develop in similar ways, given the same conditions, everywhere in the world, with similar approaches to classroom discipline aimed toward developing children's self-regulation under the banner of democratic freedom being applied?

A related question in this chapter is whether and to what extent national and local approaches to pedagogical practices, including discipline and associated understandings of democracy and power, may contribute to an alternative world-system and its accompanying cultural underpinnings? Can we really promote a more democratic participation by people in governance, for more equal and just distributions of social and economic goods globally, in and through educational institutions? Can approaches to discipline, particularly those theorised as promoting individuals' agentic potential through their acquisition of particular dispositions, overcome the almost inevitable tension of operating to construct and/or reinforce conceptions of 'others' as just another way of justifying the inequitable but purportedly meritocratic distribution of educational credentials and associated socio-economic outcomes?

Our primary purpose in this chapter is to raise these types of questions, highlighting the importance of international relations theory and world-systems analyses as a basis for research addressing such questions. Discipline policy and practice are potentially at the heart of questions like these, given their productive nature and potentially enabling or capacitating character, as elaborated in other chapters of this volume (e.g., Chapters 2, 4, 5 & 6). The task of examining the extent to which these potentials are universal and/or local, imposed globally or developed locally, mediated or conditioned by world-system level influences, will further develop our responses to these types of questions, and in so doing contribute further to our understanding of classroom discipline as a global phenomenon.

References

Arnove, R. F., & Torres, C. A. (Eds.). (2003). *Comparative education: The dialectic of the global and the local (2nd ed.)*. New York: Rowman & Littlefield.

Baker, D. P., & LeTendre, G. K. (2005). *National differences, global similarities: World culture and the future of schooling*. Stanford, CA: Stanford University Press.

Balibar, E., & Wallerstein, I. (1988). *Race, nation, class: Ambiguous identities*. London: Verso.

Beck, U. (2006). *Cosmopolitan vision*. Cambridge: Polity Press.

Benavot, A., & Braslavsky, C. (Eds.). (2006). *School knowledge in comparative and historical perspective: Changing curricula in primary and secondary education*. Hong Kong: Comparative Education Research Centre.

Boli, J., Ramirez, F., & Meyer, J. (1985). Explaining the origins of mass education. *Comparative Education Review, 29*(2), 145–167.

Boli, J., & Thomas, G. M. (1997). World culture in the world polity: A century of international non-governmental organization. *American Sociological Review, 62*(2), 171–190.

Brock-Utne, B. (2007). Worldbankification of Norwegian development assistance to education. *Comparative Education, 43*(3), 433–449.

Carney, S. (2008). Learner-centred pedagogy in Tibet: International education reform in a local context. *Comparative Education, 44*(1), 39–55.

Chabbott, C. (2003). *Constructing education for development: International organizations and education for all*. New York: RoutledgeFalmer.

Chase-Dunn, C. (1989). *Global formation: Structures of the world-economy*. Cambridge, Oxford: Basil Blackwell.

Chase-Dunn, C., & Hall, T. D. (1997). *Rise and demise: Comparing world-systems*. Boulder, CO: Westview Press.

Dale, R. (1994). National Reform, Economic Crisis and 'New Right' Theory: A New Zealand Perspective. *Discourse, 14*(2), 17–29.

Elliott, J., & Tudge, J. (2007). The impact of the west on post-Soviet Russian education: Change and resistance to change. *Comparative Education, 43*(1), 93–112.

Ginsburg, M. B., Cooper, S., Raghu, R., & Zegarra, H. (1990). National and world-systems explanations of educational reform. *Comparative Education Review, 34*(4), 474–499.

Green, A. (1990). *Education and State Formation: The Rise of Education Systems in England, France and the USA*. London: Macmillan.

Griffiths, T. (2009). Schooling for twenty-first century socialism: Venezuela's Bolivarian project. *Compare: A Journal of Comparative and International Education*. First published on: 25 November 2009 (iFirst).

Grigorenko, E. L. (2007). Hitting, missing, and in between: A typology of the impact of western education on the non-western world. *Comparative Education, 43*(1), 165–186.

Habermas, J. (1984). *The theory of communicative action. Vol. I: Reason and the rationalization of society*, (T. McCarthy, Trans.). Boston: Beacon.

Habermas, J. (1987). *The theory of communicative action. Vol. II: Lifeworld and system* (T. McCarthy, Trans.). Boston: Beacon.

Hobbes, T. (1968). *Leviathan* (edited with an introduction by C.B. Macpherson) Harmondsworth: Penguin.

Irwin, L. H., Anamuah-Mensah, J., Aboagye, J. K., & Addison, J. K. (2005). Teachers' perceptions of classroom discipline in Ghana. *International Education, 34*(2), 46–71.

Jones, P. W. (2007). Education and world order. *Comparative Education, 43*(3), 325–337.

Kant, I. (1983). *Perpetual peace and other essays.* Indianapolis, IN: Hackett.

King, K. (2007). Multilateral agencies in the construction of the global agenda on education. *Comparative Education, 43*(3), 377–391.

Klees, S. J. (2008). Presidential address: Reflections on theory, method, and practice in comparative and international education. *Comparative Education Review, 52*(3), 301–328.

Larsen, M. A. (2008). North American insecurities, fears and anxieties. *Comparative Education, 44*(3), 265–278.

Marks, G. N., & Ainley, J. (1997). *Longitudinal surveys of Australian youth: Research report number 3: Reading comprehension and numeracy among junior secondary students in Australia.* Australian Council for Educational Research.

Meyer, J. (2006). World Models, National Curricula, and the Centrality of the Individual. In A. Benavot & C. Braslavsky (Eds.), *School knowledge in comparative and historical perspective: Changing curricula in primary and secondary education* (pp. 259–271). Hong Kong: Springer.

Meyer, J. W., Boli, J., Thomas, G. M., & Ramirez, F. O. (1997). World society and the nation-state. *American Journal of Sociology, 103*(1), 144–181.

Mintrop, H. (1996). Teachers and changing authority patterns in eastern German schools. *Comparative Education Review, 40*(4), 358–376.

Ramirez, F. O., & Rubinson, R. (1979). Creating members: The political incorporation and expansion of public education. In J. W. Meyer & M. T. Hannan (Eds.), *National development and the world system: Educational, economic, and political change, 1950–1970* (pp. 72–82). Chicago: The University of Chicago Press.

Robertson, S. L. (2005). WTO/GATS and the global education services industry. *Globalisation, Societies and Education, 1*(3), 259–266.

Simola, H. (2005). The Finnish miracle of PISA: Historical and sociological remarks on teaching and teacher education. *Comparative Education, 41*(4), 455–470.

Sternberg, R. J. (2007). Culture, assessment and instruction. *Comparative Education, 43*(1), 5–22.

Tabulawa, R. (2003). International aid agencies, learner-centred pedagogy and political democratisation: A critique. *Comparative Education, 39*(1), 7–26.

Tharp, R. G., & Dalton, S. S. (2007). Orthodoxy, cultural compatibility, and universals in education. *Comparative Education, 43*(1), 53–70.

Tikly, L. (2004). Education and the new imperialism. *Comparative Education, 40*(2), 173–198.

Valverde, G., A. (2004). Curriculum convergence in Chile: The global and local context of reforms in curriculum policy. *Comparative Education Review, 48*(2), 174.

Walker, RBJ. (1988). *One world, many worlds: Struggles for a just world peace.* Boulder, CO: Lynne Reiner.

Wallerstein, I. (1994). The agonies of liberalism: What hope progress? *New Left Review,* (204), 3–17.

Wallerstein, I. (1995). *After liberalism.* New York: The New Press.

Wallerstein, I. (1996). *Open the social sciences: Report of the Gulbenkian commission on the restructuring of the social sciences.* Stanford, CA: Stanford University Press.

Wallerstein, I. (1998). *Utopistics: Or, historical choices of the twenty-first century.* New York: The New Press.

Wallerstein, I. (1999). *The end of the world as we know it: Social science for the twenty-first century.* Minneapolis, IN: University of Minnesota Press.

Wallerstein, I. (2001). *Unthinking social science: The limits of nineteenth-century paradigms.* Philadelphia: Temple University Press.

Wallerstein, I. (2003). *The decline of American power.* New York: The New Press.

Wallerstein, I. (2004). *The uncertainties of knowledge.* Philadelphia: Temple University Press.

Wallerstein, I. (2006). *European universalism: The rhetoric of power.* New York: The New Press.

Chapter XII

Utopia/Dystopia: Where Do We Go With 'Discipline'?

Rob Imre, Zsuzsa Millei, and Tom G. Griffiths

This chapter raises possible ways in which we imagine the future of discipline as a concept. This means that we are critically assessing how the concept of 'discipline' serves to represent a (possible) positive ideal, a model of perfection or its impossibility. As such we seek to examine the concept of discipline from utopian/dystopian, and world-systems inspired utopian perspectives. Here, we will use the idea of utopia, and its converse, dystopia, as a centralizing theme in order to take apart the notion of discipline in its modern institutional setting. This chapter seeks to provoke thinking about discipline in a meta-theoretical fashion so as to ask the grand questions about society as these questions might relate to what we seek to accomplish through a different approach to discipline. Rather than argue for a 'solution' to a 'problem', or demonstrate a 'better way' to approach discipline, we seek to ask a series of questions about how modern people can organise themselves, and thus what we actually 'do' with the concept of 'discipline'.

Utopia

The modern condition of theorizing about society was to present it as a utopia. This was the Enlightenment move to rip Heaven from the heavens and place it on earth, to be engineered by 'man'. The means to do this was through institutions that arose as a direct result of the industrialization of the modern world. These institutions included hospitals, schools, modern prisons, and the like. Coupled with the perfectibility of the human condition, and the idea that human beings could become an embodiment of their ideal potentialities, the idea of utopia became a powerful motivating force for modern people. One way to achieve this was to control human activity through discipline. This is how discipline in its various manifestations was also made subject to this radical concept so that through rational application of discipline we might be able to create this utopian society. This is one way in which utopian thinking thus becomes intimately entwined with modernity and the modern project. The liberal world-view then is as much about utopia as is the socialist, anarchist, and so on. These modern ideological positions are built on the premise that there is a perfectibility of social order and that perfectibility is 'at hand' in the disciplining of an ever-present 'current' generation of students. Moreover, they suggest that disciplining is achievable through those scientific mechanisms that use students' different forms of self-disciplining and that are based on their rational thinking (Millei, 2007, and see also Chapter 2). Modern ideas then claim to contain the Platonic forms that science and reason can deliver us closer to. This is the modern utopia that all forms of modern government aspire to.

Some common examples of this kind of thinking in social theory involve a number of thinkers who are foundational to our understanding of modernity and modern society. For example, Weber's rationalisation thesis fits perfectly with the use of 'discipline' here (Weber, 1904–5/1992). The modern institution, relying on discipline as an external force, one that authorities enact upon people in their respective institutions to help create socialised human beings, has a deeply ingrained moral problem. It is clear that modern societies have the capacity to create predictability, and when that predictability is 'learned' by students in institutions, they can achieve a great deal of personal freedom. However, this personal freedom is heavily conditioned in the sense that it can then only be achieved in the machine of modernity itself. This is Weber's famous 'iron cage' dilemma. If we attribute at least part of this to discipline and how it relates to utopia, then we are stuck with this dilemma: children in institutions must be disciplined in order to both navigate their way through the system, as well as to become good subjects of and successful learners within that system. As such, we look for ways out from this 'cage of reason' to live with our freedom, and for Weber, the more we are disenchanted (the less we believe in reason), the more enchanted (or mystical), or de-rationalised, we become. Weber's problem, and ours, is that perfecting our modern societies will ultimately lead to a fragmentation of reason in which we seek a way out of the utopia, thus living dystopically in the ordered modern society. This is precisely the core of the utopia with clear dystopic features: seeking a way out from rationality invokes further disciplining, spiralling towards the perfectly ordered society.

At the end of the eighteenth century a penal reform had taken place, argues Michel Foucault (1979a), through which "emerged the utopia of a universally and publicly punitive society" (p. 273) that was thought to be able to cease all practices of illegality. These processes were concentrated around first, political illegality that aimed to overthrow political power; second, revolt against the power concentrated in the new regime of landed property set up by the bourgeoisie; and third, a more specialized form of criminality associated with people on the fringes of society. The 'fear' from these forms of illegality served to support the emergence of the idea of 'delinquency' that associated criminality with the bottom of the social classes. Prisons failed to eliminate crime but produced an 'enclosed illegality' that became delinquency. Delinquency is a politically and economically less dangerous form of illegality that does not have the power to attract a great number of people, and on occasions it is usable for political aims (p. 278), such as the use of delinquents as political informers. In this way, 'delinquency', as Foucault (1979a) argues, served a strategic move to keep in check illegality by turning illegality into specified criminality described and managed by scientific knowledges and the carceral network.

With the creation of the carceral network or panoptic society the problem of illegality was addressed. While illegality is against the law, the strategic emergence of delinquency managed to keep illegality within the law. As Foucault expresses it: the carceral network "saves everything, including what…it has decided to disqualify" (p. 301). The examination of the object of delinquency produced detailed knowledges about delinquency. These knowledges prescribe norms and discipline bodies and behaviour. By the spread of their normalizing power to other institutions, such as schools, "each individual, wherever he may find himself, subjects to it his body, his gestures, his behaviour, his aptitudes, his achievements" (p. 304). Through discipline, prescriptions are made according to which to behave, thus order is kept through the prescription of orderly behaviour, while what is not discussed remains as undetermined and prohibited. In this way, in similar ways as delinquency has brought illegality within the law and what became unspoken remained outside of the law thus prohibited, discipline prescribes all possible behaviour and what is prohibited remains illicit.

Child-centred and socio-constructivist pedagogies and guidance theories of discipline prescribe particular behaviours in the classroom that are different to teacher-centred pedagogies and disciplinary practices (Millei, 2007, and Chapter 2 this volume). Instead of sitting quietly in the classroom and listening to the teacher as in classrooms where an autocratic teaching style is applied, it became accepted (prescribed in pedagogies) for children to speak out loud, raise questions, move around in the room, and talk to each other and so on through the use of child-centred and constructivist pedagogies. These behaviours are thought to be conducive to learning and as long as they signal that learning is taking place, they are allowed. In this way, the child is free to choose to speak, to question the teacher and so on, as long as s/he chooses to act as a learner and according to the behaviour prescribed in these pedagogies. The prescription of the learner is expandable, that is one can also learn from bad choices, but simply not learning is prohibited due it being undetermined. There is no literature discussing specific cases when learning does not occur in classrooms.

The medicalisation and pathologisation of human development shows us some interesting consequences of accepting this embedded utopian thinking. For example, it has been demonstrated that a regular intake of milk will improve bone density and height benchmarks for children. When these benchmarks are not reached, and the milk intake is not enough to reach the benchmarks, parents have the option to seek hormone therapy to drive their children's bodies onward to reach the benchmarks. Further, various additives are built into these foods in order to avoid disease as well as reach these benchmarks: hormones (not hormones to make animals grow and/or produce more milk/meat, etc. but rather to make children meet target growth rates), antibiotics and inoculation in order to avoid disease, vitamins so as to maximise nutritional value of the food, and so on. This is an attempt towards the fulfilment of the modern condition and thus becomes dystopic upon that fulfilment, especially with the medicalisation of discipline. It becomes dystopic not the least of which because there is no longer an acceptance of diversity and the capacity for disease. Disease and diversity become one and the same.

The administering of antipsychotic drugs to young children in the US stirred a vivid debate after a four-year old girl died due to overdose of Clonidine and two other psychiatric drugs.[1] ADHD, autism spectrum disorder, conduct disorder, authority defiance disorder and bipolar disorder are all arguably linked to disorderly behaviour and handled predominantly with drug treatment. The potential of administering drugs almost guarantees the fulfilment of the 'perfect' school child; no matter what ways that child is being constructed. These children who have been through diagnosis and treatment are subjects of institutions and, just as much as adults do, they have agency to act against doctors' decisions (Raby, 2005). Thus, we do not presume that a kind of 'docile child' is created by giving children medication, because they still have an agency to decide whether to take these drugs, but this agency is a sub-legal one in that they cannot legally defy their parental and school/institutional authorities. They can use the option of exerting influence in their social situations, thus the spread of prescription drugs occurring throughout the classroom and peer group. Indeed, the number of children taking the behaviour modification prescription drugs increases dramatically as children themselves begin to distribute these drugs to friends and peers in classrooms (http://www.methylphenidate. net/). Similar to our argument above about modified and enhanced food products, human beings in general, and children in particular, whether in social, institutional, family, or other settings, are agentic, and as such make decisions about what to do with the foodstuffs and medications they are supposed to be consuming. This is not to argue the other side of the false duality that victims do not exist, for they do, and many people are indeed victimized by such regimes of medication without the capacity to resist. Our point here is that in school settings, children in general ought to be perceived as agentic subjects of the state, rather than docile bodies of the state. We maintain, however, that this agency is restricted when it comes to children: legally, politically, economically, and socially, children do not have the agency to the degree that adults do (see Imre & Millei, Chapter 10 in this volume, as well as Millei & Imre, 2009).

Dystopia

Another way to think about the concept of discipline in relation to utopia is to claim that the closer one gets to the realization of the stated social goals for the utopian condition, the greater possibility, or likelihood there is of the radical dystopic condition. For example, one might claim that an overarching modern utopian social condition is an ordered society. So far, in the modern period, within these various social orders, moving towards perfection within an institution has also led to disastrous side effects. Exemplar factories meeting specific criteria for liberal-capitalism, have also made their workers suffer, exemplary social order achieved in classrooms using corporeal punishment have also made their students suffer (Southgate, 2003, and in Chapter 7). By suffering here, we mean to state that the production of order does not entail the production of a state

---

[1] Source: http://www.boston.com/yourlife/health/diseases/articles/2007/06/17/backlash_on_bipolar_diagnoses_in_children/

of non-suffering. Discipline in the classroom can provide a state of order, and can thus be a utopian condition in the sense that it can support students to realise their full potential as people learning in that classroom. But this condition can still entail alienation and symbolic violence for those whose subjectivities do not or cannot comply with the disciplined and ordered conditions created. Further, like workers in a factory who are able to produce and contribute to their work life, they are always limited in at least two ways: they cannot change the system externally (that is, they might be able to reform the factory from the inside, but it is considerably more difficult to own and manage it), and they cannot change the overall global system of production and exchange to which the factory is subject. Order is achieved, individuals are productive, but this is all only relevant in terms of the prevailing system.

Another example might involve the following, as we have seen in earlier chapters (Chapter 2 and 10), when ostensibly 'democratic' forms of discipline based on egalitarian approaches, children's rights, and so on become problematic. They appear to move toward a utopian state of schooling in the abstract, in which it is assumed that students have the opportunity to experience the greatest freedom in creating themselves and their knowledge, regulating themselves and making decisions regarding their lives through free choices. At the same time, as argued in Chapters 2, 3 and 7 for example, and by Millei (2007) and Pongratz (2007), this utopian condition can involve more subtle and insidious forms of control, with students' freedom and choices occurring within tightly predetermined boundaries.

Moreover, acts are explained as reactions to acts of living with this illusionary freedom. In this way, school shootings are evaluated in the media as symptomatic of this greater freedom when in fact this violence might be the representation of broader societal processes. In reaction to these 'moral panics' more and more authoritarian rules are being introduced in schools, such as the zero tolerance policies that guarantee the automatic removal of students who perpetrate acts of violence through either suspension, expulsion or transfer; the use of police officers and security guards to patrol and monitor student behaviour while school is in session, or security checks that are put in place in order to ensure 'freedom' (Pedro, 1995). Here three things happen: one, 'choice' is equated with freedom; two, drastic restrictions upon liberty are justified in the name of ensuring 'freedom' (which is really ensuring that people have a version of 'choice'); three, subjects become disciplined to choose in a general way, thus individuals are "not merely 'free to choose', but obliged to be free, to understand and enact their lives in terms of choice" (Rose, 1999, p. 87). In other words as Marshall (1995) argues, "[t]here is almost a postulation of a human *faculty* of choice, which is both part of human nature and which humans need to exercise to be 'proper' human beings" (p. 326, *original emphasis*). Moreover, choice itself becomes calculated and manipulated by working on the environment within which it is exercised (Rose, 1999). Choice and freedom, however, are two different concepts, they are imbued with quite different senses of duties and obligations in modern societies, and they can lead to very different social consequences.

We can take this idea further, and claim that the 'freedom' experienced in a contemporary school setting has been involved in a kind of postmodern process of 'folding in' the values of general society. This idea is partly discussed by Kupchik and Monahan (2006) when they discuss the folding in of the values of industrial society into the school and the outsourcing of discipline to security companies and the police. Similar to a kind of reification, or as Girard (1978/1987) puts it, a 'mimetic desire', this 'folding in' of value structures, or singular values, means that there is no journey towards an ethical position (Girard, 1978/1987). There is rather a hollowed-out version of an ethical construct that is used for the sole purpose of delivering on bureaucratic necessities: we are teaching children multiculturalism because we have filled in the forms stating that they have learned about other cultures and how to respect them, we have adopted democratic practices because we have a policy that says we have done so, we have surveys to prove that students are happy since we asked them whether or not they are happy and a majority of them have replied that they are happy. These approaches demonstrate the concept of mimesis in which an imitation of desired life becomes the norm of human activity and shows us how to develop our 'freedom'. This freedom then is nothing more than a hollowed out reflection of what goes on outside the classroom, and as such is an illusion.

Dominant, or hegemonic, value structures have been engulfed by students in classrooms, reinforced by teachers and administrators, and as such self-actualisation disappears. There might be freedom to act out reflections of this dominant culture or hegemonic value system, but there is little in the way of resistance that has the capacity to change the social order, as well as little in the way of self-actualisation in a direction that does not involve neo-liberal values if we are looking at contemporary society. Supporting this idea further by using Girard's idea of mimetic desire, freedom could be only thought about and desired in particular ways that are already enacted and witnessed. Self-creation, the desire to be someone through free acts, is already limited by experience rather than free imagination since this free imagination is curtailed and directed by the already accepted value structures.

Some postmodern thinkers have suggested that a way out of this dilemma is to embrace a kind of radical acceptance of the 'other'. This radical acceptance is meant to 're-humanise' and thus take away the power of bureaucracies to regulate human beings, to regulate life itself. Both Zygmunt Bauman (1993) and Jacques Derrida (1981a, 1981b) have claimed that the way to achieve social 'order' that takes us beyond the parameters of what modern thinking might involve, is to use this postmodern ethics as a guide to place the needs of the 'other' before our own. It is thus that modern social systems can overcome this limitation. But this radical acceptance is not a totalising solution in the case of schools, and it brings up a number of new dilemmas that are not solved, and perhaps not solvable by this approach (Bauman, 1993). For example, in Derrida's view, and Bauman would agree, the radical acceptance of the 'other', in the case of adults, has some specific examples centring around poverty and the difficulties migrants face in Europe. Part of the idea is to accept two things: a radically different culture of the 'other', and a way of life for oneself that allows for a greater distribution of resources. Typically, this means that people in modern societies need to discard a number of neo-liberal values of accumulation and consumption in order to ensure that the 'other' is placed within a construct that elevates 'them' to a status of 'trusted friend'. This is a kind of radical individualism that seeks to undo its neo-liberal counterpart by using the original version of 'deconstruction' Derrida (1981a; 1981b) discussed in his work. One can reject accumulation and consumption as markers of individual achievement and demand that social and political institutions work to accept all of the individuals we are linked with in our everyday lives. As an ethical and moral position, for both Bauman and Derrida, this postmodern approach is meant to ensure a just world, rather than an ordered one.

Children, as a human category, however are faced with two different dilemmas that postmodern ethics, as a counter to the utopia/dystopia problem, cannot solve. First, children who experience schooling are by their very nature institutionalised. This is an inescapable social fact. A large majority of children are subject to the governance imposed by these (and other) institutions. The definition of 'the child' as a social category, in all modern/contemporary societies, includes the idea that they are institutionalised, if not in school then in the family or other institutions. Second, children cannot escape the difficulties of the 'other' within the classroom, and the final arbiter on any given set of circumstances is an adult. While there is room to negotiate and room to 'play', there is not much capacity for children to engage in this radical acceptance of the 'other' unless it is pre-defined by those running the institution, such as in the case of enacting a social justice curriculum and pedagogy (and even that is questionable after Gore, 1993). They cannot decide on cultural norms and the distribution of resources. They cannot for example, reject the 'other' (which surely is a legitimate choice), as an adult can. They cannot move in to the next room, engage in asocial behaviour, disengage from public life and work privately and so on. The question in relation to discipline that we might ask is: how conducive is the radical acceptance of the 'other' for learning and what is the role of discipline that is based on normative expectations?

Further, even if we examine the exceptions to the necessity of having the institutions pervade modern human life, we are still left with the same problem. For example, there are a number of exceptions to schools and hospitals as institutions: home-schooling, and some alternative schools, rejecting hospitals for treatment of a variety of ailments and illnesses, home-birthing, and so on. All of these demonstrate ways in which people resist the control institutions place on their everyday lives, in some cases by developing another institution themselves. Perhaps this is a way out of the totalising effects of institutions, but one would need to ask what role children play in constructing this 'alternate reality' of home-schooling, home-birth, and self-healing. And indeed why it must be the 'home' that is the alternative to the institution.

Within these institutions, such as schools, children can resist this totalising control. They can ostracize and bully peers; they can use violence and force to separate themselves from others and so on. However, this is still in breech of the rules, and when the rules are breeched, there is no trial, and no right except in cases where the act exceeds everyday infractions that result in serious harm or abuse. In these cases restorative justice is used in the form of community conferencing to deal with incidents of serious harm as an additional tool to other strategies (Cameron & Thorsborne, 2001). In Australia the principles of natural justice are promoted in student welfare and discipline policy (as promoted for principals in New South Wales government schools: www.schools.nsw.edu.

au); however these strategies are rarely translated to everyday practices. Edwards (2008) discusses judicious discipline that uses rules and rights to foster students' citizenships, however he places this approach in the framework of "human growth and development, [and] learning theory" (p. 244) that potentially limits viewing children as citizens who can live with their rights at the present. Adults can claim these rights, and in many places around the world fight wars and die for them. Children in most cases are subject to the rule of authorities not of their making.

'The Perfect Flower'—Utopia in Early Childhood Education

The work of early childhood teachers is often compared to the gardener who provides care and nurturing to raise perfect flowers. This analogy is not only a Romantic ideal, but also a utopian one, since it tells as much about the imagined society this flower will grow into as about the flower itself. The analogy of the teacher as gardener is commonly found in discourses of the early years around the world. It is used in writings of Froebel, Steiner and poets of Romanticism, and it has local variations depending on ideological standpoints and intellectual traditions. Here we discuss two particular understandings of this analogy: first, in socialist Hungary and second, in liberal Australia.

In Hungary not so long after World War II, the socialist ideal of the 'perfect' adult as the aim of education was laid down building on ideas of Marxism-Leninism and overshadowed by the utopian vision of building a communist social system. As Hermann and Komlósi (1972) state in their report on Hungarian early child care:

> The socialist ideal is known by every pedagogue: the many-sided, harmoniously developed, theoretically and practically trained man [sic] who loves his work, has a socialist conception of the world and social-moral convictions, who can enjoy beauty and feels himself to be a part of the community. (p. 10)

Education was proclaimed as a means of class struggle to erase bourgeois values and ethics from people's consciousness, thus it had a strong moral element in which discipline plays a crucial part. Socialist education identified the needs of the developing socialist society in regard to the characteristics of humans and aimed to produce these individuals. As Makarenko (1948), the prominent Soviet pedagogue, states: "Where could the aims of education come from? Naturally, it cannot originate from elsewhere than from our society's needs, from the aspirations of the Soviet people, the aims and tasks of our revolutions and struggles" (p. 75). Thus, to ensure the ideal development of people, their morals and consciousness needed reformation that translated into the reformation of society through a dialectical relationship and the creation of the classless society of communism.

Moral education in the early years of socialism, following Makár's (1953) interpretation of central policy, worked through discipline and the creation and the precedence of strong community life above individuals that included being respectful towards elders, following rules, maintaining a preference for group play, the creation of common routines, cultivating a sense of duty, teaching to value and look after common and individual assets, and to work collectively. Working collectively, according to Makár, also meant to include every child, develop a love for one's community, to understand that groups can achieve higher than individuals. Discipline also worked through the community by highlighting and addressing together individual's mistakes and wrongful individual dispositions (Makár, 1953). Moral education sought to create experiences that enabled the determination of the consciousness on new grounds that prioritised the community over the individual (Hermann & Komlósi, 1972).

The utopia of communism was thought to be achievable based on the Marxist belief about the modifiability of the individual through the creation of specific experiences, and the application of moral education and discipline. One could argue that one of the manifestations of the reformation of the individual was the appropriation of the ideal and value of common property to the extent that there appeared to be no difference between individual and common property. This ideal, however, turned into a dystopic one, in which the individual justified stealing from the common goods on the grounds that 'it is owned by everybody, so every person has a right to have some of it'. It became common practice to take home some products or raw material from factories and offices to be sold or used as a bribe for other goods or services. This dystopic outcome of moral discipline enabled the emergence of the so-called second economy and, as a result, the diversification of economic and social practices similar in nature to that of capitalist systems (Haney, 2002). Further, the dystopic outcome promoted a sort of double morality within individuals, both functional for and entirely at odds with the socialist utopia.

In liberal democratic societies the ideal of the 'perfect flower' was constituted on different grounds. The Romantics, such as Rousseau (1957), regard the child as closer than the adult to real freedom, truth and beauty because s/he is uncorrupted by culture. Thus, the realisation of human progress through reason was considered to be dependent upon how children's reasoning develops from birth. Culture, in this way, undermines the human capacity to think and live in liberated ways, so to regain freedom, beauty, justice and truth, it was argued that it is necessary to enable children's natural dispositions to flourish and to keep their thinking free of corruption through education. Therefore, the gardener's role is to keep out the corrupting effects of society from children's thinking in order to raise the 'perfect' individual. This role extends arguably to the point when the teacher's role is to set aside her or his own influence or domination over children.

As it was established in Chapter 2, one of the rationalities of classroom discipline is to enable children to be free of the teacher's control. 'Democratic' or 'egalitarian' discipline theories strive to remove the teachers' dominance from over children and to enable children to participate in decisions over their lives, and thus to be independent thinkers (Porter, 2008). Outward discipline, signalling the dominance of the teacher, in this way was 'transformed' to self-discipline performed by the children themselves. This type of discipline was not considered as control anymore since it liberated children from dominance. Hence, the child was set free from adults' corrupting influences; a utopian condition was reached, with freedom itself turned on to the individual. Through this very freedom that liberated, the child was also governed. Freedom in neo-liberalism has turned out to be a technology of regulation (Rose, 1999).

The 'perfect flower' of the gardener, in the neo-liberal regime of Australian education, is provided with an increasing freedom in the classroom from teachers' domination but at the same time this freedom also means a dystopic state in which the child's soul is made the target of government (Rose, 1989). Self-discipline, as explained in Chapter 2, is closely linked to obedience. Following Foucault's (1984) argument, self-discipline invokes the child's self-examination according to particular morals and norms. Through confession to the teacher or peers, that happens through the counselling techniques of guidance approaches, the child not only carries out self-discipline, but it also becomes a way "to open up entirely to its director—that unveil to him the depths of the soul" (Foucault, 1979b).

World-Systems 'Utopistics': Discipline for an Uncertain Future

The broad theoretical perspective of world-systems analysis associated with Immanuel Wallerstein (1998) has consistently elaborated an argument about the historical development of a single capitalist world-economy and its transition toward an uncertain future. A central feature of this theorizing traces the emergence of a shared geoculture of liberalism common to capitalist and historical socialist nation-states. The shared ideology of nation-states included utopian visions of a better, more just, equal and democratic world, to be achieved at some point in the future. According to this argument, citizens of so-called socialist or liberal capitalist states were encouraged to believe that progress was inevitable, endless, and such that through the application of their labour, in conjunction with scientific and technological advances, and led by rational policy makers in government, full lives of material abundance and leisure were just around the corner (for its application to the case of socialist Cuba see Griffiths, 2005; In Press).

Taking a long-term view, a world-systems perspective links this convergence back to the French Revolution, the emergence of three competing ideologies of conservatism, liberalism and socialism, and their merger into a shared geoculture of liberalism across the capitalist world-system, which normalized this sort of progressive political change within sovereign nation-states. This in turn underpinned the subsequent 'two-step strategy' applied across the system to achieve state power and then to reform the world. Whether led by a vanguard communist party, a national liberation movement, or a liberal democratic (conservative or social democratic) party, the premise was that once in power, legislation would be enacted to achieve the legitimising goals of linear progress, development, increased consumption and material abundance, etcetera. Huge differences emerged within the socialist variant over how to achieve state power, via insurrection or electoral politics, but the premise of winning state power to legislate for a future utopia held (see Wallerstein (2002) for a concise account of this reasoning).

Wallerstein's (1998) world-systems approach also highlights the dystopian potential of such endeavours, noting that: "utopias are breeders of illusions and therefore, inevitably, of disillusions, and utopias can be used, have been used, as justifications for terrible wrongs. The last thing we really need is still more utopian visions" (p. 1). In their place Wallerstein (1998) puts forward a concept of *utopistics*, which he describes as the serious assessment of historical alternatives, the exercise of our judgement as to the substantive rationality of alternative possible historical systems…. Not the face of the perfect (and inevitable) future, but the face of an alternative, credibly better, and historically possible (but far from certain) future. (pp. 1–2)

What are the distinctive features of such a project, compared with utopian visions of liberal capitalist, socialist, or other variants of existing political regimes promising better futures for all, and what implications might a utopistic project have for the concept of discipline?

Utopistics begins with an understanding of the contemporary capitalist world-system as being in a period of empirically demonstrable transition toward something else and facing a number of crises that the current system, based on the principle of maximising the accumulation of capital, cannot resolve. These include: 1) the dilemma of capital seeking to maximise profits via higher prices and reduced labour costs, while relying on increased wages to sustain and expand demand, and state support to support higher sales prices; 2) the dilemma of capital seeking to reduce its tax bill to states to further support increased profits, while seeking increased state expenditure to support production, achieve partial monopolisation of markets, and meet the externalised environmental costs of production; 3) these dilemmas reaching their systemic limits in the face of rising wage and tax bills over the long-term across the whole world-system, while the scope to relocate capital to reduce costs is similarly reaching its limits (this basic argument is set out particularly well in Wallerstein, 1991; 1995; and 1998).

Critically for Wallerstein's (1998) world-system view, these secular trends are approaching their "asymptote" (p. 42) in the context of the collapse of liberalism as the dominant geoculture of the world-system. This collapse began with the world revolution of 1968, is marked by the end of the communisms in 1991, and is manifested in a "popular antistatism" in which populations across the political spectrum of states, whether ostensibly socialist, national liberationist, neo-liberal capitalist, or somewhere in between, have lost faith and hope in the "two-step strategy for transforming the world" and with it faith in states that had "not fulfilled their historic promise" (Wallerstein, 1998, p. 31). This marks then a disillusionment in what Wallerstein (1998) argues has been "an essential pillar of the modern world-system", the modern nation-state operating in an interstate system capable of delivering national development and progress (p. 32). With the collapsing legitimacy of liberalism and the capacity of states to deliver promised progress and development, comes a corresponding pressure on the disciplining power of this ideology.

Such a scenario underpins the utopian project, arguing that in such historical moments of systemic crisis and transition, the capacity of individual and collective agency to impact on this transition, and hence on the alternative system that emerges, is at its greatest. Hence we do not seek a normative course for utopian visions of how this alternative ought to be, with the almost inevitable dystopic results, but for the sustained and rigorous examination of credible alternatives and interventions, within the shifting conditions, to advance core principles of increased greater democracy, equality, and justice at a world-system level. This is an important distinction, advocating authentic and consequential participation by more people in shaping the uncertain future of the world-system, rather than claiming some sort of teleological vision towards which we are inevitably moving.

What are the implications of a utopistic perspective on the concept of discipline? On the one had, discipline has been used historically to support the disparate privileges and inequalities within and between nation-states, and hence between individuals within and between states, that have been characteristic of the capitalist world-system. With a world-systems critique of the Marxist-Leninist states, and so-called historical socialism more widely (Wallerstein, 1998, p. 67), comes a clear emphasis that practice in such states included state and party-based oppression, and in some cases terror, while maintaining privileges for a nomenklatura. In liberal capitalist states, examples of oppression, and terror, may also be cited. In education systems everywhere, a common form of disciplining has been through flawed notions of meritocracy that have legitimised both inequitable educational achievements, and through this inequitable social and economic realities.

The utopistic challenge of world-systems analysis then involves the search for credible alternatives, including whether and how an alternative world-system that is not based on the endless accumulation of capital could operate. Efforts to elaborate such alternatives require consideration of knowledge structures and hierarchies, and their underlying epistemologies, particularly in relation to their functioning in educational systems everywhere to divide and legitimise divisions between some groups from others. The consideration of understandings of universal and particular knowledge, their historical construction, and their relation to identifiable social groups, is not new in educational and sociological studies. From an utopistic perspective however, the focus on the analysis is driven by the potential to influence the shape and substance of a credible, alternative world-system.

In many ways this is an educational project. Wallerstein (1998) writes, for example:

> What is needed educationally is not to learn that we are 'citizens of the world' but that we occupy particular niches in an unequal world, and that being disinterested and global on the one hand and defending one's narrow interests on the other are not opposites but positions combined in complicated ways. Some combinations are desirable, others not. Some are desirable here but not there, now but not then. Once we have learned this, we can begin to cope intellectually with our social reality. (p. 63)

The point here is one of knowledge creation, however uncertain or ambiguous, that can support the creation of a viable, alternative world-system not based on the endless accumulation of capital. Utopistics is also a direct and distinctly unambiguous rejection of the disciplining power of education with respect to social and economic inequalities between and within component parts of the single world-economy. Connecting with the work elaborated in this volume on the potentially capacitating power of discipline to enhance individual and collective agency, it would therefore argue for the application of this agency in a general direction (more equality, democracy, justice), conscious of the contingent, contested nature of the results of such applications. It is not enough for discipline to produce individual subjectivities that might achieve educational and subsequent social and economic success within an unequal world-system, but rather discipline that contributes directly to the elaboration of credible alternatives, and to subjectivities with the capacity to act for their development, however uncertain and undefined these are.

Conclusion

We have undoubtedly provided more criticism than solutions in this chapter. The question of 'where do we go with discipline' is an important one to ask. It is crucial to our capacity to deliver on a future-seeking stance, to demonstrate that there are some positive possibilities, and to show that there are ways to deal with students in a manner that engages their humanity. But in this chapter we are at a loss as to how to get beyond the limitations of two fundamental things. One is the institution of the school as a producer of disciplined bodies and souls, and the other is the severe limitation on the capacity to resist from within this institution.

If we return to some of our earlier concerns and discuss the problem of discipline in schools as elaborated upon through the gardening metaphor, it provides us with a frightening conclusion that can aptly illustrate our problem with the utopian and dystopic condition of modern life. Cultivating and developing a garden, fostering life, is surely a good thing. However there have been many periods in modern history in which the right, good and just approach has yielded genocidal results. Good people who wanted a socially just society could well have, and by some accounts did, participate in removing Indigenous and Aboriginal children from their homes and families and placed them in schools run by church organizations with the sanction of the modern nation-state in Australia, Canada, and the United States. The administrators sought justice, wanted a world in which all subjects of the nation-state had equal life-chances, and would see some of their vision come to pass.

This inculcation of discipline upon those Indigenous and Aboriginal communities, however, ensured that the 'weeding out' process destroyed individuals. Bauman's 'gardening state', like Weber's (1904–5/1992) bureaucracy, is an "all-powerful, all-knowing regulator" (Baumann, 1991, p. 143) that encounters sub-cultures, anomalies in the form of individuals and groups, who do not fit in the garden of the nation-state. Maintaining the fiction of homogeneity became difficult for these nation-states, and thus the disciplining of corporeal bodies extended to the genocidal impulse of the state. So what are we left with? Is any form of discipline also a form of 'violence'? Do we do 'violence' to students by demanding they work, read, or study for no reward other than an unmeasured inner change? And does the violence then increase when we attempt to measure this unmeasurable, classify and categorize how many letters and numbers small children have tried to retain? Nearly every social and political theorist in the modern period, and a number of others in pre-modern periods all the way back to Plato and Aristotle, have discussed a version of utopia. We have merely touched on a few of the debates that are important for education and important for the problem of the concept of discipline. We hope that we have provoked rather than answered questions.

References

Bauman, Z. (1991). *Modernity and ambivalence*. Cambridge: Polity Press.

Bauman, Z. (1993). *Postmodern ethics*. Cambridge: Polity Press.

Cameron, L., & Thorsborne, M. (2001). Restorative justice and school discipline: Mutually exclusive? In H. Strang & J. Braithwaite (Eds.), *Restorative justice and civil society* (pp. 180–194). Cambridge: Cambridge University Press.

Derrida, J. (1981a). *Dissemination*. Chicago: University of Chicago Press.

Derrida, J. (1981b). *Positions*. Chicago: University of Chicago Press.

Edwards, C. F. (2008). *Classroom discipline and management*. Hoboken, NJ: John Wiley & Sons.

Foucault, M. (1979a). *Discipline and punish: The birth of the prison*. London: Penguin Books.

Foucault, M. (1979b). *Omnes et singulatim: Towards a criticism of political reason*. Retrieved August 15, 2009, from http://foucault.info/documents/foucault.omnesEtSingulatim. en.html

Foucault, M. (1984). The ethics of care for the self as a practice of freedom: An interview with Michel Foucault on January 20, 1984. In J. Bernauer & D. Rasmussen (Eds.), *The final Foucault* (pp. 1–20). Cambridge, MA: The MIT Press.

Girard, R. (1978/1987). *Things hidden since the foundation of the world*. Stanford, CA: Stanford University Press.

Gore, J. (1993). *The struggle for pedagogies: Critical and feminist discourses as regimes of truth*. New York: Routledge.

Griffiths, T. G. (In Press). 50 years of socialist education in revolutionary Cuba: A world-systems perspective. *Journal of Iberian and Latin American Research, 15*(2).

Griffiths, T. G. (2005). Learning 'to be somebody'. Cuban youth in the special period. *International Journal of Learning, 11*, 1267–1274.

Haney, L. (2002). *Inventing the needy: Gender and the politics of welfare in Hungary*. Berkeley, CA: University of California Press.

Hermann, A., & Komlósi, S. (1972). *Early child care in Hungary*. London: Gordon and Breach.

Kupchik, A., & Monahan, T. (2006). The new American school: Preparation for post-industrial discipline. *British Journal of Sociology of Education, 27*(5), 617–631.

Makár, I. (1953). Erkölcsi nevelés egy Baranya-megyei üzemi óvodában. (Moral education in a Baranya County factory kindergarten) *Neveléstörténet, 1953*(3), 66–69.

Makarenko, S. (1948). *The methods of education: Selected pedagogical studies*. (Hungarian Translation) Budapest: Uj Magyar Konyvkiado.

Marshall, J. D. (1995). Foucault and neo-liberalism: Biopower and busno-power. Retrieved August 15, 2009, from http://www.ed.uiuc.edu/EPS/PES-Yearbook/95_docs/ marshall.html

Millei, Z. J. (2007). *Controlling or guiding students—what's the difference? A critique of classroom approaches to discipline*. Paper presented at the 2007 AARE Conference Fremantle, Fremantle, WA, Australia. www.aare.edu.au/07pap/mil07410.pdf

Millei, Z. J., & Imre, R. (2009). The problems with using the concept of 'citizenship' in early years policy. *Contemporary Issues in Early Childhood, 10*(3), 279–290.

Pedro, N. A. (1995). Preventing and producing violence: A critical analysis of responses to school violence. *Harvard Educational Review, 65*(2), 189–212.

Pongratz, L. (2007). Freedom and discipline: Transformations in pedagogic punishment. In M. S. Peters & T. A. C. Besley (Eds.), *Why Foucault? New directions in educational research* (pp. 29–42). New York: Peter Lang.

Porter, L. (2008). *Young children's behaviour: Practical approaches for caregivers and teachers* (3rd ed.). Marrickville, NSW: Elsevier Australia.

Raby, R. (2005). What is resistance? *Journal of Youth Studies, 8*(2), 151–171.

Rose, N. (1989). *Governing the soul: The shaping of the private self.* New York: Routledge.

Rose, N. (1999). *Powers of freedom: Reframing political thought.* Cambridge: Cambridge University Press.

Rousseau, J. J. (1957). *Émile* (B. Foxley, Trans.). London: J.M.Dent & Sons Ltd.

Southgate, E. (2003). *Remembering school : Mapping continuities in power, subjectivity & emotion in stories of school life.* New York: Peter Lang.

Wallerstein, I. (1991). *Geopolitics and geoculture: Essays on the changing world-system.* Cambridge: Cambridge University Press.

Wallerstein, I. (1995). *After liberalism.* New York: The New Press.

Wallerstein, I. (1998). *Utopistics: Or, historical choices of the twenty-first century.* New York: The New Press.

Wallerstein, I. (2002). New revolts against the system. *New Left Review, 18*(Nov Dec), 29–39.

Weber, M. (1904–05/1992). *The protestant ethic and the spirit of capitalism.* London: Routledge.

Chapter XIII

Continuing the Conversation About Discipline as a Problem? A Conclusion

Zsuzsa Millei, Tom G. Griffiths and Robert John Parkes

In his interview with Michel Foucault (1984/1994) shortly before the French philosopher-historian's death, Paul Rabinow asked about the history of 'problematics' that Foucault claimed he had been exploring as an alternative to the history of ideas (or the analysis of systems of representation) and the history of mentalities (or the analysis of the attitudes motivating actions in particular times and places). Foucault's answer is instructive for what we have attempted to do in this volume. According to Foucault (1984/1994), and we quote at length:

> What distinguishes thought is that it is something quite different from the set of representations that underlies a certain behaviour; it is also quite different from the domain of attitudes that can determine this behaviour. Thought is not what inhabits a certain conduct and gives it its meaning; rather, it is what allows one to step back from this way of acting or reacting, to present it to oneself as an object of thought and question it as to its meaning, its conditions and its goals. Thought is freedom in relation to what one does, the motion by which one detaches oneself from it, establishes it as an object, and reflects on it as a problem. (p. 117)

In this book the various contributors have taken up 'discipline' in education as a 'problem for thought'. According to Foucault (1984/1994), "for a domain of action…[such as discipline in education] to enter the field of thought, it is necessary for a certain number of factors to have made it uncertain, to have made it lose its familiarity, or to have provoked a certain number of difficulties around it" (p. 117). Drawing on various forms of contemporary social theory, not limited to Foucauldian forms of problematisation, the contributors to this volume have engaged with 'discipline' in ways that render it both uncertain and unfamiliar. Detaching themselves from the taken-for-granted ways in which discipline is discussed in education, the authors of the various chapters in this volume have contributed to an understanding of discipline as an important 'problematic' for intellectual critique; and the success of their work will be determined by the extent to which 'discipline' becomes an 'object of thought' that may be reflected upon as a problem, for the reader of this collection.

In a similar manner, we investigated patterns of *ideas* that inhabit thinking about, and practices of, classroom discipline that give it its meaning. We examined the ordering of knowledge of classroom discipline in a way that parallels Foucault's (1970/1994) use of the analytical tool of archaeology in his book *The Order of Things: An archaeology of the human sciences*. Following the logic of Foucault's archaeological method, we can unearth two sets of patterns that compose discourses of classroom discipline: 'epistemes' and 'discursive formations'. 'Epistemes' are the underlying patterns that fix what can be said and done in a given place and period, thus, rendering other things unthinkable. 'Discursive formations' are the organising principles of an episteme that are made up of knowledge disciplines, commentary and authors. The combination of these factors allows a 'discursive formation' to exclude what does not fit, thus, creating a truth that constrains what can be said and done. In this book many of the authors were engaged in an attempt to unearth the order of the underlying knowledge of discipline in education and its set of practices, with a particular purpose in mind: to create the freedom for their readers and themselves to 'step back' from what one does and to make classroom discipline an *'object of thought'* that can be reflected upon as a problem.

Any future project on classroom discipline that considers it as a 'problem' consequently has two main streams: first, to unearth further the order underlying knowledge and practices of 'discipline' in education. Second, to reflect upon discipline in education as an *object of thought*, a problem that can be considered from new perspectives, without remaining constrained by the prior baggage the idea of 'discipline' carries, such as well-rehearsed theory, un-tested or un-acknowledged assumptions, or pre-determined possibilities for the solution of the prescribed problem. Thus, we need to direct questions at the 'politics' of discipline, as Marshall (2007) understands it:

> the social, economic and social processes found in an amalgamation of laws (Legal Acts of Education), public institutions (Education Boards, schools, universities, etc.), Board of Trustees (Governors), teachers, parents and students/children. …[they] need to be questioned along the parameters of meaning, conditions and goals by questions probing the areas of the social, the economic and the political, and along those parameters we need to look at the historical factors (p. 23).

Along these lines, we consider our work in this book to be a contribution to the task of drawing up some problematics of classroom discipline that are devoid of the 'wisdom' of recognised theories, practices and beliefs. However, the work of troubling discipline is far from complete, and we would like to end this conclusion by providing some suggestions for areas that require further investigation.

Disciplinary Regimes in 'New' Institutional Settings

Another area that could be extended in future work is discipline as it manifests in different institutional settings not previously addressed in terms of the kinds of critique offered in this volume. The current literature on education and discipline only marginally addresses routines developed in early childhood settings in relation to the regulatory power they produce, and the ways in which routines powerfully shape children's subjectivities, and regulate their behaviour and bodily functions. The early years are also important because they could be considered as the first institution of the child, other than the family, that partakes in the formation of habits: health, social, school-like and so on. For example, bathroom routines form a part of the curricula in the early years through which children learn to care for themselves. Bathrooms in preschool centres, however, are open to the public gaze in Australia, due to regulatory standards. In this way, while on the toilet, children are subjected to constant surveillance by adults and other children. These practices have far-going implications not only as ways that produce avenues for regulating children and provoke children's self-discipline, but also have far-reaching impact on their health and well-being.

Academic Disciplines, Curriculum Knowledge, and Subject Formation

According to the authors of *Knowledges: Historical and critical studies in disciplinarity* (Messer-Davidow, Shumway, & Sylvan, 1993), we are "socially and conceptually...disciplined by our disciplines" (p. vii), and in failing to see their "historical novelty" (p. vii), we are trapped inside their specific ways of producing and organizing knowledge. While there are claims widely appearing today that knowledge is increasingly interdisciplinary (Klein, 1996), most school jurisdictions maintain a curriculum that mirrors some version of the academic disciplines; according to Popkewitz (2001), school curricula operates as "a disciplining technology that directs how the individual is to act, feel, talk, and 'see' the world and 'self'" (Popkewitz, 2001, p. 153), serving the function of an apparatus for the social re/production of particular identities and subjectivities. This relationship between disciplines, identity production, and subject formation deserves to be explored further, particularly in relation to the development of professionals in the contemporary academy and 'global' citizens in schools. There are unanswered questions about the organization of knowledge within teacher education curriculum and school subjects and how this impacts upon teachers' and students' capacities as border crossers. Understanding how disciplinary boundaries are formed and maintained, crossed and disrupted, and the forms of subjectivity that are produced through subjection to different forms of disciplinary, interdisciplinary, trans-disciplinary, and meta-disciplinary study, is an important area for further social research in education.

Comparative Studies of Classroom Discipline

Comparative research is a powerful tool to help destabilize taken-for-granted understandings of the idea and meaning of discipline, its utility, the ways in which discourses of discipline construct 'the teacher' and 'the child' and invent alternative understandings and practices of classroom discipline. The exploration of similarities and differences—across times, places, spaces and ideological regimes—between particular discourses and practices of discipline have the potential to highlight rationalities of discipline that must be abandoned to make discipline the *object of thought*.

Comparative studies of educational projects designed to form particular types of citizens, with a view to enabling their contribution to the construction of future society, continue to hold particular interest in relation to thinking about discipline. The agentic potential of discipline highlighted in some of the chapters of this volume, coupled with the possible historical trajectories of our global or world-system (e.g., Wallerstein, 2004), suggest that educational discipline for subjects who might engage with the transformation of society is worthy of ongoing study. With explicit attempts at such projects continuing to develop internationally, comparative research becomes essential.

Conclusion

Like Foucault (1984/1994), the authors in this volume consider 'discipline' as it is shaped by scientific, political, and moral discourses (see p. 116). In this book we have not tried to provide formulae for more effective forms of classroom discipline. Nor have we proposed perfect political solutions to the problem of discipline in education. To the critics of the former we would remind them of Foucault's (1984/1994) response to his own detractors that "it would be wrong to imagine that politics has nothing to do with the prevention and punishment of crime, and therefore nothing to do with a certain number of elements that modify its form, its meaning, its frequency" (p. 114). To the critics of the latter we would also draw on Foucault (1984/1994) who reminds us that "it would be just as wrong to think that there is a political formula likely to resolve the question of crime and put it to an end" (p. 114). We feel this perfectly sums up the position taken towards 'discipline' in education in this book. In making 'discipline' in education an object of social inquiry, we hope to have opened up different conversations around discipline than the one typically encountered in newspapers, on the television, or in staff rooms—conversations in which our approaches to discipline are de-stabilised and disrupted, to be re-examined and re-considered, as we continue these conversations to explore discipline's problems, politics, and possibilities.

References

Foucault, M. (1970/1994). *The order of things: An archaeology of the human sciences.* New York: Vintage Books.

Foucault, M. (1984/1994). Polemics, politics, and problematizations: An interview with Michel Foucault (L. Davis, Trans.). In P. Rabinow (Ed.), *Essential works of Foucault 1954–1984* (Vol. 1: Ethics, pp. 111–119). London: Penguin Books.

Klein, J. T. (1996). *Crossing boundaries: Knowledge, disciplinarities, and interdisciplinarities.* Charlottesville: University of Viriginia Press.

Marshall, J. D. (2007). Michel Foucault: Educational research as problematisation. In M. S. Peters & T. A. C. Besley (Eds.), *Why Foucault? New directions in educational research* (pp. 15–28). New York: Peter Lang.

Messer-Davidow, E., Shumway, D. R., & Sylvan, D. J. (1993). Preface. In E. Messer-Davidow, D. R. Shumway & D. J. Sylvan (Eds.), *Knowledges: Historical and critical studies in disciplinarity* (pp. vii–viii). Charlottesville: University of Virginia Press.

Popkewitz, T. S. (2001). The production of reason and power: Curriculum history and intellectual traditions. In T. S. Popkewitz, B. M. Franklin & M. A. Pereyra (Eds.), *Cultural history and education: Critical essays on knowledge and schooling* (pp. 151–183). New York: Routledge Falmer.

Wallerstein, I. (2004). *Alternatives: The United States confronts the world.* London: Paradigm Publishers.

Notes on Contributors

Dr Ken Cliff is a lecturer in the School of Education, the University of Newcastle, Australia. His primary research areas focus on the social construction of the body and Health and Physical Education curriculum study. His recent research has included such projects as an examination of the effects of obesity discourse and related health imperatives on schools and teachers, and the emergence of a sociocultural perspective as a curriculum change in HPE. His current research examines the role of teacher preparation programmes in shaping pre-service HPE teachers' meanings and understandings of the 'obesity epidemic'.

Dr Tom G. Griffiths is a senior lecturer in comparative and international education at the University of Newcastle. His research has two major trajectories: the development of world-systems analysis as a theoretical framework for comparative research, and the study of 'socialist education' in Cuba and, more recently, Venezuela, informed by this framework. He has published this work in national and international journals, exploring the ways in which mass education might contribute to a broader project of constructing a more democratic, equal and just world-system.

Dr Rob J. Imre has recently co-authored two books examining the phenomenon of global terrorism. He is currently writing a sole-authored book on the topic of global multiculturalism as a comparative political initiative. He is also writing two other collaborative book manuscripts: one on global civil society and the governance state, and another on the problem of regime change. He has also just completed a research project examining the rise of the radical right in Central Europe. Dr. Imre has worked in a number of nation-states including South Korea, Canada, and Hungary, and is now teaching International Relations at the University of Newcastle in Australia.

Dr Zsuzsa Millei's research examines the ways in which ideologies and contemporary governance constitute the subjects of education. Based in comparative frameworks and individual case studies, her published work explores classroom discipline; government policies and initiatives; the use of political concepts in education; and curriculum and pedagogical discourses under different political ideological regimes. Zsuzsa teaches the sociology and politics of education and early childhood education at the University of Newcastle.

Dr Robert John Parkes is a senior lecturer in Curriculum Theory, History Education, and Media Literacy at the University of Newcastle. Robert's scholarship, drawing on poststructural, postcolonial, and hermeneutic theories, is built along two axes of concern focusing on 'knowledge, curriculum, and the representation problem', and 'disciplinarity, pedagogy, and self-formation'. His most recent published work theorises a curricular response to the 'history wars'; argues for the importance of historiography when teaching contested histories; challenges 'classroom management' discourse as a regime of truth in teacher education; and explores the enduring histories and micro-geographies of the (post)colonial Australian nation, as they play out in education policy change. He holds a 5th Degree Black Belt in Bujinkan Ninpo Taijutsu, and an instructor's credential in Wing Chun Kung-Fu.

Dr Rebecca Raby is a sociologist and an Associate Professor in the Department of Child and Youth Studies at Brock University. Her research interests include constructions of childhood and adolescence, theories of rebellion and resistance among adolescents/ youth and the relationship between adolescence and other (constructed) life stages. Her current research concentrates on investigating secondary school dress and discipline codes in the Niagara and Toronto regions, specifically how the rules and their application construct students' current and future subjectivities and how to conceptualize students' responses to them.

Dr Erica Southgate is a lecturer in the School of Education, the University of Newcastle, Australia. She has worked in public health, education and community development. Her research interests include social disadvantage and marginalisation, child protection, queer history, qualitative research methods, and theories of risk and power. She has published a book, *Remembering School: Power, Subjectivity and Emotion in Stories of School Life* (2003). She has also authored several book chapters and numerous peer-reviewed articles and reports on drug use and public health.

Dr Affrica Taylor is a senior sociology lecturer in the Faculty of Education, University of Canberra. She teaches undergraduate and postgraduate sociology of education and early childhood courses in Australia and in China. She is a founding member of the Centre for Research in Education, Poverty and Social Inclusion and is currently researching and writing across the disciplinary fields of early childhood studies, Australian identity politics, queer and posthumanist theory and cultural geography.

Dr Megan Watkins is Senior Lecturer in Literacy and Pedagogy in the School of Education and a member of the Centre for Cultural Research at the University of Western Sydney. She is the author of Discipline and Learn: Lessons on Embodiment (2010 forthcoming) and co-author of Genre, Text, Grammar: Technologies for Teaching and Assessing Writing (2005). Megan has recently produced reports for the Australian Research Council on Cultural Practices and Learning: Diversity, discipline and dispositions in schooling (2008) and Parents, Diversity and Cultures of Home and School (2009) and has also published widely in the areas of affect, desire and the role of the body in learning.

Index

OMPLICATED

A BOOK SERIES OF CURRICULUM STUDIES

This series employs research completed in various disciplines to construct textbooks that will enable public school teachers to reoccupy a vacated public domain—not simply as "consumers" of knowledge, but as active participants in a "complicated conversation" that they themselves will lead. In drawing promiscuously but critically from various academic disciplines and from popular culture, this series will attempt to create a conceptual montage for the teacher who understands that positionality as aspiring to reconstruct a "public" space. *Complicated Conversation* works to resuscitate the progressive project—an educational project in which self-realization and democratization are inevitably intertwined; its task as the new century begins is nothing less than the intellectual formation of a public sphere in education.

The series editor is:

> Dr. William F. Pinar
> Department of Curriculum Studies
> 2125 Main Mall
> Faculty of Education
> University of British Columbia
> Vancouver, British Columbia V6T 1Z4
> CANADA

To order other books in this series, please contact our Customer Service Department:

> (800) 770-LANG (within the U.S.)
> (212) 647-7706 (outside the U.S.)
> (212) 647-7707 FAX

Or browse online by series:

> www.peterlang.com